UNDERSTANDING
A/S LEVEL GOVERNMENT
AND POLITICS

MANCHESTER
UNIVERSITY PRESS

UNDERSTANDING POLITICS

Series editor **DUNCAN WATTS**

Following the review of the national curriculum for 16–19 year olds, UK examining boards introduced new specifications, first used in 2001 and 2002. A level courses are now divided into A/S level for the first year of sixth-form studies, and the more difficult A2 level thereafter. The **Understanding Politics** series comprehensively covers the politics syllabuses of all the major examination boards, featuring a dedicated A/S level textbook and three books aimed at A2 students. The books are written in an accessible, user-friendly and jargon-free manner and will be essential to students sitting these examinations.

Already published

Understanding political ideas and movements
Kevin Harrison and Tony Boyd

Understanding British political issues
Neil McNaughton

Understanding American government and politics
Duncan Watts

Understanding
A/S level
government
and politics

A guide for A/S level politics students

CHRIS WILSON

Manchester University Press

Manchester and New York

distributed exclusively in the USA by Palgrave

Published by Manchester University Press
Oxford Road, Manchester M13 9NR, UK
and Room 400, 175 Fifth Avenue, New York, NY 10010, USA
www.manchesteruniversitypress.co.uk

Distributed exclusively in the USA by
Palgrave, 175 Fifth Avenue, New York,
NY 10010, USA

Distribued exclusively in Canada by
UBC Press, University of British Columbia, 2029 West Mall,
Vancouver, BC, Canada V6T 1Z2

British Library Cataloguing-in-Publication Data
A catalogue record for this book is available from the British Library

Library of Congress Cataloging-in-Publication Data applied for

ISBN 0 7190 6081 8   *paperback*

First published 2003

11   10   09   08   07   06   05   04   03   10   9   8   7   6   5   4   3   2   1

Typeset by Northern Phototypesetting Co. Ltd, Bolton
Printed in Great Britain
by Bookcraft (Bath) Ltd, Midsomer Norton

Contents

List of figures and tables

Figures

Tables

Acknowledgements

Many thanks to Duncan Watts, the Editor of the Politics Association Resource Centre, whose support and patience were extraordinary. Many thanks also to Linda Koncewicz, whose encouragement and ideas were invaluable.

THE POLITICS ASSOCIATION

is a registered educational charity, committed to the diffusion of political knowledge and understanding. It produces a wide range of resources on government and politics, and on citizenship. Members receive the journal, *Talking Politics*, three times a year.

Further details can be obtained from the Politics Association, Old Hall Lane, Manchester, M13 0XT, Tel./Fax.: 0161 256 3906; email: politic@enablis.co.uk

Part I

INTRODUCTION

The context of politics in the United Kingdom

In simple terms, the United Kingdom consists of four nations. The mainland includes England, Scotland and Wales, which are known as Great Britain. The remaining part of the United Kingdom is Northern Ireland.

Uniting the kingdom

Over the centuries, England brought the constituent nations of Britain under its control.

- Wales
  1536 – Act of Union with England, having previously been conquered.

- Scotland
  1603 – Union of the crowns of England and Scotland under King James I.
  1707 – Act of Union with England.

- Ireland
  1800 – Act of Union with England.
  1921–22 – Partition of Ireland into the Republic (26 counties) and Northern Ireland (six counties).

Unitary state

One important consequence of English dominance has been the creation of a **unitary state**. The Parliament at Westminster has been sovereign so that laws passed there have applied to the whole of the country. As such, the country has been governed from London. In addition, the Westminster Parliament has been constitutionally supreme.

Distinctive administrative arrangements for Scotland, Wales and Northern Ireland were later developed, along with structures of local government. These did not really challenge the **sovereignty of Parliament**. What has threatened parliamentary sovereignty from 1973 has been Britain's membership of the European Economic Community (now known as the European Union). Entry

> **unitary state**
> A state in which sovereignty is vested in a single, national institution which, at least, in theory, possesses supreme legislative authority. In the UK, this is Parliament which has the power to create or abolish any local or devolved body.

has meant that European law has often prevailed over British law.

A unitary state does allow for the possibility of devolution. Devolution provides for a measure of self-government within the context of the United Kingdom. Since 1998, devolved assemblies have been created in Scotland, Wales and Northern Ireland.

> **parliamentary sovereignty**
> Sovereignty means supreme, unrestricted power. In this case, the absolute and unlimited authority of Parliament which can in theory make, repeal or amend any law.

History

Continuity and tradition have been important aspects of British history. Britain has not been conquered since 1066, although there have been several occasions when there was an external threat, most recently in the Battle of Britain, in 1940. Not since the seventeenth century has the country been undermined by civil war or revolution.

In Britain, political change has come about gradually. This is especially true of the Crown, Lords and Commons. Following the 'Glorious Revolution' of 1688, an equal balance was established between all three elements and subsequent changes in the balance of power took place gradually over the next 230 years. Such gradualism helps to explain why Britain has no written constitution. In other countries, successful invasion or internal disorder have made it necessary to make a fresh start. As part of this, they have found it necessary to re-write their constitutions.

A number of other broad historical trends have had a considerable impact too. Britain had the world's strongest industrial economy and by far the largest overseas empire for most of the nineteenth and early twentieth centuries. Since the Second World War, the collapse of empire, and especially economic decline have been the focus of debate in British politics. It can be argued that Britain 'won' the war but lost the peace as a consequence. Because Britain, as a nation state, did not lose the war and stood firm and alone in 1940, successive governments clung to the view that as a nation state Britain could succeed in the peace, forgetting that the war had been won only with the significant support of the superpowers – the USA and the USSR. One outcome of this is that while other European countries began to draw more closely together, eventually creating the European Economic Community (EEC), Britain delayed entry until 1973. The debate over the extent of Britain's involvement with the EU continues today.

Neither was there substantial change in economic and financial policy for many years after the Second World War. Radical change only came about under the Thatcher governments (1979–90). Not until the mid-1990s did 'modernisation' and 'renewal' become part of the language of politics, with the advance of New Labour politics.

Society

Since 1945, Britain has become an increasingly heterogeneous (socially diverse) society. Both before and after the Second World War, the stability of British politics has owed a great deal to an overall cohesion in society and an absence of critical issues – of class, religion, or ethnic origin – that might have destabilised the political system. Essentially, the forces of integration have prevailed over the forces of division.

About 80 per cent of the British population live in urban or suburban areas, share similar life styles, use the same public services, earn their livings in similarly conventional ways, broadly acquiesce to the political system and are subject to the same mass media influences every day.

This does not mean that differences are absent. In Northern Ireland, religious and constitutional issues have been a deep source of division and violence, but this is scarcely the case elsewhere. Minority nationalist parties developed in Scotland and Wales, but they basically conformed to the rules of the political game. Class differences have been profound but as occupational patterns have changed so the class structure has become infinitely more complex and there is greater social mobility than ever before. Ethnic minorities make up only about 5.5 per cent of the population, although concentrations of particular groups live in some parts of large towns and cities. This has had a political impact as, for example, Muslims have demanded their own schools in the last decade. It has also led to occasional racial tension and disturbances, as in Brixton and Liverpool in 1981, London and Birmingham in 1985, and Oldham and Burnley in 2001, and subsequent discussion over how to improve race relations. Regions too have their own traditions and histories, with the North–South divide frequently quoted.

In this context, mention must be made of religion. The impact of religion as a source of values is an important component of **political culture**. Certainly, since 1945 Christianity in its varied forms has occupied a diminishing role in personal, social and political life in Britain with the exception of Northern Ireland. Although this process of secularisation has been acknowledged with deep regret, for example by the Archbishop of Canterbury in 2001, it is clear that Christian values still pervade our institutions and society. Non-Christian religions in the United Kingdom – especially the Islamic religion – have become an increasingly important component in Britain's political culture.

political culture

'The sum of the fundamental values, sentiments and knowledge that give form and substance to political processes.'[1] In other words, people's political attitudes, beliefs, symbols and values. As such it is different from public opinion, in that it has developed out of long-term values rather than simply people's reactions to particular issues. In simple terms, public opinion is the majority on a particular issue at a particular time. There may be one public, but there are many opinions; there may be several minority views.

Political consensus and the moderation of governments since 1945

It is essential here to distinguish between political consensus on policy matters and political consensus on procedural matters. See also Chapter 9.

Political consensus on policy matters

Following the immediate post-war period, it has been argued that for about 25 years there was a broad consensus on policy matters by successive governments whether Conservative or Labour. In the 1970s this consensus was called into question and in the 1980s it collapsed, with the election of three Thatcher governments and a profound swing to the left by Labour and its only gradual return to the centre. Polarisation replaced consensus. From the late 1980s to the present day, some commentators have argued that a new consensus has emerged.

Political consensus on procedural matters

From 1945until the 1970s, public confidence and trust in Britain's political system was strong. Since then, there has been a considerable decline in confidence in both governments, institutions and politicians, leading to the growth of pressure-group activity. In recent decades this has been accompanied by direct action in some cases. For example, between 1989 and 1992 there were anti-poll tax demonstrations and widespread refusal to pay. Such actions indicate not just a widespread distrust of political institutions and elected representatives, but also illustrate the disappearance of **deference**. Historically, Britain's political culture has been more evolutionary than revolutionary and social deference may have been one explanation for this.

> **deference**
> Respect. In this case, the willingness of the many to accept the views of their supposed social and political superiors.

Moderation of governments

This basically, may be explained by two factors. Firstly, the majority of British people have long preferred cooperation to confrontation and party politicians once in office have acknowledged this. Their view may be summed up in Bismarck's phrase that 'politics is the art of the possible'. Secondly, in an increasingly complex and interdependent world, parties once in power have realised that their capacity to implement major change is severely limited by both internal and external factors; **globalisation** has become synonymous with the latter.

> **globalisation**
> The emergence of a world economy and a network across the planet of instant communication and rapid transport.

Political parties

The development of highly centralised and disciplined parties strongly linked to their local associations in the constituencies has become a dominant factor in British politics and British political culture. In the twentieth century, the strength of the Conservative party, the decline of the Liberal party and the rise of the Labour party perpetuated an essentially two-party system. This may ignore the growth of smaller parties and in particular the re-emergence of the Liberal party but it does clarify a major trend in British politics. Today and in recent decades, the spectrum of British political opinion has become far more complex. However, to return to the two major parties, even in the 2001 general election it was still essentially 'New Labour' and Conservative who were competing to form a government even though the Liberal Democrats had become an increasingly significant force.)

The people and politics

The British public might accept the British political system, with some reservations, but they are not active participants. For most, voting at general elections has been activity enough, but in 2001 41 per cent of the electorate did not turn out. Most people do not vote at local and European elections, and the political parties have struggled to keep their members. Pressure group activity is the one area of expansion.

The standard of living of the vast majority of people is far higher than in the 1950s. However, the gap between the richest and poorest has widened, society has become more fragmented and concerns about job and financial security have grown since the recession of the late 1980s and early 1990s.

The European Union

Delayed entry to the European Economic Community (1973), scepticism about the extent of Britain's involvement following the Maastricht Treaty (1992) and free debate about the prospect of joining a single European currency have all been evidence of a negative British approach to Europe. On the other hand, supporters of the European idea – both in Britain and among Britain's European partners – have favoured increasing both economic and political union. These differences have cut across party lines and especially in the 1990s became a topic of fierce debate.

The future – post-materialism and globalisation

The concept of **post-materialism** is seen as a key factor in accounting for changes in the political culture of a country among the population and its political elite. Inglehart[2] says that following a period of unprecedented economic growth in the Western world, and relative peace from 1945 to the early 1970s, a 'silent revolution' began in the political cultures of Western democracies. Previous emphasis on economic achievement and welfare-state provision began to give way to 'quality of life' issues. This took place in the 1950s and 1960s among the new generations who questioned pre-war emphases on political rules and sexual morality, and were less loyal to traditional political parties. These generations have had no experience of world war, are well-educated and have focused on particular issues – nuclear disarmament and feminism are examples of their progressive views.

Post-materialists are active and opinion-leading, and some are moving into positions of political power. Given the above, it could be argued that Tony Blair (born 1953) and the creation of New Labour can be viewed in this context (see Chapter 9), as well as injecting the concept of 'Cool Britannia' into British political culture.

materialism

Materialists Shared a commitment to living standards, welfare state provisions to ensure personal security, and strong adherence to conventional forms of political authority and religious teaching.

post-materialism

Post-materialists Following the spread of affluence, and relative peace and security especially amongst those educated from the 1960s in well-established democracies, share a commitment to 'quality of life' issues such as the environment.

The future of world peace

Huntington[3] has argued that culture based on civilisations rather than countries would be a dominant source of future world conflict. He points to six main groups – Western, Japanese, Islamic, Hindu, Slavic-Orthodox and Latin American. Political culture within the state has been the focus of this section but it clearly has a global perspective too. This was reinforced by the Islamic terrorist attacks on the United States (11 September 2001).

The main elements of British political culture: a summary

1 an island race;
2 a heterogeneous and multinational people (i.e. dual loyalty such as British/Scottish: presence of ethnic minorities);
3 gradualism of political change; post-1945, the politics of economic and international decline;
4 consensus and moderation in policy and procedures;
5 dominance of 'party' but shortage of public involvement;
6 an end to deference;
7 decline of trust in politicians and government pledges;
8 widespread support for the political system;
9 sense of unity;
10 post-materialism;
11 globalisation.

REFERENCES

1 L. Pye, *The Encyclopaedia of Democracy*, Routledge, 1995.
2 R. Inglehart, *Modernisation and Postmodernisation: Cultural, Economic and Social Change in 43 Societies*, Princeton University Press, 1997.
3 S. Huntington, *The Clash of Civilisations* and *The Making of World Order*, Simon and Schuster, 1996.

2

Key concepts in British politics

AIMS OF THIS CHAPTER

➤ To explain the concept of politics from a number of points of view.

➤ To explain a basic understanding of the concept of government.

➤ To distinguish between the concept of 'state' and government.

➤ Via 1, 2 and 3 to introduce other key elements and the nature of political activity.

➤ To provide, via a revision exercise and a case study, a short programme of work to reinforce the contents of the chapter.

What is politics? Possible background for Year 12 students

On television:
- Prime Minister's questions: Tony Blair v Iain Duncan Smith;
- Italian police clashing with anti-capitalist protesters in Genoa July 2001;
- Rory Bremner impersonating politicians.

Newspaper headlines:
- the Millennium Dome;
- political sleaze;
- political cartoons – e.g. Steve Bell in the *Guardian*;
- *Sun* headline 'Two Jabs': 17 May 2001 – John Prescott punches egg-thrower.

Other sources:
- newspaper/magazine articles and reports;
- pre-Year 12 curriculum – political content in previous courses – e.g. GCSE History;
- school debates;
- informal discussions with parents, friends, teachers.

All of the above and more, hopefully in many cases, provide a background for Year 12 students embarking on an A/S Government and Politics course. Unlike most other A/S subjects, Government and Politics does not have a place of its own in the school curriculum before Year 12. As a consequence, students have acquired an 'informal' political education prior to Year 12. All the more reason to focus first on the question:

What is politics?

There is no simple answer to this question. Much has been written on this subject but it is necessary to try to keep the issue as simple as possible to have some idea of the nature of the subject we are studying. It is safe to say that 'politics' is a many-sided concept which may be best understood if viewed from various angles. A brief consideration of the following views seems worthwhile:
1 politics as the peaceful resolution of conflict;
2 politics as the art of government and the activities of the state;
3 politics as the authority to govern;
4 politics as the struggle for power and influence;
5 politics as deception.

Politics as the peaceful resolution of conflict

This is the view put forward most famously by Professor Bernard Crick[1]. It stresses the resolution of conflict via peaceful and legal means. As John Kingdom[2] emphasises, 'it defines the pure essence of politics'. This notion of politics therefore excludes resolutions of conflict by force, as is used in regimes such as military or one-party dictatorships where force is often used. On the other hand, this notion can be applied on any scale. In human society, individuals live, work and share leisure time together in groups. Thus, where people form groups, group decisions need to be made. Such decisions may produce conflict as individuals have different beliefs, value systems and interests (see Example: football club).

Example: football club

A village football team need to make decisions about spending for the season. A number of items are on their list but there is insufficient money for all of them now.
- new kit for the team;
- modernisation of the clubhouse;
- paying for new groundsman;
- buying/hiring a minibus for away matches.

In modern societies as a whole, the problems may be similar but on a much larger and more complex scale because of the sheer number of people and groups involved. At the same time, there is a need to ensure that peace and harmony are sustained. The example below of the National Health Service is of just one national issue.

> **The National Health Service**
>
> Evidence from opinion polls and, indeed, the general election campaign in 2001, indicates that the vast majority of the population of the United Kingdom value the National Health Service.
>
> Nevertheless, there is much debate at all levels of society about how the NHS may be made more efficient and how it should be financed. There is an unlimited demand for good health, but there is a limit to the supply of funds available.

Many conflicts by their very nature cannot be resolved, so that politics is about 'the art of the possible'.

Politics as the art of government and the activities of the state

Unlike the previous view, this notion involves just the organisation and running of the **state**. Michael Oakeshott,[3] the twentieth-century British political philosopher argued that politics is limited to this. He means – in contrast with the wide-ranging nature of Crick's view – that most human activities are 'outside' politcs. In essence, politics is to do with the art of government and the activities of the state alone.

> **state**
> This is the permanent entity or political association that exercises sovereign power over groups and individuals via permanent institutions and within a defined territory.

Politics as the authority to govern

Here, politics is viewed as an activity for the people as a whole and is associated with the conduct and management of the community's affairs. David Easton,[4] an American political scientist, argued that politics was concerned with the 'authoritative allocation of values'.

> **authority**
> This is power with consent – i.e., power is exercised with the general approval of the governed.

The key concept here is **authority**, i.e., in this case the right of say, a monarch or government to make decisions affecting the community. So 'authority' is **power** with consent; in other words, those who are governed acknowledge the right of **government** to govern.

> **power**
> The ability to make others do as one wishes, without their consent.

Authority has its origins in legitimacy which essentially means rightfulness. It involves a willingness to comply with a system of rules by the people as a whole. The most widely accepted basis for legitimacy is consent.

> **government**
> Put simply, the body of persons authorised to administer the laws and to rule and control the state.

These concepts of consent and legitimacy, especially the latter, present us with a number of problems which need be considered only briefly here. It can be credibly argued that the governments of the UK and USA exercise legitimate authority i.e., the rightful use of power because the population has elected them. Moreover, the life of a government is limited to a set period of

> **liberal democracy**
> A form of democracy based on regular elections and representative institutions. It lays great stress on individual freedom and a limited role for government (see democracy, p. 19).

time after which the population may elect it again or elect an alternative government. Such **liberal-democratic** systems are our main concern in this book (see p. 20).

However, what constitutes legitimate rule is a matter of hugely varied opinion; for instance, in the Islamic regime in Iran, religion is the basis of government.

The concept of consent can prove problematic. New Labour won the general election in June 2001 with 42 per cent of the total votes cast (excluding Northern Ireland) and formed a government with a massive overall majority in the House of Commons. However, 58 per cent of those people who voted, voted against New Labour. In addition, only 59 per cent of the electorate voted so that New Labour's total votes (10.7 million) represented only about 24 per cent of the electorate (excluding Northern Ireland) as a whole. Does this amount to popular consent? The issue of consent becomes even more problematic where governments are not subject to general elections. Adolf Hitler's Nazi government was initially elected, but became a one-party dictatorship and seems to have sustained strong popular consent from 1933, probably until 1940.

The second point we need to turn to in this view of politics concerns legitimacy and is well made by John Kingdom: 'of course, to say that a government enjoys legitimacy does not necessarily imply that it is *good* government; legitimacy merely resides in popular consciousness. Hence, political regimes will devote considerable time and energy . . . to the shaping of attitudes – the process of legitimisation.'[5]

Clearly, 'politics as the authority to govern' is a key consideration for us. Nevertheless, governments do not maintain legitimacy all the time. Easton's authoritative allocation of values definition is extremely helpful but we now need to dig a little deeper.

Politics as the struggle for power and influence

In simple terms, whereas the previous view provided us with the formal and legalistic elements of politics, this view looks beneath these surface trappings of state.

The book *Politics: Who Gets What, When, How?* (1936), by the American political scientist Harold Lasswell, provides a starting point. According to this view the essence of politics is power, the struggle for power in government and society, and how that power is used.

By focusing on power and, according to this view where real power resides, we need to return briefly to the concept of authority and make the distinction between **de jure** authority and **de facto** authority:

So where does power lie? – With the Prime Minister, Parliament, the public? With the media or City of London financiers? With organisations that cut across national boundaries, such as Microsoft or Nato? This view focuses on power and the distribution of power. We would do well, given this view of politics, to follow the example of former Labour MP, Tony Benn, who habitually asked the following questions on meeting a person holding high office: 'What power have you got? Where did you get it from? In whose interests do you exercise it? To whom are you **accountable**? How do we get rid of you?'

> **influence**
> The ability to shape a decision or outcome by permission, pressure or both.

> **de jure**
> This is legal authority – i.e. according to rules/laws/procedures/constitution, etc. – who has it and over what issues?

> **de facto**
> This is authority in reality – i.e. authority in practice that cannot be traced back to rules/procedures etc. In effect, power.

> **accountability**
> Being answerable to a higher authority.

Politics as deception

Whereas the first view of politics in this section – the peaceful resolution of conflict – contains in its purist form a vitally moral sense, this view clearly does not. Here we are into a world of intrigue and deceit by politicians pursuing self-interest. As David Lloyd George (1863–1945) British Prime Minister (1916–22) is believed to have said: 'If you want to succeed in politics, you must keep your conscience well under control.'

Kingdom[6] points out that deception takes place at the micro-level – e.g. intrigue and competition between those cabinet ministers such as Gordon Brown and Peter Mandelson in the first New Labour government. However, he argues that it is far more important at the macro-level – i.e. on a national and international scale – for example, via government secrecy or by manipulation of the media.

The distinction between 'state' and 'government'

In considering the nature of politics, the terms 'state' and 'government' have frequently occurred and it is important to distinguish between the two.

The state

The state refers to those permanent institutions which exercise a sovereign power over all individuals and groups within a defined territory. It is an abstract and permanent institution which does not change when a new government is elected or when political leaders are replaced. It has the power to use consensus or, if necessary, coercion. Institutions included in this are, Parliament, civil service, government itself and the bodies administering the law – e.g. police, courts and the armed services.

Summary: key elements of the state

- **Territory**: A state has clearly defined geographical boundaries and is treated internationally as a self-contained unit.
- **Sovereignty**: The state exercises sovereignty within its territory, holding ultimate legal power over its citizens. As such it may be an instrument of domination.
- **Legitimacy**: The state possesses legitimacy so that its decisions are usually seen as binding on all its citizens as it represents the permanent interests of society.
- **Citizens**: All members of the population become citizens at birth.
- **Institutions**: The state delegates its power to particular institutions – e.g. Parliament, police, etc., which are recognisably 'public' by contrast with the 'private institutions' of civil society, e.g. clubs, businesses, etc.
- **Constitution**: Every state has a constitution – i.e. the basic rules or laws, conventions and customs defining and limiting the powers and composition of the state institutions, their relationship with each other and their relationship to individual citizens whose rights and freedoms are often stated. Most constitutions, e.g. the US, are written and codified in a single document, but in the United Kingdom it is partly written and uncodified.
- **Nation**: This is simply a body of people identified by a common descent, language, culture and/or historical tradition whether or not bound by the defined territorial.
- **Civil Society**: This is usually now viewed as distinguishable from the state, reflecting the public/private divide. Sometimes seen as a political community – a society within and under the authority of the state.

The government

The concept of 'government' refers to an elite group with the authority to run the state (see above). Thus, the government is the agent of the state and, unlike the state, is transient, representing a temporary majority derived from a Parliament voted in at the previous general election. The government has gained a majority of the votes from the electorate and has therefore been given a temporary **mandate** to administer or change existing laws, introduce new laws and control the permanent institutions of the state in accordance with its promises within the **manifesto**. In effect, while a government serves its period of office, 'it is the state'. While this is basically the case, one or two reservations need to be noted:

- The United Kingdom's membership of the European Union means that in some areas of policy, it is the Council of European Ministers whose decisions are paramount. (e.g. the environment).
- Parliament may veto the government's legislation but rarely does so.

Core functions of government

In his book *The Spirit of the Laws* (1748), the Frenchman Baron de Montesquieu popularised the theory of **the separation of powers**. This was advocated before the 1789 French Revolution in which the monarchy was overthrown. The monarchy had held such power in France that Louis XIV had been able to say with a great deal of truth, 'L etat c'est moi' (I am the state). In other words, absolute power lay in his hands. He was the legislature, executive and judiciary. Although this is oversimplified, it helps to explain Montesquieu's advocacy of the separation of these powers in order to ensure that the nation had safeguards against such a tyranny.

> **mandate**
> The approval and authority given by the electorate to the policies contained in the manifesto of the party that is elected to office. In other words, manifesto pledges are given an electoral mandate by the voters to the party forming a government. This is like a binding contract.

> **manifesto**
> The document produced by each political party prior to a general election, containing the policy proposals to be introduced if it forms a government.

> **the separation of powers**
> The principle that executive, legislative and judicial power should be separated, via the construction of three independent areas of governmental activity.

A separation of powers is a key element in any democratic system. It ensures checks and balances between different parts of the system, and ensures freedom for the citizen.

> **The Legislature** creates the law via debate, amendments and voting. In the United Kingdom this is Parliament, i.e. House of Commons, House of Lords and Crown.

> **The Executive** puts forward most bills to Parliament and implements the laws. Consists of Crown, Cabinet, PM, ministers, civil service and partly local government.

> **The Judiciary** interprets and enforces the laws.

Figure 2.1 The three elements of the British system of government

In the American system of government, there is extensive separation of powers (see Figure 2.2).

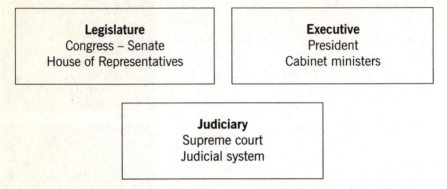

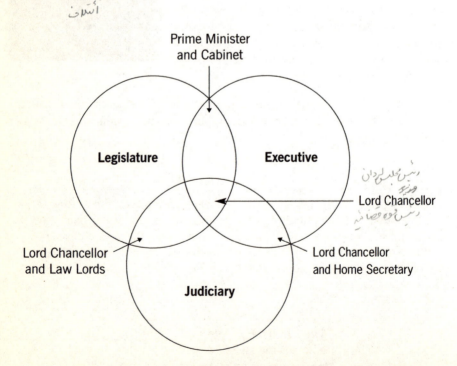

Figure 2.2 Separation of powers in the USA: basic elements

In the United Kingdom, there is a degree of separation between the powers of the three branches, but there are also overlaps, the most important of which is between the legislature and the executive. This overlapping of functions is known as <u>fusion</u>.

اِنَّسَف

Figure 2.3 British system of government, showing overlap or fusion of the three powers

Democracy

The United Kingdom claims to be a democracy. The word 'democracy' is derived from the two Greek words, *demos*, 'the people', or 'the many', and *kratos*, 'rule' or 'power'. Thus, literally, 'democracy' means 'rule by the people' or 'rule by the many'. This concept may be extended by Abraham Lincoln's Gettysburg Address of 1864, when he spoke of democracy as being 'government of the people, by the people, and for the people'.

Two types of democracy can be distinguished:
- **direct democracy:** government by the people;
- **indirect or representative democracy:** government for the people.

In addition, 'government of the people' shows that democracy involves a vital link between government and people.

Two other concepts need to be introduced at this stage. The Greek philosopher Aristotle, in the fourth century BC attempted to distinguish between different political systems when he wrote *Politics*. Here, he defined the following:
- **oligarchy:** rule by the few;
- **monarchy:** rule by one;
- **democracy:** rule by the many, as defined above.

Direct democracy

From the sixth to the fourth century BC, a form of direct democracy operated in the independent city state of Athens. It was possible for all citizens to meet in one place, and to deliberate on the issues of the day. This process is sometimes called 'marketplace democracy'.

All citizens had the right to attend meetings of the Assembly, which met over forty times per year. Each citizen had the right to speak and vote, and so determine directly the laws of the city state. There was also a council of 500, so called because each citizen belonged to one of ten 'tribes', from which fifty were chosen by lot to serve for one year. The Council prepared the agenda for each meeting of the Assembly; and chose a Presiding Committee of fifty which, in turn, chose a presiding officer by lot; the latter could only ever hold this office for one day in his life. Full-time public officials were held accountable to the Assembly. Overall, then, all jobs in government were served out by lot, the only exception being the election of ten military generals, who were eligible for re-election.

It must be emphasised, however, that out of a population of 250,000, only men born in Athens, aged 20 or over, qualified as citizens – a total of about 40,000; thus, women, children, slaves, and residents from elsewhere did not qualify. Nevertheless, because written evidence of this early experiment in democracy survived, and became the subject of much debate during the Renaissance, it has continued to influence political thought until the present day. Some key elements are:

- the concepts of popular participation and political equality (at least for citizens);
- responsible government, i.e. one that is accountable to the people;
- the concept of majority voting.

On the other hand, modern democracies differ from the Athenian model in a number of ways, the most obvious of which is due to the number of citizens within the nation state. Whereas Athens had 40,000, the United Kingdom has 40 million, hence the need for **representative democracy**. Nevertheless, direct democracy is present to some extent within the United Kingdom today (see pp. 71–4, covering the nature and use of referendums).

> **representative democracy**
> Citizens elect representatives to act on their behalf in an assembly.

The possibilities of using communications technology as a method for promoting direct democracy are certainly increasing. The most obvious would be via citizens voting on home computers over specific issues or proposed laws. New Labour set up a People's Panel, in conjunction with MORI, the opinion poll and marketing organisation, to gauge the reaction of its 5,000 members, randomly selected, to proposed policies.

Indirect or representative democracy

We have seen that in a direct democracy, as in ancient Athens, all citizens may act on their own behalf by participating in debates and voting on issues and policies in an assembly. This is, by and large, not possible today for modern nation states where citizens are numbered in millions, rather than in thousands. Hence, in the United Kingdom, voters elect Members of Parliament to represent them in a national assembly, i.e., the House of Commons. All MPs may speak and vote on proposed laws. If a proposed law gains a majority of MPs' votes, then it becomes an actual law.

Citizens vote for their representatives and, as a consequence, they hand over responsibility to make decisions or vote on their behalf. However, this does not give representatives absolute freedom to make decisions or vote any way that they choose. Representatives are elected for a limited period – in the UK for a maximum of five years – after which they must seek re-election. The representative are accountable for their behaviour. They must make decisions or vote in accordance with the majority view of their electorate, otherwise they are likely to be defeated on seeking re-election.

Liberal democracy

The United Kingdom and the other democracies of western Europe, North America, Australia and New Zealand are all called 'liberal democracies'. Andrew Heywood has explained the concept well: 'The liberal element in liberal democracy is a belief in limited government, the idea that the individual should enjoy some protection from an arbitrary government. The second element, democratic government, reflects the idea that government should, in some way, be tied to the will of the people.'[7]

Essentially, his definition breaks down into two elements: limited government; and democratic government.

Limited government

The central preoccupation of liberalism concerns the individual's position in society – i.e., the safeguarding of individual freedom, as well as the creation of a society in which individual interests can best be achieved. Government is viewed as a necessary evil. In other words, governments always have the potential to act in an arbitrary manner if their powers are not checked. The ultimate consequence of this is a tyranny, or dictatorship, in which the rights of the individual are not protected. Thus, the power of government needs to be checked in a number of ways:

- **Constitutionalism**. Government is based upon clear, formal and enforceable rules, which set a limit on its political power.

- **Protection of the rights and freedoms of the individual**. Essential rights and freedoms guaranteed by law or contained in a bill of rights.

- **Rule of law**. The doctrine that the law of the state is just and impartial, and that the governments, as much as the individuals, are subject to it, and so must conduct themselves accordingly, and are restricted in their use of discretionary powers.

- **Pluralism**. A healthy civil society in which organised and diverse groups and interests are able to compete for economic and political power, thus ensuring that government does not dominate.

- **Separation of powers** (see p. 15).

- **Decentralisation** of governments. e.g., devolution or federalism.

- **Institutional fragmentation**. Like the division of the legislative into two assemblies, i.e., bicameralism, as well as other checks and balances.

Democratic government

- **Liberal democracy** is a type of representative democracy, and, as such, means that the people participate in the political process by electing representatives.
- **Regular elections** should be held on the basis of universal suffrage and on the concept of 'one person, one vote'.
- **Elections** should be competitive; there should be a choice of candidates and parties, with a range of ideologies and policies, and free from intimidation and corruption.

Types of liberal democracy: presidential and parliamentary government

There are two types of liberal democracy, the presidential model and the parliamentary model:

The presidential model. This model, for which the USA is a good example, is characterised by a separation of powers between the executive, legislative and judicial branches. Here the legislature is elected separately from the head of the executive, that is the president, who is not directly accountable to the legislature and is independent of it in the constitution.

The parliamentary model. In the United Kingdom, we have a system of parliamentary democracy. Here, elections to the legislature and executive are not independent of one another. Indeed, there is overlap or fusion of these two powers which arises from this process.

General elections take place to the House of Commons following which, the political party with the majority of Members of Parliament in the Commons forms a government. The leader of this party becomes the Prime Minister and he makes the choice of personnel to include in his administration.

As a consequence of this parliamentary system of democracy, the executive requires the support of the legislature, if it is to continue to govern. One traditional criticism of parliamentary democracy of the British type is that Parliament is dominated by the government. Lord Hailsham, in his 1976 Dimbleby lecture, coined the term 'elective dictatorship', suggesting that governments with large Commons majorities were subject to very few checks on their power.

Most liberal democracies, ranging from Australia to Sweden, from India to New Zealand, have some kind of parliamentary government.

Liberal democracy, especially since the collapse of Communism in Europe, has become pre-eminent in the developed world. Its success, historically, has been its association with the development of capitalism, and the eventual growth of consumer prosperity. Another reason for its success has been its ability to respond to the needs of individuals and groups within society – i.e., between the governors and the governed. In 1989, its success led Francis Fukuyama[8] to argue that its triumph as 'the final form of human government' was strong evidence in support of his 'end of history' theory.

There are various criticisms of liberal democracy. They may be summarised as follows:

- **Marxists** argue that those with wealth hold power, and that liberal democracy, with its façade of political equality, merely serves to cover this up. Thus, the power structure of liberal democracies helps to preserve and perpetuate the interests of a dominant economic class (as opposed to a political elite) to the exclusion of the majority in society.

- **Radicals** argue that popular political participation is essentially limited to general elections, and that substantial reform is vital to redress this balance, and allow for more openness, and reductions in the powers of the state, for example, devolution and freedom of information.

- **Feminists** argue that, as a system, it has sustained male dominance in all walks of life, not least in government.

- **Elitists** argue that liberal democracy, while it might shift power within the existing political elite from time to time, does not allow for the reform of the elites themselves. These political elites, regardless of party labels, share a common interest in preserving the power structure that supports them, even though they are a very small minority of the population. This is a criticism made by some of the UK's system.

REVISION AND TASKS

A Check that you understand each of the concepts in Table 2.1

Table 2.1 Separation of powers

State	Separation of powers
Government	Legislative
Authority	Executive
Power	Judiciary
Influence	Democracy
Legitimacy	Constitution
Legitimation	Parliamentary system
Sovereignty	of government
De Jure	Fusion =
De Facto	Mandate =
Nation	Manifesto
Civil Society	Citizen
Territory	Consent

B Case study

1 Using the index and any other reference books, check the following terms: Lord Chancellor, shadow cabinet, hereditary peers, life peers.
2 Using Chapter 15 for more detail, write down the powers of the House of Lords over bills passed by the House of Commons.
3 Read the case study below with the five views of politics in mind.
4 Which of the five views of politics is not applicable to this case study?
5 For each of the four that are applicable, give two reasons (using the case study) to justify your choice.

Case study: reform of the House of Lords 1998–99
Adapted from *Servant's of the People* by Andrew Rawnsley, Penguin, 2001 (pp. 201–3)

Situation: New Labour government
• 'New Labour' was elected with a huge House of Commons majority in May 1997.
• In its general election manifesto it pledged to 'end the hereditary principle in the House of Lords'.
• With its huge majority, it could claim that it had a mandate from the electorate to fulfil all of its election pledges. As such, it had many bills to push through Parliament.

House of Lords
• The House of Lords has power to delay bills passed by the House of Commons.
• The hereditary peers were mostly Conservative and were understandably reluctant to see all of their number ejected from the Lords

Act one Sometime in the summer of 1998
Scene: Lord Chancellor's apartments.
Characters: Lord Chancellor, Derry Irvine (New Labour), Conservative leader in the Lords, Viscount Cranborne.
Irvine (on the telephone to Cranborne): I'd like to talk about our mutual problem. Would you like to come and see me – secretly of course – to discuss the matter?
Cranborne (in reply): Certainly.

Some time later: same scene
Irvine: It would be good if we could avoid a row' (*offering Cranborne a glass of white burgundy and pouring one for himself*).
Cranborne: 'I think it would be good too'
Irvine: 'I'm not in the business of bargaining . . . What about ten hereditaries remaining?
Cranborne: Not enough. (*He had consulted with his colleagues and the minimum he was to accept was one hundred.*) We want one hundred and fifty to remain.
Irvine (chuckling slighly): What about fifteen?
Cranborne: No deal.
Irvine: I'm not bargaining!
Cranborne (Icily): Right then. It's the battle of the Somme and Passchendaele. It's the complete buggerisation of your legislative programme! (*Cranborne walks out.*)

Act two October 1998 – same scene
['Characters: Cranborne and Irvine (knowing the government was getting increasingly anxious about its legislative programme)]

Irvine: We really do want a deal.

Cranborne: So do we. We want one hundred to remain.

Irvine: I can offer seventy-five but no more.

Cranborne: I think I can sell that to my colleagues, thank you. But, would it be possible to allow the fifteen hereditaries who hold office to remain as well?

Irvine: I'll talk to young Blair.

Next day – same scene
The telephone rings.
Irvine: Hello.
Cranborne: Done.

Act three 26 November 1998

Scene: Prime Minister's flat in No. 10.

[Characters: Cranborne (having been smuggled in), Tony Blair, Derry Irvine, Jonathan Powell (PM's chief)]

Blair: Will Hague back this?

Cranborne: (*who still had not told Hague of his activities. Hague and his shadow cabinet were opposed to any deal.*): If he has any sense he will . . . He can have some fun at your expense on the grounds that the government has done a huge U-turn.

Same scene: 30 November

[Characters: Cranborne, Alistair Campbell (press secretary to the PM)]

Campbell: We'll get Lord Wetherall (*a former Speaker in the Commons*) to propose this compromise in a press release. Won't Hague go ballistic when he hears this?

Cranborne: I'll take the risk.

The end

Subsequent events: Hague did go 'ballistic' and sacked Cranborne as leader of the Conservatives in the Lords. Hague then had to back down fearing a rebellion of Conservative peers who wanted the deal. The crisis among the Conservatives distracted media attention from the government's compromise over its manifesto pledge. In November 1999 (see Chapters 15 and 17) 650 hereditary peers left the Lords but 92 remained following the Wetherall amendment to the bill.

REFERENCES AND FURTHER READING

1 Crick, *In Defence of Politics*, Harmondsworth, Penguin, 1964, p. 141.
2 J. Kingdom, *Government and Politics in Britain: An Introduction*, Polity, 1991.
3 M. Oakeshott, *Rationalism in Politics and Other Essays*, Methuen & Co., 1962.
4 D. Easton, *The Political System*, Knopf, 1953.
5 J. Kingdom, as note 2.
6 J. Kingdom, as note 2.
7 A. Heywood, 'Liberal Democracy', *Talking Politics*, vol. 3: 2, 1990–91.
8 F. Fukuyama, *The End of History and the Last Man*, New York Free Press, 1992.

FURTHER READING

I. Adams and B. Jones, *Introducing Concepts and Doctrines in British Politics*, Politics
    Association/SHU Press, 1996.
A. Heywood, *Politics*, Macmillan, 1997.
A. Heywood, *Key Concepts in Politics*, Macmillan 2000.

Part II

PARTICIPATION

می‌کوکه تا شمهابش از این گور بگذرد
تا آفتابش از شب آن گور بگذرد .

روح ما را به روح تو نزدیک می‌کند
حتی اگر صدای تو از دور بگذرد .

Political participation and citizenship

3

AIMS OF THIS CHAPTER

➤ To examine the concept of citizenship in a liberal democracy.

➤ To outline the different interpretations of citizenship from the perspectives of the Conservatives, Labour and Liberal ideologies.

➤ To examine the types and levels of political participation in a liberal democracy.

➤ To outline the debate about developing citizenship and **political participation** in Britain.

Political participation in a direct democracy

In the direct democracy of ancient Athens (see p. 17) all citizens had the opportunity to participate in political decision making. Indeed, there was every motivation to participate if they wished to have their views and particular vested interests considered. Failure to participate could produce victory for one's opponents. Political apathy could lead to political punishment with startling immediacy.

> **political participation**
> Citizen involvement in politics intended to influence those who govern, or the decisions taken by governments – e.g. voting, party activity, group activity (see opposite).

Political participation in an indirect/representative democracy

In a modern representative democracy, most citizens do not have a direct input into political decision making. The United Kingdom in 2001 had an electorate of approximately 44 million. As we have seen in Chapter 2, we elect representatives to participate and vote on our behalf.

Types of participation

In a representative democracy there are many types of political participation. It is important to remember that this is of a voluntary nature. By contrast, in a **totalitarian** state, non-voluntary participation takes place. For example, individuals under threat of punishment are found to vote for one party or leader, or are intimidated into attending a political rally. This type of participation was common among the communist states of Eastern Europe from 1945 until the collapse of the Iron Curtain, and the destruction of the Berlin Wall in 1989, as well as in Fascist Italy (1922–43) and Nazi Germany (1933–45). Nevertheless, our main concern here is political participation in liberal democracies by citizens. At this point, it is therefore essential to consider the concept of citizenship.

totalitarian
In simple terms 'total rule'. Such a state has an all-encompassing system of rule that is sustained by an official ideology and control over the media and armed forces. It operates under one-party government with an all-powerful leader and terroristic policing.

'Civis Romanus sum' (I am a Roman citizen – St Paul when faced by persecution as a Christian [*New Testament*]).

'And so my fellow Americans, ask not what your country can do for you – ask what you can do for your country.' (President J.F. Kennedy's Inaugural Speech, January 1961)

A **citizen** is a member of a state. **Citizenship** refers to the relationship between the citizen and the state. The relationship between the two is based on reciprocal rights and duties. **Subjects** are not the same as citizens. Subjects are individuals who live in a state where **duties** are imposed upon them but no **rights** are granted in return. Examples include the totalitarian regimes mentioned previously and autocratic monarchies like that of Henry VIII in Britain (1509–47).

rights
Entitlements to behave and be treated in a particular way (see below for types of rights).

duties
Obligations, in other words things that we must accept that we have to do.

Voluntary political participation: types of activity

1 **Voting** – in local, general and by-elections; in Scotland, Wales, Northern Ireland, London for devolved assemblies.
2 **Active membership** – of a political party or a pressure group.
3 **Seeking election** – to local council, UK Parliament as an individual or member of an organization, e.g. political party/pressure group/trade union.
4 **Membership of any voluntary organisation** – e.g. political party/pressure group/trade union/local-national protest, e.g. anti-war or anti-terrorism.
   • attending meetings;
   • joining protests/demonstrations;
   • leaflet distribution;
   • canvassing public to vote a particular way/support a cause;
   • writing to elected representatives/newspapers/government.
5 **Direct action** – e.g. sit-down protests.
6 **Political violence** – as in Northern Ireland.
Note: All of the above involve contact with the political system. However, remember that on the most informal level, e.g. within a family or in a group political activity may take place.

Citizens possess rights and freedoms but, at the very least, limitations must be placed upon them otherwise the rights and freedoms of other citizens will be infringed. The possession of rights is conditional upon the performance of duties. No citizen can expect rights, freedoms and interests to be respected unless he or she respects those of other citizens. Further, citizens in a democracy must accept majority ruling and also respect the rights of minorities. Equally, citizens must accept their duties under the law, e.g. accept a properly constituted authority and pay their taxes.

Rights

The basic definition of rights given above now needs to be explored in more detail. 'Rights' may be divided into two broad categories, moral and legal.

Moral

These are claims made on moral grounds for human beings. *Natural* rights and *human* rights are essentially moral rights. Natural rights were the predecessors of human rights as they were believed to be given by God. Human rights are seen as universal and fundamental entitlements for all human beings, regardless of ethnicity, nationality or religion. They are also viewed as inalienable, i.e. entitlements that all human beings should possess regardless of the nature of the state. They were recognised in the USA's Declaration of Independence from British rule (1776):

> We hold these truths to be self-evident, that all Men are created equal, that they are endowed by their Creator with certain inalienable Rights, that among these are Life, Liberty and the pursuit of Happiness – That to secure these Rights, Governments are instituted among Men, deriving their just Powers from the Consent of the Governed, that whenever any Form of Government becomes destructive of these Ends, it is the Right of the People to alter or to abolish it, and to institute new Government, laying its Foundation upon such Principles, and organising its powers in such Form, as to them shall seem most likely to effect their Safety and Happiness!

Similar principles were stated in the Universal Declaration of Human Rights adopted by the United Nations in 1948.

Legal

These are the **liberties** which the **law** allows us. They are recognised by the machinery of the state and are enforceable, for example, freedom of speech and freedom of religion. Unlike human/moral rights, legal rights are not universal, but proceed from the society in which we live and therefore vary from one country to

liberty
Interchangeable with freedom: the extent to which one may behave or think as one wishes.

law
The law consists of a set of rules that are public and that are enforceable in a state.

the next. In turn, it is possible to distinguish in this broad category two types of right:

1 **Economic and social rights:** i.e. those relating to standards of living and life style;
2 **Civil rights**: those necessary for complete citizenship.

Of the two, it is the second group – Civil Rights – which are our prime concern. These are the rights which are granted to citizens and are usually defined in the constitution of the state.

Civil rights

These rights, as previously stated, are necessary for complete citizenship. In written and codified constitutions, they are set out in one document (see Chapter 10 on the constitution). Being a citizen of a democratic country does

---

Political ideologies and citizenship

Differing party ideologies contain variations of view about citizenship and the right and duties of citizens.

The Right/Conservatives
- are usually sceptical about abstract concepts like universal human rights;
- have thought of rights as traditional in that they should be viewed within the circumstances of a particular society;
- believe that rights therefore evolve within society so this is not a view that sees rights as unchanging;
- are more likely to talk of duty and stress that people should obey the law, be self-reliant as individuals and support and be responsible for their own family, etc.

For **Liberals**
- the rights of the individual in society are their basic starting point, the word 'liberal' deriving from the Latin *liber*, meaning free;
- there is little justification for limiting individual rights, except in so far as they affect the rights of other individuals;
- human rights are seen as universally applicable.

The Left/Labour has
- stressed collective rights;
- emphasised the role of the state in facilitating collective action;
- emphasised the need for positive and collective help for those in need, and for those who are disadvantaged (e.g. Labour governments created the National Health Service (1945–51) and introduced laws to end racist and sexual discrimination (1964–70 and 1974–79);
- more recently stressed economic and social rights (e.g. the right to work and to a good education);
- under Tony Blair's leadership, attached more importance to duties than is traditional on the Left.

not lead to automatic possession of all these rights. In Australia and New Zealand, women gained the vote at the beginning of the twentieth century, but in Britain, women over the age of 30 gained the vote in 1918, and over the age of 21 in 1928.

It is useful to differentiate between civil rights and civil liberties: **Civil rights** provide protection for the citizen (e.g. from arbitrary arrest, innocent until proven guilty). **Civil liberties** provide citizens with the freedoms to participate in the political system (e.g. freedom of assembly).

Political participation, in detail

We now need to return to political participation in more detail. The key issues are:

1 What types of participation occur?
2 Who participates and at what levels?
3 What changes have taken place in political participation since 1945?
4 What specific measures have been taken to expand political participation?
5 Reasons for/against more political participation in the UK and in liberal democracies generally.

What types of participation?

Voting

Voting is the most basic type of political participation in the liberal democracies and by far the one that involves most citizens. Any other form of political participation in the United Kingdom and elsewhere remains very much a minority activity. Voting in national general elections is the only form that engages the majority of citizens, but it takes place in a variety of forms such as national and local referendums, and those for devolved and European elections.

Until the 2001 general election (see Chapter 4) voting had involved about 73 per cent of the electorate. In local government elections and elections to the European Parliament, turnout has been significantly lower.

Table 3.1 Voting in local elections

	Turnout %
Luxembourg	93
Italy	85
Belgium	80
Denmark	80
Germany	72
France	68
Spain	64
Portugal	60
Netherlands	54
United Kingdom	40

Source: Adapted from the *Guardian*, 22 April 1998.

Political parties

Membership of a political party, no matter how active or passive the individual member happens to be, indicates a higher level of political commitment than voting as does membership of a cause or pressure group (see next section). Membership of political parties in the United Kingdom, overall, has declined significantly since the high point of the 1950s and as a percentage of the population is now significantly less than in some other Western European countries.

Table 3.2 Membership of political parties

Year	Conservative	Labour[a]
1953	2,805,832	1,005,000
1969	1,200,000 approx.)	681,000
1975	1,120,000 (approx.)	675,000
1982	not known	274,000
1997	250,000	401,000
2001	310,000 (estimate)	not known
Average age of members in 1990s	62	48

[a] Individual Labour members i.e. does not include those affiliated to a trade union.

Source: *Adapted from D. and G. Butler,* Twentieth Century British Political Facts 1900–2000, *MacMillan, 2000.*

Table 3.3 Party membership as percentage of population

	% of population
U.K.	1.6
Germany	2.3
Italy	7.4
Sweden	14.7

Source: Adapted from I. Morgan, *Power and Politics*, Hodder & Stoughton, 1999.

As Charles Kennedy remarked on television some years ago, the overall membership of the three main political parties remains consistently less than that of the Royal Society for the Protection of Birds (RSPB) – 850,000 in 1999. One set of explanations for this includes the marginalisation of members. The increased role of the media in communicating between party leaderships and the electorate, the use of direct mail and the increasing use of expert advice rather than grass roots opinion, are other explanations.

Pressure groups (see also Chapter 6)

Membership of political parties has declined but the reverse is the case with pressure groups. It has been estimated that at least 60 per cent of adults belong to at least one pressure group. In 1999, membership of environmental pressure groups – including Greenpeace, Friends of the Earth and the RSPB – was estimated at over 4.5 million.

The above are the main areas in which formal political participation takes place apart, of course, from those citizens who seek election as local councillors, MPs etc.

Studies of participation

Among the studies which attempt to establish different levels of political participation in democracies, the results of two are helpful.

L. Milbrath and M. Goel,[1] working in the USA, took the model of Roman gladiatorial contests to establish labels to apply to the population of the USA (see Figure 3.1). There are
- **Gladiators**: activists who are committed to political participation, i.e. 5–7 per cent;
- **Spectators**: voters only, i.e. who watch the political contest but only participate by voting (60 per cent approx);
- **Apathetics**: non-participants, i.e. those who do not even watch the contest and are indifferent to it.

In 1985, Parry *et al.*[2] began a survey of 1,578 respondents throughout Britain. The survey was multi-dimensional in that it included a list of 23 different political actions ranging from attendance at meetings to contacting an MP. The findings are shown in Figure 3.2.

They found that only one quarter of the citizens engaged in significant political activity. The rest who were almost inactive or just voters accounted for 3 out of 4 citizens. Their key findings were that:
- participation increased with wealth except for direct action where it was 'the poor who protest';

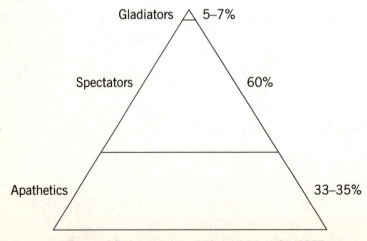

Figure 3.1 Levels of participation in the USA, 1977

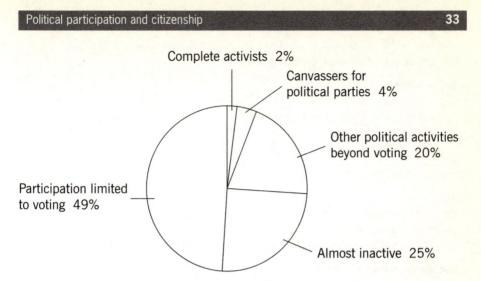

Complete activists 2%

Canvassers for
political parties 4%

Other political activities
beyond voting 20%

Participation limited
to voting 49%

Almost inactive 25%

Figure 3.2 Types of political participation in Britain

- graduates have high levels of participation. Those with no qualifications have low levels of participation;
- there is a 'life-cycle effect', leading to peak participation in middle age;
- men were traditionally more active than women, but this gap was narrowing: single women were more politically active than single men: and women were more likely to vote than men.

Factors affecting political participation: who are the activists?

Parry *et al.* found that the politically active minority of the population was not representative of the nation as a whole. Using their survey and others, we can formulate a checklist of relevant factors in participation.

With voting at general elections, some broad trends are evident.

- **Age:** In the 1997 election, Labour captured 57 per cent of the 18–29 age group vote with the Conservatives on 22 per cent and the Liberal Democrats on 17 per cent. With the 65 and above age group, the Conservatives had 44 per cent, Labour 34 per cent and the Liberal Democrats 16%. The evidence of this *Sunday Times* survey (May 1997) suggested that:
  1 as voters get older, more vote Conservative, fewer vote Labour, while the Liberal Democrat vote remains approximately the same;
  2 on the other hand, Labour gained great support from those in the 18–44 age group and was still 10 per cent better than the Conservatives in the 45–64 age group.

- **Sex:** Using surveys completed by the *Guardian* and the *Daily Telegraph* concerning sex and party choice over the 1987, 1992 and 1997 general elections, in each election, the percentage of men and women voting for each party was mostly similar or the same. For example, the 1997 election:

Factors affecting political participation

Social class
Higher Education ⎤
high income   ⎬ very strong determinants
wealth   ⎦

Gender
Men still at an advantage

Age
Young people now less likely to be active in political parties and pressure groups than middle-aged and older people. Youth wings of main parties are low in numbers. Under 35s are more interested in direct action, e.g. for animal rights, the homeless

Socialisation and personality
Outgoing individuals
Shared in making family decisions as children ⎬ very strong determinants
Born into politically active families

Location of residence
Rural locations – low level
Urban locations – higher level
inner cities with high population turnover – low level

Ethnic origins
Jewish – high electoral turnout
Afro-Caribbean – low level electoral turnout
Asian – moderate to high turnout

Adapted from G. Parry, *Political Participation in Britain*, Cambridge University Press, 1991 and M. Evans, *Political Participation* (*Developments in British Politics No. 5*), Macmillan, 1997.

	Conservatives	Labour	Liberal Democrats
Men	31	44	17
Women	32	44	17

- **Race:** Evidence from various surveys shows that black and Asian voters support Labour rather than the Conservative Party. Labour can usually expect to gain over 70 per cent of the votes from these two groups.

See Chapter 4 for factors influencing voting behaviour, especially social class.

Citizenship and political participation, 1988 to present day

From the late 1980s a debate developed about citizenship. This in part stemmed from concerns about the supposed erosion or destruction of the basic rights of citizens in the 1980s. Concerns arose among pressure groups and opposition parties about the erosion or even destruction of rights and freedoms of citizens by Conservative governments from 1979–97. Evidence in support of these concerns included the way in which the police prevented miners from travelling freely during the coal strike of 1984–85 and the *Criminal Justice Act*, 1994. It led to action by Conservative governments, notably under John Major (1990–97), and to a more wide-ranging approach by the first New Labour Government 1997–2001.

Actions by government to improve political participation and develop citizenship

Even before the extraordinarily low turnout for the 2001 general election, a number of measures were introduced to try to develop and improve political participation and encourage more active citizenship, with varying results. They include the following.

Education Reform Act, 1988

In part, this measure attempted to increase parental participation and choice. Local management of schools (LMS) meant that schools became much more independent of local authority control. Parents had the right to vote for grant-maintained status which involved direct funding from central government. This policy was ended by New Labour. The act overall attempted to encourage parental involvement (e.g. parent governors to be elected) but turnout for such elections was disappointingly low. On the other hand, schools had to be much more accessible to parents and potential students.

Citizen's Charter, 1991

Introduced by John Major's government, this aimed to give more power to citizens by making them better informed (e.g. schools were required to publish exam results), and included pledges to reduce National Health Service waiting lists. The other aim here was to develop active citizenship in society as a whole. The emphasis was on citizens taking responsibility within their communities – for example via charitable work and neighbourhood watch schemes – in the belief that this would be far more effective than government intervention. This clearly was consistent with Conservative ideology.

The impact of both measures was to focus on the citizen as a consumer with rights to efficient public services. Any wider obligations of citizens, beyond their families, for example, were scarcely emphasised. As Morgan[3] says: 'The position of the apostrophe (Citizen's Charter rather than Citizens' Charter) reflects an individualistic perspective on politics; the citizen was viewed as a consumer rather than as a member of a collectivity.'

Citizenship education: Report of the Advisory Group on Education for Citizenship and the Teaching of Democracy in Schools, 1998

This report was the latest of several over the past thirty years or so on this subject. It defined citizenship as 'the knowledge, skills and values relevant to the nature and practices of participative democracy . . .' Its outcome was that from 2002, it has been compulsory for pupils from the age of eleven to be taught citizenship in secondary schools.

Arguments surrounding greater political participation

'It is necessary only for the good man to do nothing for evil to triumph.' (Attributed to Edmund Burke, a key figure in the development of conservative thought and himself an MP until 1797.)

Those who support widespread political participation see it as a vital component of democracy. For example, John Stuart Mill in *On Liberty* supported political debate: ' . . . the general or prevailing opinion in any subject is rarely or never the whole truth; it is only by the collision of adverse opinions that the remainder of the truth has any chance of being supplied.' Similarly, Adlai Stevenson (1900–65) an American Democratic politician who twice ran for the US Presidency in the 1950s said, 'A free society is a society where it is safe to be unpopular.' The former quotation basically argues that widespread political debate raises the level of political education, makes holders of political office more accountable and improves decision making. The latter is one yardstick by which a democracy may be evaluated.

The above are general reasons and considerations, but what about the motivation of particular individuals? Those who have a strong set of political beliefs may wish to persuade others and may believe that those political beliefs may be fulfilled via political processes. Others may have a particular cause or interest to promote – either to help themselves or others, or both. Others may just want power and see politics as a means to that end. Many may have a mixture of both motives.

Those who support greater participation in political processes at whatever level, would almost certainly agree with the following: 'In the political tradition stemming from the Greek city states and the Roman Republic, citizenship has meant involvement in public affairs by those who hold the rights of citizens, to take part in public debate and, directly or indirectly, in shaping the laws and decisions of a state' (Report of the Advisory Group on Education for Citizenship, 1998). As such, political participation is viewed as both a right and a duty of citizenship.

Participation is part of the foundation of a democratic society and a vital safeguard in its protection and preservation. There are many arguments to support this for example.

1 It is vital to prevent the growth of extremism – racism, fascism etc.

2 To neglect the encouragement of participation is to risk increasing alienation and **political exclusion** of certain groups in society.

3 It is ultimately the people who hold governments to account. This should not just take place at elections.

4 Group action as much as individual action is vital to safeguard democracy (see Chapter 6).

> **political exclusion**
> This refers to those people who, because they occupy a marginalised position in society are, in effect excluded from collective decision making (e.g. stereotypically young men from ethnic minorities with few/no educational qualifications living in inner cities). Such groups may be attracted to extremist/anti-democratic politics.

- Devolution, European Union, Globalisation, etc. These and other factors have made democratic society increasingly complex. Participation should be encouraged to reduce ignorance, anxiety, apathy and alienation.

- Citizenship education, compulsory in secondary schools from 2002, should be politically encouraged in order to promote participation by children and students and so, later by adults. This should be facilitated by: promoting a more democratic culture in schools; and developing political knowledge, concepts and skills to motivate participation.

Counter-arguments concerning political participation

The following counter-arguments in some cases reject the notion entirely that political participation is vital for democratic society or cast doubt on the previous arguments in favour.

- 'Much of the division on the subject comes down to a fundamental value judgment about the place of politics in a fulfilled human life. Is political action the highest possible calling or is it just sitting in boring meetings.'[4]

- Those who support pluralist theories believe that unusually high levels of participation are signs of crisis – the less political participation, the greater satisfaction of the population with the political system. Some 'New Labour' ministers viewed the low turnout in the 2001 election as a sign of 'contentment'.

- Some argue that formal measures to encourage political participation have little impact e.g. parental involvement in schools (see government measures p. 35).

- Others argue that declining political participation has been exaggerated because the forms of participation have changed (i.e. declining political party membership, disillusionment with the political system, etc. have been compensated for by increased pressure group activity).

- Citizenship Education. Many cast doubt on the efficacy of this innovation. Their arguments include the following.

1 Schools as micro-political systems are too authoritarian to teach citizenship in a meaningful way.

2 An already crowded curriculum means that citizenship education will be peripheral in schools if it is not studied for external examinations – insufficient resources, teachers and students willing to take it seriously.

3 Those who would benefit most have already, and are already being socially – and therefore politically – excluded by factors external to the schools. As a consequence, such students would be the least likely to accept democratic values.

4 There are concerns from some about 'indoctrination' and undue influence by teachers with a strong political agenda.

5 The impact will be to exacerbate an increasingly individualist/consumerist approach to politics, i.e. students will 'cherry pick' what they want – their rights – while ignoring the duties and responsibilities that ideally should be incumbent on citizens. Evidence for this is shown by the growing number of litigation cases now taken out by individuals against, for example, hospitals, doctors, schools and teachers.

REFERENCES

1 L. Milbrath and M. Goel, *Political Participation: How and Why Do People Get Involved in Politics?*, Rand McNally, 1977.

2 G. Parry, G. Moyser and N. Day, *Political Participation in Britain*, Cambridge University Press, 1991.

3 I. Morgan, *Power and Politics*, Hodder & Stoughton, 1999.

4 *The Concise Oxford Dictionary of Politics*, 1996.

Elections and voting

4

AIMS OF THIS CHAPTER

➤ To examine the different types of election in Britain.

➤ To consider the factors influencing turnout in elections.

➤ To examine the nature and style of election campaigns.

➤ To examine opinion polls and the issues associated with them.

➤ To consider the factors influencing voting behaviour and four academic models of voting behaviour.

➤ To assess the differing theories about the influence of the mass media on political attitudes and beliefs.

➤ To examine case studies on each general election from 1979 to the present day.

Types of elections

General elections

The maximum term of office for a government is five years. Formally, Parliament is dissolved by the monarch on the advice of the Prime Minister. The Prime Minister can call a general election at any time during this five-year period. If a government loses a vote of confidence in the House of Commons, as Labour did in 1979, then it is duty bound to call for a general election. This rarely happens. Prime Ministers are usually able to choose the time that is best for their party. During the general election campaign, senior civil servants take over the running of government departments. If an emergency occurs, the Cabinet is recalled.

Since the 1930s, Thursday has been the customary polling day, whereas in many other European countries voting takes place at the weekends. The result of a general election is usually clear by Friday. If a government has been voted out, as in 1997, those ministers living in official residences move out. Over the weekend, the Prime Minister appoints Cabinet ministers and the rest of the government. By Monday, all of them should be at their desks.

By-elections

If a sitting MP retires or dies before Parliament is dissolved, then a by-election is called in the now vacant constituency. By-elections often attract much media attention, as leading figures of the major parties visit the constituency and assist their candidate's campaign. The result is often taken as a measure of the government's popularity as well as that of the other parties.

Table 4.1 The Ogmore by-election, 14 February 2002: a case study

Candidate	Party	Votes obtained obtained	% share of vote
Huw Irranca-Davies	Labour	9,548	51.96
Bleddyn Hancock	Plaid Cymru	3,827	20.83
Veronica Watkins	Lib Dem	1,609	8.75
Guto Bebb	Conservative	1,377	7.49
Chris Herriot	Socialist Labour	1,152	6.27
Jonathan Spink	Green	250	1.12
Leslie Edwards	Loony	187	1.02
Capt. Beany	Bean	122	0.66

Electorate 51,325, Turnout, 18,376 (35.8 per cent)

Ogmore is in South Wales. It is a safe Labour seat. The by-election was called following the death of Sir Raymond Powell (Labour) who had held the seat for 26 years. It attracted little national attention in the media, except on polling day and to announce the result. At the general election in 2001, the turnout was 58.2 per cent (just below the UK average). Labour's majority in 2002 was 5,721, in contrast with 14,574 in 2001, and its percentage share of the vote was down by 9 per cent. The Plaid Cymru percentage share was up by 6 per cent on the general election. Including Ogmore, Labour has held all ten seats it has defended since the 1997 election.

European elections

Since 1979, elections in the United Kingdom for the European Parliament have taken place every five years. In 1979 and 1994, the simple plurality system (see p. 79) was used for England, Scotland and Wales. In Northern Ireland, the Single Transferable Vote (STV) was employed. For the 1999 elections, to bring the United Kingdom into line with the EU, a Closed List system was used for England, Scotland and Wales, but Northern Ireland continued to use STV.

Under the Closed List system, England is divided into eleven very large constituencies, whilst Northern Ireland, Scotland and Wales are each classed as one constituency. The size of the constituencies in England varies. The North West (the largest area along with the South East) returns 11 MEPs. Northern Ireland, Scotland and Wales return 3, 8 and 5 respectively.

Turnout in British elections

Turnout refers to the number of people who turn out to vote at an election, expressed as a percentage of the total number on the electoral register. In the 2001 election, there was a turnout of 59.4 per cent in the United Kingdom. By comparison with previous post-war general elections, even the low figure of 1997, this was a significant drop. Overall, after the high turnouts of the 1950s, the trend was fairly consistent until 1997 and 2001 respectively. This is, of course, on a national level. On the other hand, it is important to realise that there may be high variations between constituencies and between regions. For example, in 2001, the turnout in Liverpool, Riverside was 34.1 per cent; and in Winchester, 72.3 per cent.

For many commentators, a high turnout is seen as healthy for democracy. For others, like Jack Straw after the 2001 election, the low turnout was evidence of contentment.

Table 4.2 Electoral turnout

Year	Electorate (millions)	Total votes cast (millions)	% Turnout
1945	32.8	24.1	73.3
1950	34.2	28.7	84.0
1951	34.6	28.6	82.5
1955	34.8	26.7	76.8
1959	35.3	27.8	78.7
1964	35.8	27.6	77.1
1966	35.9	27.2	75.8
1970	39.3	28.3	72.0
1974 (Feb)	39.7	31.3	78.1
1974 (Oct)	40.1	29.2	72.8
1979	41.1	31.2	76.0
1983	42.2	30.7	72.7
1987	43.2	32.5	75.3
1992	43.2	33.6	77.7
1997	43.7	31.3	71.5
2001	44.4	26.4	59.4

Source: Based on D. Butler and D. Kavanagh, *The British General Election of 2001*, Palgrave, 2002.

Factors influencing turnout

Low turnout
- The result is seen as a foregone conclusion – e.g. 1983, 1997 and 2001.
- The election is portrayed by the media as boring – e.g. 1997 and 2001.
- The state of politics and politicians are perceived negatively – e.g. MORI found Labour with a +2 rating in 1997 on keeping its promise, but on a –23 one in 2001.
- Partisan dealignment (see p. 53): in 1997, MORI found that 75 per cent of people questioned had a strong or fairly strong attachment to 'their' party. In 2001, it was 70 per cent.

High/higher turnout

- The result is likely to be close – e.g. February 1974, following the Miners' Strike and Three-Day Week, 1979 and 1992.
- Campaigns in marginal constituencies may attract a turnout that is higher than the national average. These constituencies often attract more media attention, and visits by party leaders, and voters believe that their vote will be more influential.

The 2001 election

Turnout for the 2001 general election fell everywhere and the overall figure was 59.4 per cent. Basically, two in every five people did not vote. This was a record low since 1918, and a considerable drop from 71.5 per cent in 1997. This means that nearly 5 million fewer people voted in 2001. A gap of 12 per cent between 1997 and 2001 is considerable but the 1997 figure was itself a record low since 1918. In all regions except Northern Ireland, the fall in turnout varied between 11.6 per cent and 13.1 per cent. In Northern Ireland, it increased slightly to 67.8 per cent. Not surprisingly, Pippa Norris[1] could describe the election outcome as 'an apathetic landslide'.

A number of factors may be offered to explain this decline but the influence of each one on the overall figure varies:

- Before 7 June, every opinion poll showed Labour with a lead of between 11 and 28 per cent. The result was a foregone conclusion so why bother to vote? This was true for many voters in 'safe seats'.

- Many seemed to think that the 2001 general election was not very important. Other general elections might be, but this one was not. An ICM/BBC poll showed that among those 'unlikely to vote', 77 per cent did not mind who won.

- Perhaps the most significant group are those who might have voted but were frustrated by the information they received via the media and the parties. This group was *not* bored.

- *But*, the campaign was presented by the media as boring. Certainly, the campaign was less active especially in those seats not targeted by the parties.

- Poll figures indicate that more voters find there to be little difference between the major parties. The attachment to parties is also in decline. A MORI poll on the eve of the 1997 election showed that 75 per cent felt attached to their party. In 2001, the figure was 70 per cent.

- The electorate's perception of politics and politicians continued to decline. In 1997, MORI found Labour with a +2 rating to keep its promises but in 2001 it was −23.

- The 18 to 24-year-old age group were notable for their absence at the polling stations (MORI). Only 39 per cent voted. This was one of the most worrying aspects.

- There were also those with strong political views that were unlikely to vote.

Worcester and Mortimore concluded that 'the 2001 election did not connect with people and made them view it differently to previous ones. Certainly, it seems it was more short-term factors than a long-term decline that were the immediate cause of the fall in turnout.'[3]

Election campaigns

Campaigns and campaigning are an integral part of the democratic process. Those who organise campaigns need to ensure that the electorate is well-informed about party policies and that they achieve their maximum potential turnout on the day. The length of the campaign is usually about 30 days. The 1997 campaign of 45 days was unusually long, and although this gives the parties more time to get their message across, it can induce boredom.

SPENDING LIMITS IN ELECTION CAMPAIGNS

Election expenses per candidate in Parliamentary constituencies: 1997 election

For funding purposes, constituencies are defined as county or borough ones:
- County: £4,956 plus 5.6p for every voter entered on the electoral register;
- Borough: £4,956 plus 4.2p for every voter entered on the electoral register.
County constituencies receive more due to extra expenses required to meet rural constituents. The maximum spend, using the above formulas in that election, were:
- County £8,941;
- Borough £7,825.

The Political Parties, Elections and Referendums Act, 2000

The report of Lord Neill's Committee on Standards in Public Life (1998) included a raft of recommendations on election expenses and party funding at national and local level, many of which were incorporated in the 2000 Act. They included:
- a £20m limit on national campaign expenditure by each political party contesting 600 seats or more;
- limits for the elections to the devolved assemblies of £1.5m for Scotland, £600,000 for Wales and £300,000 for Northern Ireland;
- a £100,000 limit for by-elections;
- a national limit for £3.5m for elections to the European Parliament. There were no separate limits on candidates or regional lists.

By-elections

£19,863 plus 22.2p (county) and 16.9p (borough) for every voter entered on the electoral register.

(*NB*: Greater expense is allowed at by-elections, as they attract national attention.)

New styles of campaigning

1959 was the first election in which television was used. Ever since then, new styles of campaigning have developed, so that there have been innovative polling techniques, a wider use of focus groups, the introduction of professional advisers and an emphasis on the training of candidates. Such increased professionalism has been a feature of campaigns in all political systems, as has been an increasing emphasis on the qualities of the candidates rather than the party.

The parties now have sophisticated electioneering organisations, using advertising agencies, consultants and 'spin doctors' to manage the campaign. The Conservatives were in the forefront of the attempt to manage the media and to display their best image to the voters. One of the most significant innovations since 1945 was their use of a major advertising agency, Saatchi and Saatchi, prior to the 1979 election. By 1987, Labour had followed suit. It built a 'presidential' campaign around the figure of Neil Kinnock and made skilful use of party election broadcasts. In 1997, Labour had reinforced its electioneering machine by following the example of Bill Clinton and the Democrat Party in the USA. Clinton had created a massive system of media monitoring and briefing designed to counter-attack the Republicans and any media bias against them.

Electioneering in the age of television

Election campaigns are made for television and television has significantly altered the ways in which they are conducted. Television dictates the form and style of electioneering and in addition has a significant influence over the daily agenda for discussion. Producers have a chance to draw attention to issues they believe to be interesting and contentious, and so they help determine the topics which are considered and highlighted in the campaign.

Whereas by other means of electioneering such as political meetings, party leaders can only connect with a small percentage of the electorate, television enables them to address millions of voters at one time. Moreover, television has also changed the nature of the message politicians convey and the type of politician chosen to convey it. The modern tendency is to 'presidentialise' the campaign around the figure of the leader, so that in choosing their leader they bear in mind the need for the person to look 'good on television'. Appearance and manner are important, so that intelligence and experience alone may not be sufficient qualities. In choosing Tony Blair, Labour voters in the party electoral college (see p. 120) knew that they were voting for someone who seemed young and in touch, and who possessed easy charm.

Politicians are now better placed to know what the voters think about issues, via opinion polls and focus groups. Their advisers devise new ways of addressing popular anxieties or demands. They do so in a way which recognises the nature of television, which is a visual medium, primarily concerned with entertainment. If politicians are to compete with other programming, they have to be interesting. Their media advisers help them to put their message across convincingly and in a way which has appeal. They recognise the need to speak in relatively easy-to-understand language, using simple, memorable slogans which are often repeated. Tony Blair used the sound bite 'tough on crime, tough on the causes of crime' to good effect in the 1997 election.

> **opinion polls**
> Opinion polling is a method of market research used, for example, by companies to estimate the popularity of their products. A political opinion poll is an estimate of public opinion made by questioning a representative sample of the population.

Butler and Kavanagh summed up the impact of the media in 1997 election in their election study. They might have been talking about any recent election:

> More than ever, election campaigns are managed and orchestrated. Each party attempts to shape the agenda so that the media reflects its views on favourite issues ... An election campaign is increasingly seen by those in charge as an exercise in marketing and many of the skills of selling goods and services to customers are now applied to the electorate.[4]

Opinion polls and polling methods

There are a number of organisations that carry out political **opinion polls**, including Gallup, MORI, NOP and ICM. These are surveys of a sample of between one and two thousand voters, usually from a range of different constituencies. Sampling is done by one of two methods:

1 **Quota**: a quota sample is obtained by finding voters who together match the known age, sex, social class and other characteristics of the population as a whole.
2 **Probability**: a probability sample is obtained by taking, for example, every 50th name on the electoral register.

The quota method has been dominant since 1937. However, in the 2001 general election campaign, random digit dialling was used for the great majority of polls. Only MORI continued to use face-to-face interviewing.

Opinion polls: 1945–2002

Political opinion polls are not just carried out during general election campaigns. They are taken from time to time between general elections, asking a variety of questions. They might include:
- Which of the three main party leaders would be the best Prime Minister?
- Which of the three main parties is the most competent to manage the economy?

- If there was to be a general election today, which party would you campaign for?

General election campaigns, however, produce the greatest number of polls during a few weeks: 1992, 57; 1997, 44; 2001, 31.

These were nationwide polls. The much reduced number in 2001 reflected reduced media interest. The four main pollsters were each commissioned by the media: Gallup, *Daily Telegraph*; ICM, *Guardian*; MORI, *The Times*; NOP, *Sunday Times*.

The amount of polling in recent general elections may have declined, but this does not detract from the polls' importance. In 1992, the result was difficult to forecast, whereas in 1997 and certainly in 2001 a New Labour win, if not the scale of the victory, was predictable.

Issues concerning opinion polls

1 *Role*

Opinion pollsters are major players in the electoral process. Their findings help shape the mood of the voters and the parties. Their main income may come from market research, but 'election forecasting . . . is their most publicised activity'.[4]

2 *Accuracy*

In general election campaigns, the pollsters emphasise that there is a margin of error of plus or minus 3 per cent in predicting the parties' share of the votes (for by-elections, polls are much less accurate because of voter volatility). The accuracy of the polls in predicting winners has been reasonably good, but the elections of 1970, February 1974 and 1992 especially undermined their credibility. In the 1992 general election campaign, more polls than ever were taken across the five main polling organisations. Labour had a lead of 1.3 per cent over the Conservatives. A hung parliament was predicted. However, the Conservatives gained a 7.6 per cent win, an 8.5 per cent margin of error by the pollsters.

The Market Research Society investigated and found four main reasons for such a large margin:
- There was a late swing to the Conservatives that the pollsters did not identify.
- There was a disproportionate number of Conservative voters not prepared to admit their allegiance.
- Non-registration of voters, especially Labour, reduced the Labour vote
- Faulty sampling.

In the 1997 election, the polling organisations came within a 3 per cent margin of error for each party's vote share. On the other hand, 4 out of the 5 overestimated Labour's percentage share of the vote and there was a 12 per cent range in Labour's lead over the Conservatives, as Table 4.3 shows:[5]

Table 4.3 Final poll figures for 1997 (%)

Organisation	Conservative	Labour	Lib Dem	Other	Lab lead
NOP	28	50	14	8	22
MORI	29	47	19	5	18
Harris	31	48	15	6	17
Gallup	33	47	14	6	14
ICM	33	43	18	6	10
Average	31	47	16	6	16
Actual result	31	44	17	7	13

Final poll figures for the 2001 election show better accuracy, (see Table 4.4). However, follow-up surveys by MORI for the Electoral Commission and a survey for the Labour Party suggest that there was a gap of nearly 20 per cent between respondents claiming to have voted – 78 per cent – and the actual turnout of 59 per cent.

Table 4.4 Final poll figures for 2001 (%)

Organisation	Conservative	Labour	Lib Dem	Lab lead	Error on Lab lead
MORI *Times* 7 June 01	30	47	18	15	+6
Gallup *Telegraph* 7 June 01	30	45	18	17	+8
ICM *Guardian* 6 June 01	32	43	19	11	+2
NOP *Sunday Times* 4 June 01	30	47	18	17	+8
Rasmussen 6 June 01	33	44	16	11	+2
Average	31	45	18	14	+5
Actual result	33	42	19	9	

3 Saying and doing

Opinion polls measure what people say. Voting is what people do in secret. Given these two elements, it is always likely that discrepancies will occur between polls and votes. In the 1992 election campaign, the Conservatives appealed to the self-interest of voters, while Labour and the Liberal Democrats adopted more altruistic stances. Some argue that this partly accounted for Labour's unexpected defeat.

4 *Do the polls influence the electorate?*

The 'bandwagon' and 'boomerang' effects have been the subject of much debate, there being two relevant terms:
- **Bandwagon**: If a party is popular in the polls, then more of the electorate may be tempted to vote for it.
- **Boomerang**: This is where a party that is faring badly in the polls picks up a sympathy vote, while the party in the lead suffers from a low turnout of its supporters.

There may be some evidence to show that the polls damaged Labour's lead in the late stages of the 1992 election. Last minute fears about a possible Labour government, especially its perceived lack of competence in managing the economy, may have reinforced this trend.

Opinion polls within a constituency allied to the previous election result may lead to 'tactical voting'. In the 1997 election, many Conservative-held constituencies were lost to the party previously in second place, which received votes not only from its own supporters but also from the party previously in third place.

5 *The publication of opinion polls*

There is a possibility that the polls influence voting behaviour. Some argue that in the United Kingdom – as in some other countries such as Germany – there should be a ban on publication for a period of a few days or a week before polling day. As we have already seen, the case that polls help to determine voting behaviour is unproven either way and even if it were the case, some would argue that it does not matter too much; people can be influenced by a whole variety of considerations. Furthermore, a ban could be considered both illiberal and impractical. It is illiberal to ban the taking or publication of a poll, in itself a socially harmless occupation. It is impractical – because as has happened in Germany – the likelihood is that survey work will be undertaken anyway and the results published abroad; they can then be made known via news bulletins in Britain.

6 *The polls and the parties*

Politicians do take opinion polls seriously. In public, they may say that they never pay any attention to them, but in private the reverse is true. The parties increasingly conduct private opinion polls between elections and during election campaigns. During the hectic and exhausting days of an election campaign, a good showing in the polls improves party morale from leader to party workers.

The voters

Table 4.5 Changes affecting the franchise in Britain

1832	**Great Reform Act**	The vote was extended to the middle classes. The number of adult males in Britain entitled to vote rose from approximately 478,000 to 813,000 (total population of Britain was approximately 24m).
1867	**Second Reform Act**	Male householders in the towns gained the vote – i.e. the 'respectable' working class. Number of voters rose from approximately 1,360,000 to 2,460,000.
1872	**Ballot Act**	Open voting was abolished and the secret ballot introduced.
1883	**Corrupt Practices Act**	A maximum limit on expenditure was established and the problems of bribery and corruption tackled.
1884	**Third Reform Act**	Male householders in the countryside gained the vote – the 'respectable' working class. Two in three male adults now had the vote.
1885	**Redistribution of Seats Act**	647 single member constituencies were created out of a total of 670.
1918	**Representation of the People Act**	All remaining categories of men aged over 21 and women over 30 obtained the vote.
1928	**Equal Franchise Act**	The voting age for women was reduced to 21; all women now had the vote.
1948	**Representation of the People Act**	Single member constituencies were created across the UK and plural voting was abolished.
1969	**Representation of the People Act**	The voting age was lowered to 18.
1985	**Representation of the People Act**	Principle of voting rights for British residents abroad was agreed (initially for up to five years.)
1989	**Representation of the People Act**	Voting rights for British residents abroad extended to twenty years.

Those eligible to vote include people who are:
- aged over 18;
- on the electoral register;
- British, Irish or Commonwealth citizens;
- EU citizens (able to vote in local, devolved assembly and Euro elections).

Those not eligible include:
- peers, who are disqualified from voting in parliamentary elections only (they already sit in the Lords and therefore do not need representation);
- the mentally ill – this is an imprecise common law category, but it usually involves those living in institutions;
- convicted prisoners;
- bankrupts;
- those convicted of a corrupt or illegal electoral offence within the last five years.

Voting behaviour

Psephology is the study of elections and voting behaviour (in ancient Athens, pebbles – psepholos – were used to vote in elections). This branch of political science has developed strongly in the post-war period and a mass of academic work has been produced.

A changing electorate 1945–2001

The electorate since 1945 has been subject to constant change:
- **demographic** change – i.e. not only the size, density and distribution of population, but also the relative numbers according to, for instance, age, gender, ethnicity;
- changes in **attitudes, values and behaviours** in the long and short term.

A simple comparison of the 1950s electorate with that of the June 2001 general election provides a useful starting point. People born in 1900, and voting in the 1950s, would have lived through the First World War, may have suffered during the depression of the 1930s, the Second World War and the period of post-war austerity. Scarcely any would have voted in 2001. At the 2001 election, young first-time voters would think of the Falklands War as history and their most recent experience of a government would be that of 'New Labour'. The political agenda for 2001 by contrast with that of the 1950s was significantly different too. On the other hand, people born in 1945, and voting in 2001, would be well aware of these changes.

Political socialisation

'Socialisation' refers to the way in which individuals, through interaction with other individuals and groups, come to absorb and understand the culture of their society. **Political socialisation** is the way in which individuals acquire, absorb and understand the political culture of the society in which they live. In short, people are not born with political attitudes and values, but acquire them. But when? Two models have been developed in an attempt to explain the process of political socialisation – the primary model and the recency model.

> **political socialisation**
> The process through which individuals acquire an awareness of politics and develop political beliefs, attitudes and values.

- **The primary model**. This model focuses on influences in childhood. For example, Butler and Stokes[6] in 1963 interviewed 2009 voters in 80 constituencies in the United Kingdom. In research of this kind, it was found that the political orientation of teenagers was very close to that of their parents.
- **The recency model**. Writers such as Kavanagh[7] have suggested that the impact of more recent experience in adulthood is most influential in determining political socialisation. He notes the importance of events, issues and key political figures.

The agencies of political socialisation

The sources which influence the political orientation of an individual are known as the agencies of political socialisation. They are the family, peer groups, the church, education and the media.

1 **The family**. The family is positioned within the social structure and provides an ethnic, class and religious identity. In turn, it shapes the attitudes of the child to many issues in the outside world (e.g. authority and gender) as well as particular values (e.g. tough-minded/tender-minded). As a group, the family may operate in different ways.

2 **Peer groups**. These are groups of individuals who associate with each other, both in childhood and adulthood. Whether in school or work, each peer group provides terms of reference for individual members and so may be influential.

3 **The church/religion**. Whether it be church, chapel, synagogue or mosque, religion has a place in political life. It attempts to influence attitudes, values and behaviour.

4 **The education system**. Education is compulsory from the age of 5 to 16. More people now stay on at school after 16 and attend a hugely expanded university system. Before the age of 16, politics is rarely found on the curriculum. On the other hand, educational institutions from infant school to university all provide an element of political socialisation because individuals have to adapt to life within an organisation with a hierarchy, a bureaucracy and a set of rules.

5 **The mass media** (see pp. 57–9). The mass media provides both child and adult with the means to see the world beyond their immediate experience.

Newspapers, radio, films and particularly television have an impact on the attitudes and behaviour of individuals and groups.

Political socialisation: a summary

- The agencies of political socialisation overlap each other.
- No one agency completely determines the political outlook of an individual.
- The agencies themselves are subject to change. For example, with increasing divorce rates, births outside marriage, the traditional concept of the family has been weakened. People now live in different forms of the 'family'.
- The 'primacy' and 'recency' models provide useful insights but the relative influence of childhood and adulthood experience are very difficult to determine in relation to political socialisation.

Voting trends 1950 to 2001

Two-party system 1950–70

1950 saw the first 'normal' post-war general election as nearly 3 million electors were registered as service voters in 1945. Both class alignment and partisan alignment were believed to be strong determinants of voting behaviour (see box on voting behaviour, p. 53).

In the seven general elections during this period, the Labour and Conservative parties always gained at least 40 per cent each of the total votes cast. The third party, the Liberals, were constantly reduced to a single figure percentage share; the one exception was in 1964. Combining the percentage of votes cast in the following way for the seven elections produces the figures shown in Table 4.6.

Table 4.6 1950–70: % share of votes

Conservative and Labour	91.77
Liberals	6.77
Other parties	1.46

In turn, these totals were turned into a disproportionate share of seats in the House of Commons. The highest number of MPs achieved at a general election by the Liberals was 12 in 1966. Over the twenty-year period the average return of Liberals was 7.7 MPs.

Overall, the evidence of this twenty-year period was characterised by the following elements:
- voting patterns remained stable;
- loyalty to one of the two major parties and social class voting were key determinants of voting behaviour;
- class was a key determinant in party allegiance;
- voting for a particular party at a general election was habitual;

- election results were largely determined by 'floating voters', especially the undecided electors in marginal constituencies;
- basically, most of the working class voted for Labour and most of the middle class for the Conservatives. In the 1950s approximately two-thirds of the working class voted Labour and four-fifths of the middle class voted Conservative. There was of course some deviant voting, for instance some did not support the party appropriate to their social class (e.g. middle-class Labour voters).

Key concepts in voting behaviour

Partisan alignment (or party identification). This is the attachment of people to one political party over a long period of time.

Partisan dealignment. This is the steady loss of once reliable support by those who had previously identified with one political party.

Class. Definitions of this concept vary. In the context of voting behaviour, the most helpful is 'The Market Researcher's View' (see p. 61) in which the economic and social status of individuals is linked to occupations.

Class alignment. This is an explanation of voting behaviour. Class was aligned/linked to voting. So the majority of the working class voted Labour and the majority of the middle and upper class voted Conservative.

Class dealignment. The theory that from the 1970s, the link between social class and voting weakened. One outcome was increased working class voting for the Conservatives.

Floating voter. A member of the electorate who is likely to change party allegiance easily.

Tactical voting. This is where voting for a candidate who is not the voter's first choice takes place with the aim of keeping out a less-preferred candidate.

Late deciders. A member of the electorate who is likely to decide on which party to vote for during, or even in the last few days of, the election campaign.

Instrumental voting. The product of rational thinking.

Expressive voting. The product of emotion.

Decline of the two-party system 1974–2001: 'The era of dealignment'

The general elections of February and October 1974 provided a significant turning point. Some of the trends evident then have certainly continued. For instance, there has been a decline spread over eight general elections of the percentage share of the total votes cast for the Conservative and Labour/New Labour parties. In Table 4.8, showing general election figures, note the emergence and decline of the Social Democrat party, the rise, decline and re-emergence of the Scottish and Welsh nationalist parties and the presence of MPs from Northern Ireland following the return to direct rule from Westminster. Nevertheless, the evidence in Table 4.7 – by contrast with the period 1950–70 – is indeed significant.

Note that in the 1970 general election the combined percentage vote for Conservative and Labour had been 89.4 per cent and for the Liberals

Table 4.7 1974–2001: % share of total votes cast

Conservatives and Labour/ New Labour	74.5
Conservatives	38.3
Labour/New Labour	36.2
Liberal/Liberal Democrats	16.3

7.5 per cent. In February 1974, the respective figures were 75.06 per cent and 19.3 per cent.

Given the nature of the simple plurality system used at general elections to the House of Commons this increased percentage for the Liberals has not converted into a proportionate number of MPs throughout the period. However, the 1997 and 2001 election returns of 46 and 52 respectively are certainly a considerable advance.

Two of the main reasons suggested for the decline of the combined Conservative/Labour vote have been class dealignment and partisan dealignment (see academic models of voting behaviour below). Given these two factors it has been suggested that electoral volatility has increased. Evidence from surveys done over the election campaigns from 1983 to 1997 show an increasing number of 'late deciders'. For example, at the 1983 and 1987 general elections, only about 1 in 5 voters were 'late deciders' whereas in 1992 it was 1 in 4. In the 1997 campaign 3 out of 10 Labour voters and 4 out of 10 Conservative voters were 'late deciders'. Since 1979, also, an increasing amount of 'split ticket' voting has taken place, that is supporting different parties in local and general elections.

Political scientists have attempted to explain these trends by developing a number of academic models or theories of voting behaviour.

The party identification model

The party identification or partisan alignment model originated from research in the USA in the 1950s. Essentially, it describes a psychological attachment to a particular political party. The argument for this model is that:
- Individuals identify themselves with a political party.
- This sense of identity is strong and long term.
- This sense of identification influences voters' approach to politics as a whole.
- It has much to do with the image and beliefs of the party.
- Partisan alignment directly affects voting behaviour.
- It contrasts with the rational choice model by which voters 'critically assess' the various parties in competition at the general election in terms of their policies, leadership and other factors.

In a sense this concept was summed up as follows in the *Times Higher Educational Supplement*:[8]

> Football fans do not decide who to go and watch on the basis of which team has the best tactics. Rather, they watch their 'own' team, even if they are at the bottom of the league. Butler and Stokes suggested voters form just the same emotional attachments to a political party . . . where does football partisanship come from? Passed on from generation to generation as father introduces son to the terraces. So equally, Butler and Stokes argues political partisanship is passed from mother to daughter as they talk in the home.[9]

Further, this model does not exclude the notion of tactical voting. This clearly happened significantly in the 1997 general election. For instance, in constituencies where the Liberal Democrat was second to a Conservative at the 1992 election and with the Labour candidate a distant third, switching of votes from the latter to the Liberal Democrat took place; Cornwall South-East provided a good example of this.

Partisan dealignment

The evidence for partisan alignment before the early 1970s and for partisan dealignment since for both the Conservative and Labour parties has already been considered (see section on voting trends 1950–2001, p. 52) in terms of vote share at general elections. There is general agreement that this has basically been the case, but it was the publication in 1983 of *Decade of Dealignment* by Bo Sarlvik and Ivor Crewe[10] which highlighted the developing trend.

In a party system that is changing slowly, it remains true that long-term identi-fication with Conservative and Labour exists and is a strong psychological element among the British electorate. But the 1970s saw a turning point. Look for yourself and compare the figures before and after the two general elections of 1974 (see p. 63).

The reasons for partisan dealignment

Several causes of partisan dealignment have been suggested by political scien-tists. Most have, in varying measure, played a part in the process:

- **Class dealignment** (see box p. 53): Most political scientists accept the connection between class dealignment and partisan dealignment. As the social structure of Britain became more complex in the second half of the twentieth century, social class allegiance to particular political parties declined. In addition, both major parties made great efforts to attract the support of people outside their natural class support (for more on this see: social structure model p. 59).

- **Expansion of education**: The expansion of education since 1945 has produced an electorate that is better educated, so that more individual voters are likely to make independent, rational choices at elections.

- **Age**: Between general elections, the composition of the electorate changes. While new, and mostly young voters (aged 18 since 1969) come onto the electoral register others, mostly older, die (for more on this see 'the social structure model').

- **Media**: Combined with the expansion of formal education, the impact of the expanding media – particularly television – is believed to have had an impact on partisan alignment. For example, the political interviews on television in the 1950s and early 1960s were highly deferential, while those of today (e.g. Jeremy Paxman on *Newsnight*) have gone to the other extreme. This is just one example of the way in which politicians and party loyalties have been subject to increasing scrutiny. In addition, the tradition of political satire on television – beginning with *That Was the Week That Was* on BBC1 in the early 1960s – has continued with *Spitting Image* and now the *Rory Bremner Show*. At the very least these programmes provoke a 'questioning' approach, while very often they reflect and reinforce a growing cynicism among the public about politicians.

The rational choice model

As both partisan and class alignment seemed to become reduced in their significance as determinants of voting behaviour, political scientists turned to theories of the voter making a rational choice. This model focuses on instrumental voting, the product of an assessment of the relative merits of each political party, rather than expressive voting, based on emotional attachments. Basically, the voter adopts a consumer approach in choosing the 'best buy'. Harrop and Miller sum it up in this way: ' . . . most citizens treat elections like a shopping expedition; they are on the look-out for fresh ideas and new parties as well as old favourites. Although the voters information may be skimpy or even wrong, elections are at least making a conscious, individual and instrumental choice.'[11]

There are a number of variations of the rational choice model. These variations are based on the type of thinking believed to most closely determine voting behaviour. Some suggest that voters make a judgement on the past performance of a particular administration. Others that the judgement may be more related to the prospects for the individual or his family under any alternative one. Whatever the case, the voters make their decisions in the light of what they think the parties can offer them. They are decisions based more upon a perception of self-interest in the short run than on longer-term factors. Parties have to sell their wares to the consumer, for they can no longer count on their habitual loyalty.

Some studies advanced in the 1980s and 1990s have cast doubt on the rationality of the choices that voters make. If voters are exposed to a slanted presentation of news and current affairs via the media, then their judgements are vulnerable to any misleading impression given to them.

The dominant ideology model

Dunleavy and Husband[12] argue that a number of powerful institutions in society influence the attitudes, values and behaviour, and subsequently voting behaviour of the electorate as a whole. In their view, the place of the individual voter within the social structure has a bearing on voting behaviour, but the dominant ideological messages of these institutions (in effect, the Establishment) on the electorate as a whole are more significant.

These institutions are:
• the government;
• political parties and leaders;
• the business community;
• the mass media.

Of these, they emphasise especially the role of the mass media in reflecting the dominant prevailing ideology. Traditionally, it was the Conservative party that gained most political advantage in so far as it was supported by the business community and most of the national daily and Sunday newspapers (the television and radio stations operate under a legal requirement to be unbiased). However, 'New Labour' had usurped the Conservative Party's position by the time of the 1997 general election.

The two writers claim that media misrepresentation distorts individual choices. They note that the media help to determine the agenda for debate and consciously or unconsciously provide a partial coverage of the news. This is more important in an age of dealignment, for in the absence of traditional factors such as class and party loyalties, voters are more likely to be swayed by what they hear, see and read. Whether or not you believe that voters are likely to surrender their reason in the face of a barrage of media manipulation is a matter of opinion. It may be that many people are entirely capable of thinking for themselves and making up their own mind. On the other hand, the extent to which the main parties devote so much of their time to 'news management' (i.e. getting their message across at the most appropriate time), suggests that they think that the media have powerful effects. The following section on the media may help you make up your own mind about its effects.

Differing views about the influence of the mass media on
political and social attitudes

There are several difficulties in assessing the extent of media influence on public attitudes on political and social issues. Individuals are exposed to a range of other influences such as:

- their age, education and social class;
- other people – family, friends and work colleagues.

It is difficult to distinguish the influence of any one particular form of influence, such as the mass media.

Manipulative theory

Some writers of the manipulative school claim that the media has an all-powerful role and influence on a public that is incapable of resisting the message it conveys. The effect is similar to that of an injection from a hypodermic syringe. Their arguments apply particularly to totalitarian dictatorships in which the state has total control of the media and its output; but in liberal democracies the media is varied and diverse, and the public is free to respond if it so wishes. This theory is less fashionable today, having been advanced between the wars at a time when dictatorships existed in several countries and the media were being used to propagandise (e.g. in Nazi Germany).

Reinforcement theory

Pluralists argue the case for reinforcement theory, which developed in the USA after the Second World War and was fashionable for many years after. They stress that in western societies there are many forms of media and that several views can be expressed via programmes and publications. They accept that elements of the media such as the tabloid press are biased and may have influence, but believe that this bias is countered by the views expressed through other sources. They do not see the media as injecting views into a passive audience or readership. Rather, they believe that the effect of the media is to reflect and reinforce the views that people already hold about particular issues. They do not change opinions, but tend to confirm individuals in their existing thinking.

This idea of reinforcement is underpinned by the theory of cognitive dissonance which enables viewers and readers to cope with material with which they are not predisposed to agree; in other words, information which is dissonant or discrepant to their way of thinking. According to this, people's ideas and attitudes are created and influenced by a variety of factors, psychological, social and cultural. So before they read a newspaper or watch television, they will bring this baggage with them. On confronting information, they may go through three processes which enable them to filter out that with which they do not agree.

- **Selective exposure**. People tend to choose those communications whose views they are likely to find acceptable (for example, Centre Left supporters may read the *Guardian*, Conservatives the *Daily Mail*; similarly, Conservatives may not watch Labour's election broadcasts, or if they do so it may be only to disagree with or mock them).

- **Selective perception**. People perceive what they want to see; in a newspaper report, they take notice of those pieces of information which gel with their own preconceived ideas and expectations, and filter out the rest.

- **Selective retention**. People retain and remember only the 'agreeable' information and forget that which is unpalatable to their way of thinking.

Agenda-setting theory

A more recent theory about the influence of the media is that of agenda setting. The media determines what the public reads, hears or sees, by the topics it includes for discussion in news bulletins and current affairs programmes. At election time, journalists have a strong influence about the subjects which politicians find themselves discussing throughout the campaign. As an example, in 1997 journalists were keen to talk about sleaze, not the issue which Conservative ministers wanted to spend their time upon. In 2001, on 24 May, front pages of newspapers ran diverse stories under headings such as 'Meltdown: euro row shatters Tories' (Mirror), 'Scandal of the Lottery fatcats' (Express) and, 'I've got 'em by the ballots' (Star).

As a result of agenda setting, the public assumes that what is offered is a fair representation of the world at large and of what is important. Some issues rarely get aired and therefore individuals do not get presented with information about them.

Independent effects theory

Currently, this is the more fashionable model of media influence. Supporters of this idea believe that class and partisan dealignment, combined with the growth of media (especially television) output, have undermined traditional post-war reinforcement theory. They are convinced that the media do have an impact, but the effects are variable on different people and groups. They are difficult to prove, but whether or not newspapers and television make much difference in the short term, it is likely that over a long period of exposure there is an important influence.

The social structure model

Whilst this model includes a number of important elements, the main focus of debate has been on 'class' which was for many years considered to be the most important factor influencing voting behaviour. Peter Pulzer[13] summed up this view pithily: 'Class is the basis of British party politics; all else is embellishment and detail.' Approximately two-thirds of the working class were said to support Labour, while four-fifths of the middle and upper classes were said to support the Conservatives. This view was largely unquestioned before the general elections of 1974.

Two problems arise.

1 If the majority of the electorate were working class before 1974, why was it that Labour lost elections in 1951, 1955 and 1959, won only narrowly in 1964 and lost again in 1970? Mackenzie and Silver[14] provided an answer. They drew attention to the phenomenon of the working-class Conservatives who made up nearly half of all Conservative voters. They distinguished between two types:

• **Deferentials**: those who believed that Conservative leaders were 'born to rule' and so should be voted for out of social respect and admiration for their superior capacities, and because they had the right governing qualities;

• **Seculars**: those who supported the Conservative Party on the basis of a practical assessment of their policies.

2 The second problem concerned middle-class voters who supported Labour. Parkin[15] surveyed such 'deviant' voters. In a study of Campaign for Nuclear Disarmament (CND) marchers in 1965 he found that this group of voters were drawn mostly from public-sector workers, such as teachers and social workers. This model also includes elements such as ethnicity, sex, religion, age and regionalisation which may influence voting behaviour in both the periods of alignment (1950–70) and dealignment (1974 to the present).

Class dealignment

A number of political scientists have argued that since the early 1970s, there has been a weakening in the relationship between class and party allegiance and, as a consequence, class and voting behaviour. This view was first developed by Ivor Crewe and others at the University of Essex in 1977. Other research supported this view subsequently. Nevertheless, whilst acknowledging this trend, Crewe[16] still argued in 1993 that class was still the most important single factor determining voting behaviour.

The case for class dealignment was contested by Anthony Heath *et al.*[17] from 1985. According to this view, there was no direct evidence that the classes had weakened in cohesion. The fall in support for the Labour party of 3.8 million votes from 1964 to 1983 could be explained by the reduction in numbers of the manual working class and the poor political performance of the party. Equally, they argued that support for the Conservative Party remained strong among the middle classes.

Why has class dealignment occurred? On this assumption, a number of explanations have been suggested, among them:

Analysing class

The market researchers' classifications

		% of heads of household (1991)
A	Upper middle class (e.g. professional, higher managerial, senior civil servants)	3
B	Middle class (e.g. middle managers)	16
C1	Lower middle class (e.g. junior managers, routine white collar or non-manual workers)	26
C2	Skilled working class (e.g. skilled manual workers)	26
D	Semi-skilled and unskilled working class (e.g. manual workers)	17
E	Residual (e.g. those dependent on long-term state benefits)	13

Source: National Readership Survey, NRS Ltd, July 1992–July 1993

The Goldthorpe seven-class schema (class classifications from British general election surveys, by respondent)

		1964 %	1992 %
I	Higher salariat	7.0	11.6
II	Lower salariat	12.3	16.3
III	Routine clerical	16.5	24.2
IV	Petty bourgeoisie	6.6	7.1
V	Fireman and technicians	7.6	4.8
VI	Skilled manual	17.8	10.8
VII	Unskilled manual	32.4	25.1

Source: Dr A. Heath, Nuffield College, Oxford (from Adonis and Pollard, 1997)

The decline of manufacturing industry

There has been a decline in manufacturing industries – especially during the 1980s – which in turn has produced class dealignment. In particular, it is argued, the close links between employees in these industries and the Labour party – via their trade unions – has been undermined by this decline. Between 1979 and 1996, there was a reduction of almost 50 per cent in trade union membership, from approximately 13 million to 7 million. The growth of occupations in the service and hi-tech industries did not carry with them significant trade union membership, so that the links with Labour were weakened, and class dealignment was a consequence.

Embourgeoisement and social change

The Labour party experienced four successive general election defeats – 1979, 1983, 1987 and 1992. After Labour's huge defeat in 1983, Ivor Crewe developed

Table 4.8 Votes and seats, 1945–2001 (seats in italics)

	Turnout (%) and electorate	Total votes cast	Conservative[a]	Labour	Liberals[b]	Welsh and Nationalists	Communist	Others (mainly N. Ireland)
1945[c]	73.3% 32,836,419	*640* 24,082,612	39.8% *213* 9,577,667	48.3% *393* 11,632,191	9.1% *12* 2,197,191	0.2% *0* 46,612	0.4% *2* 102,760	2.2% *20* 525,491
1950	84.0% 34,269,770	*625* 28,772,671	43.5% *299* 12,502,567	46.1% *315* 13,266,592	9.1% *9* 2,621,548	0.1% *0* 27,288	0.3% *0* 91,746	0.9% *2* 262,930
1951	82.5% 34,645,573	*625* 28,595,668	48% *321* 13,717,538	48.8% *295* 13,948,605	2.5% *6* 730,556	0.1% *0* 18,219	0.1% *0* 21,640	0.6% *3* 159,110
1955	76.8% 34,858,263	*630* 26,760,493	49.7% *345* 13,311,936	46.4% *277* 12,404,970	2.7% *6* 722,405	0.2% *0* 57,231	0.1% *0* 33,144	0.8% *2* 230,807
1959	78.7% 35,397,080	*630* 27,859,241	49.4% *365* 13,749,830	43.8% *258* 12,215,538	5.9% *6* 1,638,571	0.4% *0* 99,309	0.1% *0* 30,897	0.5% *1* 145,090
1964	77.1% 35,892,572	*630* 27,655,374	43.4% *304* 12,001,396	44.1% *317* 12,205,814	11.2% *9* 3,092,878	0.5% *0* 133,551	0.2% *0* 45,932	0.6% *0* 169,431
1966	75.8% 35,964,684	*630* 27,263,606	41.9% *253* 11,418,433	47.9% *363* 13,064,951	8.5% *12* 2,327,533	0.7% *0* 189,545	0.2% *0* 62,112	0.7% *2* 201,032
1970	72.0% 39,342,013	*630* 28,344,798	46.4% *330* 13,145,123	43% *288* 12,178,295	7.5% *6* 2,117,033	1.3% *1* 381,819	0.1% *0* 37,970	1.7% *5* 486,557
Feb '74	78.1% 39,770,724	*635* 31,340,162	37.8% *297* 11,872,180	37.1% *301* 11,646,391	19.3% *14* 6,058,744	2.6% *9* 804,554	0.1% *0* 32,743	3.1% *14* 958,293
Oct '74	72.8% 40,072,971	*635* 29,189,178	35.8% *277* 10,464,817	39.2% *319* 11,457,079	18.3% *13* 5,346,754	3.5% *14* 1,005,938	0.1% *0* 17,426	3.1% *12* 897,164
1979	76.0% 41,093,264	*635* 31,221,361	43.9% *339* 13,697,923	37% *269* 11,532,218	13.8% *11* 4,313,804	2% *4* 636,890	0.1% *0* 38,116	3.2% *12* 1,001,447
1983	72.7% 42,197,344	*650* 30,671,136	42.4% *397* 13,012,315	27.6% *209* 8,456,934	25.4% *23* 7,780,949	1.5% *4* 457,676	0.2% *0* 53,848	2.9% *17* 890,875
1987	75.3% 43,181,321	*650* 32,536,137	42.3% *376* 13,763,066	30.8% *229* 10,029,778	22.6% *22* 7,341,290	1.7% *6* 543,559	0.3% *0* 89,753	2.3% *17* 762,615
1992	77.7% 43,249,721	*651* 33,612,693	41.9% *336* 14,092,891	34.4% *271* 11,559,735	17.8% *20* 5,999,384	2.3% *7* 783,991	0.5% *0* 171,927	3% *17* 1,004,765
1997	71.5% 43,757,478	*659* 31,286,597	30.7% *165* 9,602,857	43.2% *418* 13,516,632	16.8% *46* 5,242,894	2.5% *10* 782,570	0.2% *0* 63,991	6.6% *20* 2,077,653
2001	59.4% 44,403,238	*659* 26,368,798	31.7% *166* 8,357,622	40.7% *412* 10,724,895	18.3% *52* 4,812,833	2.5% *9* 660,197	0.6% *0* 166,487	6.2% *20* 1,646,764

Notes: [a] Includes Ulster Unionists 1945–70.

[b] Liberals 1945–79; Liberal-SDP Alliance 1983–87; Liberal Democrats 1992– .

[c] The 1945 figures exclude university seats and are adjusted for double counting in the 15 two-member seats.

a revised version of the **embourgeoisement** thesis that others had put forward in the 1960s. Crewe argued that the traditional working class was decreasing – Labour had previously been able to rely on the support of this group. However, that was cold comfort to them in the 1980s, by which time a new working class was said to have

embourgeoisement
A term used to describe the way in which working-class people were becoming relatively more affluent and developing life styles previously associated with the middle class.

emerged especially in the south, the C2s who were skilled, home-owning and employed in the private sector. As they gained the trappings of greater affluence, these people were becoming more like the middle class and acquiring their values. In the Thatcher era, they were being seduced by Thatcherite support for tax cuts, and shared certain Conservative attitudes on issues such as the position of the trade unions and crime.

The evidence from the elections of 1997 and 2001 suggests that Labour realised the dangers presented by its shrinking social base. While gaining strong support from the D, E and C2 groups (about 60 per cent of the working class as a whole), it also made successful inroads into the middle class vote, in other words the groups A, B and C1.

Some factors other than class in the social structue model

Gender

In recent years, there has been evidence of change in the pattern of gender and voting. Writing in 1967, Pulzer noted 'overwhelming evidence that women are more conservatively inclined than men'.[18] The reasons were said to be, for example, that as many women stayed at home they were likely to have more traditional values linked to the family, that they were more religious and more deferential, and less exposed to work in tough conditions in manufacturing industry.

In the 1970s, the gender gap fluctuated but between 1979 and 1987 it narrowed and disappeared altogether. The gap widened again in 1992 but closed to 1 per cent in 1997. New Labour made strenuous efforts to attract the votes of women, for instance by fielding more female candidates. Women may also be more attracted to Labour because of its association with 'caring' values and interest in issues such as education and health.

Age

There has been a long-standing belief that with increasing age, voters are more likely to vote Conservative. Reasons suggested for this are that as people grow older they acquire more property and as their families grow up and move away, important aspects of the welfare state are of less concern. The evidence of the 1997 and 2001 elections suggests that young voters are more likely to vote 'New Labour'. This was very much the case in 1997 and somewhat less so in 2001.

Table 4.9 Other results for 2001

Party	Votes	% share	Average vote %	Candidates	Lost deposits
UK Independence	390,575	1.5%	2.1	428	422
Greens	166,487	0.6	2.8	145	135
Scottish Socialist	72,279	0.3	3.3	72	62
Scottish Alliance	60,496	0.2	1.8	98	95
Socialist Labour	57,536	0.2	1.4	114	113
British National	47,129	0.2	3.9	33	28
Liberal	10,920	0.0	3.2	9	8
ProLife Alliance	9,453	0.0%	0.7	37	37
Independent	127,590	0.5%	2.2	139	128

Ethnicity

Just 5 per cent of Britons come from an ethnic minority. The evidence of research suggests that black and Asian voters mostly vote Labour (see p. 245).

There are a number of reasons suggested for this:
- Most ethnic voters live in a limited number of urban, particularly inner-city constituencies. Historically, such constituencies are Labour strongholds and this has been perpetuated by the forging of close links between the party and the ethnic communities.
- Labour is usually perceived as being more liberal on race issues especially race relations and immigration.
- Social class is the reason often provided by ethnic minorities for voting Labour – Labour is for the working class and that is how most see themselves. However, this simple class explanation ignores the fact that significant proportions of black and Asian people are in the AB categories.

Religion

With the vital exception of Northern Ireland, religious affiliation is not considered to be a significant factor in voting behaviour. Indeed, researchers mostly omit this factor. However, the work of A. Heath *et al.*[19] found evidence of certain links between religious affiliation and party voting, while acknowledging the general decline of religion in Britain. For example, members of the middle class who regularly attended the Church of England usually voted Conservative.

Regional variation

The term North–South divide was frequently used to describe the broad areas of declining regional support for the Labour and Conservative parties. Basically this meant: Declining support for the Conservatives in the north of England, Scotland, Wales and, for Labour in the south of England.

The 1997 general election saw a continuation of these broad trends. Labour gained 60.9 per cent of the vote in the north and only 26.4 per cent in the south-west, while the Conservatives gained 41.4 per cent of the vote in the south-east and 17.5 per cent in Scotland. At the same time, there were significant exceptions for 'New Labour'. It won 49.4 per cent of the vote in Greater London and 32 per cent in the south-east (a gain of 11.1 per cent over 1992). Broadly, these regional variations were sustained in the 2001 general election.

Tactical voting

This is where people vote not for their preferred party, but for another party in the hope that this will help to defeat their least favoured party.

Miller[20] used data from by-elections to show that there are four types of voter:
- Core (i.e. have a preferred party) 39 per cent
- Tactical 37 per cent
- Abstainers 15 per cent
- Floaters 9 per cent

Tactical voting has been important at by-elections for many years. A mid-term by-election might show a considerable swing of opinion against the party in power. In July 1993, the Liberal Democrats won Christchurch only for the Conservatives to recover at the general election in 1997.

Tactical voting takes place at general elections too, as recent research shows. Butler and Kavanagh[21] state that tactical voting reduced the Conservative majority by half. In Conservative-held marginals where Labour was second, there was evidence of the Liberal Democrat vote swinging to Labour. Even more so in 1997, voters opted for whichever of the two opposition parties seemed best placed to defeat the sitting Conservative. The same writers state: 'In 1992, Labour had benefited in marginal seats; on this occasion, it benefited in supposed safe seats as well. At least 15 and maybe as many as 21 seats were won by Labour from the Conservatives as a result of tactical switching, compared with between 6 and 8 in 1992.'

In 2001, Labour benefited from tactical voting by some Liberal Democrat voters in Labour-held marginals, but there was little evidence that the third party benefited significantly from it. In the marginal seats where the Conservatives were defending and the Liberal Democrats were second, the Labour vote held up surprisingly well. The party's voters did not switch to the Liberal Democrats in sufficient numbers to secure victories for them.

Some case studies: general elections since 1979

Some writers have distinguished between different types of election, especially between the maintaining ones in which the party in power continues to hold the reins, and realigning ones in which voters opt for a change of direction. In the post-war period, there have been elections which have produced – or promised to produce – a critical realignment. These were:

- **1945** – the election of the Attlee Labour Party which was committed to greater social justice and more extensive state control;

- **1951** – the election of the Churchill Conservative government, in which the party was committed to 'setting the people free' after years of rationing and restriction. In actual fact, the Conservatives accepted the broad lines of Labour policy on welfare and did not seek to undo the measures of nationalisation several of which it had once contested;

- **1964** – the return of a Labour government after thirteen years of Tory rule, although this election did not lead to the radical initiative hoped for by Labour supporters;

- **1979** – the election of Margaret Thatcher's Conservative Party (see below);

- **1997** – the return of a Labour government with a landslide majority, introducing a period of Labour dominance (see p. 68).

The 1979 election

The Labour government led by James Callaghan (1976–79) was beset by a range of serious difficulties. Lacking a Commons majority, it faced problems over its handling of the economy. The Conservatives ran an effective poster advertising campaign in 1978, entitled 'Labour Isn't Working'. The message seemed even more appropriate by early 1979, for by then there was a spirit of revolt within the trade union movement over pay policy. In the so-called 'Winter of Discontent' of 1978–79, there was a series of strikes, mostly in the public sector. They received massive and damaging media coverage. The Prime Minister had been expected to call an election in the autumn, but eventually was forced to do so after the government was defeated in a Vote of Confidence in January 1979. In the campaign which followed, the polls pointed to a clear Conservative victory.

Under Margaret Thatcher, the Conservatives won a comfortable majority, with 71 more seats than Labour. Their programme – based on New Right policies (see pp. 135–6) – marked a decisive break with the policies which had gone before. There was a real change of direction, in reaction to what the Conservatives perceived as the failure of governments of all parties in the post-war era. Lower taxes, an assault on union power and less state control were seem as desirable goals after 1979, and the new policies moved the centre of gravity in British politics sharply to the right. John Cole, a former political editor, has written of the mood at that time, observing that 'if a tide is running – as in 1906, 1945 or 1951 – what happens in the election campaign scarcely matters. The country feels in its bones that it is time for a change.'[22]

1983

Monetarist policies and world recession produced the worst depression in Britain for fifty years. Hundreds of companies went bankrupt in the early 1980s, more than 3 million people were unemployed and much manufacturing capacity was destroyed. Yet the Conservatives won a 'landslide' victory in 1983 and Labour slumped to its worst result since 1918. The Alliance (formed by the breakaway Social Democrats and Liberals) polled nearly as well as Labour, even it its efforts won only 23 seats.

How could the Conservatives win at a time when for many people there was no 'feel-good' factor? The government in general and the image of Margaret Thatcher in particular had benefited from victory over Argentina in the Falklands War. Labour, in contrast, was at a low ebb. Having lost some members of its more pro-European right to the Social Democrats, it was firmly in the hands of the left. Its manifesto, dubbed by one Labour MP as 'the longest suicide note in history', included commitments to withdraw from the EEC, adopt unilateral nuclear disarmament, abolish the House of Lords (without any replacement) and extend nationalisation. Led ineffectually by an elderly left-winger from the past, Michael Foot, it seemed unfit for office. Its election campaign was little short of disastrous, in particular the way in which the leader shunned opportunities for television exposure.

The outcome showed that as long as enough people were in work and doing well, a party could win handsomely and command their support. The Conservatives had gained support from the skilled working class (C2s, see p. 61) in 1979 and continued to do so in large numbers in this election. As a result of her party's electoral success, Margaret Thatcher was able to take the opportunity to introduce wide-ranging changes and transform some long-unchallenged features of our national life.

1987

In the mid-1980s, Labour began to put its house in order. Led by Neil Kinnock, the party was rescued from its low point of 1983 as he embarked upon a transformation of its image and organisation, and began to shed unpopular policies. By the time of the election, Labour was in better shape and it fought a strong campaign, built around the leader. There was a new professionalism, as was evident in the party election broadcast later dubbed 'Kinnock – the movie'.

By comparison, the Conservative campaign was slow to get off the ground and lacked the style and appeal shown in the previous two elections. But if the Conservatives lost the campaign, they won the war. Many voters still had doubts about whether Labour had really changed its old attitudes and preferred the Thatcherite approach on issues such as trade union reform and privatisation. After all, large sections of the working population (but not those in the public sector) had prospered as a result of Conservative policies, especially those in the Midlands and South. The result was never really in doubt and although their share of the national vote declined the Conservatives again won a handsome victory. Labour made a modest gain of twenty seats, but was left with only 31 per cent of the popular vote. The Alliance did well, but less impressively than in 1983.

1992

By the time John Major became Prime Minister, the country had entered into the second Conservative recession. In 1991, 48,000 businesses went bankrupt, unemployment was again high and there were record numbers of house repossessions as people defaulted on mortgage payments. The Prime Minister was personally popular, however, and was widely seen as having handled the Maastricht negotiations within the European Community rather well. Labour had continued the process of party renewal and after the Policy Review had revised its policies in several areas. At last, there seemed to be a viable opposition and the polls indicated a very close race, with Labour slightly ahead.

The outcome was a fourth successive Conservative victory which was remarkable in itself, but especially so in the midst of a recession. The 'time for a change' argument did not operate to Labour's advantage as much as might have been expected, perhaps because there had already been a change of prime minister. Whereas many voters seemed to be turned off by Neil Kinnock, they liked John Major and were willing to give him a longer innings. The tabloid press was very anti-Labour, as in 1987, and exploited any Labour weaknesses ruthlessly. The attacks on Kinnock were highly personal and damaging, but there were deficiencies in Labour's tax policies which were also exploited. Kinnock had made Labour electable, but when it came to polling day the prospect that he might win helped to galvanise the Conservatives to a last-minute effort. They won a narrow victory, on a high turnout. The polls had been proved wildly wrong.

1997

Soon after the 1992 election, the Conservatives ran into a series of difficulties over such issues as ratification of the Maastricht treaty and European policy in general, taxation and sleaze (the personal morality – both sexual and financial – of some of its MPs) which dogged the administration throughout its existence. The rot had set in when as a result of a run on sterling on Black Wednesday (16 September 1992) Britain withdrew from the Exchange Rate Mechanism (ERM). The cornerstone of the Government's economic policy had been removed at a stroke and ministers never recovered from its handling of the humiliating withdrawal. The Conservatives' reputation for economic competence had been shattered and they never led in the polls after Black Wednesday. John Major, whose 'niceness' had worked to their advantage in 1992 was now widely perceived as weak and dithering, although in fairness he led a cabinet which was very disunited and whose members often seemed unwilling to accept the need for unity – even in public. By-election defeats and defections meant that by late 1996 the slim majority won in 1992 had all but disappeared.

By contrast, Labour had put its house in order. Led after 1994 by Tony Blair, the party had swiftly moved to improve its image and performance. He showed his determination to modernise Labour by revising Clause Four of its Constitution (the commitment to nationalisation or public ownership – see p. 151) and by distancing it from the unions. He recognised the need to expand Labour's appeal by seeking support from among the aspirational voters who wanted a better life for themselves and their families, and a chance to acquire the trappings of a comfortable existence. Labour had lost touch with these people in the 1980s and early 1990s, and Tony Blair saw that it would not be successful at the polls unless it expanded its shrinking social base and appealed more widely to Middle England. He rechristened his party as New Labour, just as Bill Clinton had turned the US Democratic Party into the New Democrats a few years earlier. There were other signs that Labour had learned from the electoral success of the Democrats in 1992 and modernisation in the style of Bill Clinton was a recurring theme in its new approach.

Many voters felt that it was 'time for a change' after eighteen years of Conservative rule. As Anthony King observed, the result, a Labour landslide of massive proportions, '[gave] the lie to the old saying that oppositions do not win elections, Governments lose them. The Tories certainly lost, but Labour won.'[23] The Conservatives recorded their worst performance since 1906, slumping to only 165 seats and around 30 per cent of the popular vote. The Liberal Democrats won a healthy 46 seats, their best result since 1929.

2001

After four years of Labour rule, the economy was strong, with inflation, interest rates and unemployment low and the growth rate healthy. Labour had proved its economic competence and introduced a wide-ranging programme of constitutional and other reforms. At first, money for public spending on education and health was kept under very strict limits and there was much disillusion both within the party and beyond because things did not improve as fast as they had hoped. But despite the disappointment of some activists and trade unionists with the government's performance, Tony Blair's personal popularity remained strong. Not for nothing was he labelled by some commentators as 'Teflon Tony'. They noted that whatever scandals arose and however unpopular aspects of the government's policy, his reputation seemed to be unstained.

Labour's continuous lead in the polls throughout the administration was not just brought by voter contentment. The Conservatives under William Hague had inflicted little damage, as the new leader took up a variety of populist concerns, but showed little consistency in their approach. It was too soon for them to provide any convincing alternative, for they remained vulnerable to the accusation that if there were better policies than those being pursued by ministers, then the Conservatives could have introduced them during their long period in office. The public had not forgotten the less glorious days of Conservative rule and was disposed to give Labour longer to solve the country's problems.

The election campaign was widely perceived as dull, with the press playing a role in encouraging this perception. There was never any doubt that Labour would win, as every poll pointed to another Labour landslide. The party had an average lead across the polls of 18 per cent at the start of the campaign, and finished with one of 14 per cent. In the event – and as had happened in 1992 and 1997 – Labour strength was overestimated by the pollsters, but there was no doubt that the Conservatives were about to get a further hiding. In the event, they had a net gain of only one seat, the Liberal Democrats of six, and Labour suffered a net loss of only six.

The one aspect which commentators were quick to point out was the disappointingly low turnout on polling day. At 59 per cent, it was far below the figures recorded in any post-war election. Many voters were disappointed that more progress had not been made in improving public services and could not summon up the enthusiasm to go out and vote for Labour. They saw the outcome as a foregone conclusion and were uninspired by the choice available to them. In particular, Labour supporters in areas such as the northeast, stayed away in large numbers. The government had again done well in winning the support of Middle England, but large elements of the working class – Labour's core support over the years – were disenchanted with Blairism.

Table 4.10 The outcome of the 2001 election in figures

Party	Number of votes	% of votes	Number of seats	% of seats
Labour	10,740,168	42.0	413	62.7
Conservative	8,352,845	32.7	166	25.2
Lib Dem	4,815,249	18.8	52	7.9
SNP	464,314	20.0	5	6.9
Plaid Cymru	195,892	14.0	4	10.0

So why did Labour win again? A summary

Several factors explain the handsome Labour victory, among them:

The strength of the economy. Many voters were doing well, enjoying the consumer boom which gathered pace in the months prior to polling day. The economy was stable, with low levels of unemployment, inflation and interest rates. Many people had reason to 'feel good' about their prospects and polls suggested that Labour was trusted on the economy more than the Conservatives.

The public services. Many people were disappointed that things had not got better in the way they had anticipated in 1997. Labour had not been able to deliver a magical improvement in the provision of education, health and transport, but there was a general feeling that it needed a second chance after the long era of Conservative government. The Opposition had little to say on the public services (more on Europe, taxation, and law and order) and voters seemed to think that there was more chance of Labour effecting an improvement, once the funding began to flow more generously.

The Conservatives were in poor shape. William Hague had carried out a certain amount of organisational modernisation but there remained much work to do to improve the party's image and overhaul its policy. It was divided, not just over Europe but over the sort of party which it wished to be; it was still looking for an identity after its heavy defeat in 1997. Moreover, Hague himself was unable to win public approval. Leading an unpopular party can be difficult, especially when it is as demoralised as his troops were in opposition. He never emerged as a sympathetic figure to many voters. It seems to have been more his manner (appearance, accent etc.) than his inexperience which made him unappealing.

Referendums

A referendum is usually a ballot in which the electorate concerned votes on a single issue 'yes' or 'no', although multi-outcome referendums occasionally take place. The issue may be referred to the people by the government (e.g. Britain's continued membership of the EEC in 1975) or a proposal, passed by parliament, may be submitted to them (e.g. a devolved parliament for Scotland). Referendums are one method of 'direct democracy' and political participation between general elections. Unlike an 'initiative' which stems from the people, a referendum derives from government.

Table 4.11 Experience of national referendums in United Kingdom, 1973–2002

Year	Topic	Turnout (%)	Outcome
1973	Border poll in Northern Ireland: electorate asked if they wished to remain a part of the UK or join the Republic of Ireland.	61	Massive majority to remain in UK
1975	UK's membership of EEC: electorate asked if they wished to stay in the Community or withdraw from it.	64	2/3 majority to stay in (43 % of whole electorate)
1979	Devolution to: Scotland Wales (Each electorate was asked if it wanted a devolved assembly.)	62.8 58.3	Narrow majority for Majority against
1997	Devolution to: Scotland Wales (Each electorate was asked if it wanted a devolved assembly.)	60.1 50.1	Strong majority for Very narrow majority for
1998	Good Friday Agreement on Northern Ireland: voters north (and south) of border asked to endorse the package.	81	Overwhelming majority in favour

Usage

See Table 4.11. The first referendum ever to be held in Britain was in 1973. Since then, several more have taken place. All of them concerned constitutional issues but only one of them directly affected the entire United Kingdom. In 1998 a referendum was held on the future of London government (whether there should be an elected mayor and a Greater London Assembly) and the device has been used to resolve other local issues such as the future of different types of school and council estates, and the linked issue of the level of Council Tax and the provision of services. In the next few years, it is likely that there will be a referendum about whether or not the United Kingdom should join the euro.

There are several reasons why referendums have been used more in recent years:

1 The creation of newly-elected assemblies – whether in London, Scotland, Wales or Northern Ireland – required the support of the voters to provide legitimacy.
2 They seem to be popular with voters who tell the pollsters that they would like to have one on certain issues.
3 If the government is divided on an issue, then a referendum may be used to allow the people to decide; this was the case in 1975, when members of the Labour government were at odds over membership of the EEC.

This does not mean that they receive universal approval. Their merits have been much debated, as we see below.

The case against

1 **They undermine the sovereignty of Parliament.** The voters elect their representatives and a government is formed. This process means that the voters have given their consent to the party in power, authorising it to make decisions on their behalf. Some politicians dislike decisions being taken out of their hands.
2 If the government decides when to hold the referendum, then **it may do so to produce the result it wants**.
3 **The wording of the question is important.** Again, it may be phrased in such a way as to produce the result the government wants.
4 **A balanced debate.** There is great difficulty here, because the opposing sides are unlikely to have the same amount of money and resources.
5 **Information for the voter.** Sufficient information for both cases may be lacking. The Neill report (October 1998) suggested that governments, with so much in the way of resources and influence, should remain neutral.
6 **Referendums are simplistic.** They reduce an issue to a simple 'yes' or 'no'. The issue may be too complex for such a simple response.
7 **Which issues?** There is no limit on how many referendums may be held. Governments have decided to have them on Europe and other constitutional issues. There is no constitutional principle at work here, only the fact that ministers choose the issue and when to hold the vote. Other issues could be the subject of a referendum – eg capital punishment.
8 **Turnout.** This has been low in cases such as the future of Wales and London. A low figure calls into question the legitimacy of the outcome. 'Voter fatigue' is likely if we have too many referendums.

The case for

1 **Participation.** Referendums encourage political participation.
2 **Education.** The campaign prior to a referendum provides a forum for information and education of the citizen.

3 **Decision making**. Referendums resolve major issues by allowing the voters to decide.

4 **Legitimacy**. The result of a referendum is more likely to receive popular support than if the decision is made by Parliament.

5 **Popular support**. Referendums encourage support for the political system by giving voters the opportunity to get involved.

6 **Constitutional issues**. A referendum can reinforce a constitutional change, as with devolution. This is particularly important as such changes are likely to be long term.

7 **Interactions between politicians and the public**. Referendums ensure that politicians engage with the public and the public mood, and do not live in a kind of monastery at Westminster.

Postscript

In February 2002, one political journalist on BBC News 24 suggested that a referendum on the euro might take a different form to the one generally expected. This would be what might be called an **enabling referendum** – i.e. the government asking for the electorate's consent to enter the European common currency when ministers believe that the time is ripe. A referendum like this, if the answer was 'yes', would not lead to automatic adoption of the euro as the national currency.

REFERENCES

1 P. Norris, *Britain Votes 2001*, Oxford University Press.
2 R. Worcester and R. Mortimore, *Explaining Labour's Second Landslide*, Politico's, 2001.
3 D. Butler and D. Kavanagh, *The British General Election of 1997*, Macmillan, 1997.
4 D. Butler and D. Kavanagh, *The British General Election of 2001*, Palgrave 2002.
5 As note 3 above.
6 D. Butler and D. Stokes, *Political Change in Britain*, Macmillan, 1996.
7 D. Kavanagh, *British Politics: Continuities and Change*, Oxford University Press, 1985.
8 *Times Higher Education Supplement*, 18 November 1994.
9 As note 6 above.
10 B. Sarlvik and I. Crewe, *Decade of Dealignment*, Cambridge University Press, 1983.
11 M. Harrop and W. Miller, *Elections and Voters: A Comparative Introduction*, Macmillan, 1987.
12 P. Dunleavy and C. Husbands, *British Democracy at the Crossroads*, Allen & Unwin, 1985.

13 P. Pulzer, *Political Representation and Elections in Britain*, Allen & Unwin, 1968.

14 R. MacKenzie and A. Silver, *Angels in Marble*, Heinemann, 1968.

15 F. Parkin, *Middle Class Radicalism*, Manchester University Press, 1965.

16 I. Crewe, 'Voting and the Electorate' in *Developments in British Politics 4*, Macmillan, 1993.

17 A. Heath *et al.*, *Understanding Political Change: The British Voter 1964–1987*, Pergamon, 1991.

18 As note 13 above.

19 As note 17 above.

20 W. J. Miller, *Voting and the Electorate* in Dunleavy *et al.* *Developments in British Politics 3*, Macmillan 1990.

21 As note 3 above.

22 J. Cole, *As it Seemed to Me*, Weidenfield & Nicholson, 1995.

23 A. King, *Daily Telegraph*, 3 May 1997.

USEFUL WEB SITES

BBC vote 2001: **www.news.bbc.co.uk/vote2001/** This contains comprehensive coverage of the general election in 2001 including the main issues, key seats and prominent personalities. It also includes audio and video clips.

BBC vote 2001: **www.news.bbc.co.uk/vote2001/results_constituencies** This provides full results by party and by constituency of the June 2001 general election.

SAMPLE QUESTIONS

1(a) Why are elections important in a democracy?

(b) Why has the turnout in British elections been in decline in recent years?; or Why was the turnout in 2001 so low in the British general election?

2(a) Using Table 4.12 (overleaf), explain why an electoral system based on pure proportionality might have resulted in a hung Parliament.

(b) Using the table, as well as your own knowledge, consider reasons why the Liberal Democrats have been among the most consistent supporters of electoral reform)

(c) Consider arguments for and against retaining 'first past the post' for use in British general elections.

Table 4.12 Seats won in the 2001 general election

Party	Seats won under the existing simple plurality system	% of votes cast	Seats that would have been won under a strictly proportional system
Conservatives	166	31.7	209
Labour	412	40.7	268
Liberal Democrats	52	18.3	121
Others	29	9.3	61

Note: the seats that would have been won have not been calculated according to particular electoral system, but according to pure proportionality throughout the UK.

Electoral systems

AIMS OF THIS CHAPTER

➤ To consider the key concepts that shape the various types of electoral system.

➤ To assess the possible requirements of any electoral system.

➤ To examine the workings of each of the available systems and their perceived advantages and disadvantages.

Types of electoral system

Globally, there are many types of electoral system. They can be classified into four main groups:
- simple plurality;
- majoritarian;
- proportional;
- hybrid.

Simple plurality

Simple plurality systems operate within single member constituencies. To get elected, a candidate is required simply to gain just one more vote than any of the other candidates (see Table 5.1) Such systems operate in the United Kingdom, USA and Canada.

Table 5.1 Voting proportions under the simple plurality system

Votes cast	% of votes cast
Candidate A – 40,000	40
Candidate B – 39,000	39
Candidate C – 21,000	21
Total – 100,000	100

Majoritarian

Majoritarian systems usually operate with single member constituencies. 'Majority' means 'the greater part, the bulk . . . ' As the word 'majoritarian' suggests, the aim is to ensure that the winning candidate possesses an absolute majority of the votes cast – more than 50 per cent of the votes in the constituency. This total is therefore greater than the sum of the votes cast for all of the other candidates.

The aim of such systems is to avoid the biggest limitation of simple plurality whereby a candidate may be elected by merely gaining one more vote than his/her nearest competitor (see Table 5.2).

Table 5.2 Voting proportions under the majoritarian system

Votes cast	% of votes cast
Candidate A – 51,000	51
Candidate B – 40,000	40
Candidate C – 9,000	9
Total – 100,000	100

The three types of majoritarian systems to be covered here are:
- the alternative vote;
- the supplementary vote;
- the second ballot.

Proportional (proportional representation)

In systems of proportional representation (PR), the aim is to create an elected assembly in which the seats won by the political parties are in proportion to the total votes cast for each party in the country as a whole. In its purest form, this system would use the whole of the UK as a single constituency. In addition, the political parties would have each produced their list of candidates in order of preference. Such a basic model of PR in the 1997 UK general election would have produced the result shown in Table 5.3 in the competition for 659 seats.

Table 5.3 Voting proportions under the proportional representation system

	% Vote	Proportion of seats	Actual seats
Labour	43.2	286	418
Conservative	30.7	202	165
Lib Democrat	16.8	110	46
Others	9.3	61	30
Total	100	659	659

The second aim of PR systems is to provide voters with a choice at local or regional level between different individual candidates and different political parties. As a consequence PR systems use multi-member constituencies.

These two aims of proportional representation and voter choice are ideals. However, the inherent tensions between these two conflicting aims results in compromises in the PR systems. For example on the one hand, the division of the country into multi-member constituencies provides the voter with choices

within the constituency. However, on the other hand, this compromises the ideal of electing an assembly that provides each political party with a proportionate number of seats in relation to the votes it has gained throughout the country. The systems that will be covered here are:
- The closed list;
- The open list;
- The single transferable vote.

Hybrid systems

These electoral systems usually combine the characteristics of the **simple plurality** and **proportional** systems. The two most well-known are:
- The additional member;
- The alternative vote plus.

Requirements of an electoral system

The rest of this chapter on electoral systems may be used as an exercise for Assessment objective AO2. Turn to p. 87 and complete the exercise[1]. Having done so, analyse and evaluate tthe electoral systems that follow in relation to the requirements listed in the exercise. You could also consider them in relation to the issue of electoral reform in the UK (chapter 17).

Simple plurality system: single member

This system is used for elections to the House of Commons and in local government. Each constituency in the United Kingdom elects one candidate to sit as a Member of Parliament. In the 1997 general election, 659 MPs were elected. The candidate with the most votes wins the seat. Therefore with the three main parties usually competing in each constituency, it often happens that the winning candidate may secure less than 50 per cent of the votes cast. The system is sometimes called 'first past the post' (FPTP), although there is no clearly defined post. More accurate is single member, simple plurality (SMSP), though the label 'winner takes all' sums up what actually happens.

For
- It usually results in strong, stable, single-party government: for example, Labour gained a majority of 179 in the 1997 general election.
- It preserves a strong link between the MP and his constituents.
- It is simple, efficient and easily understood.
- It sustains an essentially two-party system which is a traditional element in British politics
- It gives a clear mandate to a party which has won outright to implement the policies in its manifesto (this would not be the case with a coalition government).

Against
- Every party elected to form a government since 1945 has had less than 50 per cent of the total votes cast in the general election (see Table 4.8).
- 'Wasted' votes abound.
- Some MPs win their seats while gaining less than 50 per cent of the votes cast in the constituency.
- At national level, the winning party gains more seats than its total number of votes justifies; for example, in 1997 Labour gained 419 seats out of 659 (63 per cent of the seats) but gained 43 per cent of the total votes cast.
- Third parties in the UK are unfairly treated. For example, in 1997 the Liberals won 46 seats out of 659 (only 7 per cent) but gained 16.8 per cent of the total votes cast.
- The system perpetuates two-party and adversarial politics.

Majoritarian

The alternative vote (AV)

This system elects a single member for the constituency (as in SMSP) but demands that he or she secures 50 per cent or more of the votes cast. It is used in elections to the Australian House of Representatives.

On the ballot paper, the voters may list their preferences although they are not obliged to. If a candidate receives 50 per cent or more first preferences, he or she is elected. If not, the candidate with the lowest number of first preferences is eliminated, and his or her votes are redistributed to the other candidates. If no candidate achieves 50 per cent of the votes after this, then the candidate with the next lowest number of votes after this redistribution is eliminated and his/her second preferences are redistributed. This procedure is continued until one candidate gains 50 per cent or more of the vote.

For
- It retains constituency representation.
- It ensures that the winning candidate has a majority of the votes cast in the constituency.
- It is simple and easily understood.
- It provides the voters with choices.
- It reduces the number of 'wasted votes'.
- It makes strong government likely, without the need for coalitions.

Against
- It does not guarantee a proportional result.
- It results in disproportionate support for centre parties – often the voters' second choice.
- It can produce disproportionate results.

The supplementary vote (SV)

In this system the voter is allowed only two preferences. As with AV, a candidate winning 50 per cent or more of the first preferences in the initial ballot is automatically elected. However, if no candidate gains 50 per cent or more first preferences, the two candidates with the highest number of first preferences stay in the race but the rest are eliminated. The second preferences from the eliminated candidates are redistributed among the two leaders. The candidate now gaining the greater number of voters secures the seat even if he or she does not gain 50 per cent or more of the votes cast.

For (similar points to the AV system)
- It is easy to understand.
- It retains constituency representation.
- It avoids a third-placed candidate emerging, as only the top two candidates are retained after counting first preferences.
- There are fewer 'wasted votes' than in simple plurality.
- It is likely to produce strong government.

Against (similar points to the AV system)
- It does not ensure a proportionate result.
- It would give some 'help' to third parties, e.g. Liberal Democrats, but not to any great extent.

The second ballot

Two separate votes take place. In the first ballot, the voters have one vote, that is, for their first choice candidate. If no candidate gains 50 per cent or more of the votes cast then a second ballot is held, usually a week or few days later. There are possible variations in procedure for this – in some cases, only the winner and the second placed candidate in the first ballot are allowed to stand (ensuring an absolute majority for the winner of the second ballot), in others there may be a threshold in the first ballot – perhaps 10 per cent – to allow the candidates achieving this figure to stand in the second ballot.

The second ballot is used in France for general elections; the threshold for candidates in the first ballot is 12.5 per cent. It is also used in some presidential elections, as in Austria.

For (similar points to the AV system)
- It allows for increased voter choice, because there are two separate votes.
- It ensures that successful candidates represent a majority choice.
- It retains constituency representation.

Against (similar points to the AV system)
- It does not produce a proportionate result.

- It is still unfair to small political parties.
- It can encourage pacts between parties; after the first ballot, parties may withdraw their candidate in the hope that votes will go to an ally.

Proportional

Party lists in general

Lists may be closed or open. Both systems operate using large multi-member constituencies. Each party submits a list of candidates for each constituency. In a country with a small population (e.g. Israel, with 5 million people) the whole country may be regarded as a single constituency. For larger countries such as Sweden, the whole country is divided into multi-member constituencies; in the case of Sweden, on average, eleven members are returned per constituency.

A percentage threshold may be in place. In Sweden a party must gain either 4 per cent of the national vote or 12 per cent of the vote in a constituency before it gains a seat.

Closed party lists (as used in South Africa, Spain, Argentina and Israel)

The ballot paper consists of a number of parties and one vote is cast for the preferred party. The votes are totalled for each party and seats are allotted according to the proportion of votes cast. If a party gains 40 per cent of the total votes, then it is entitled to 40 per cent of the seats. The candidates on each party's list will have been placed in the party's order of preference and the top 40 per cent will be elected.

For
- It produces a proportionate result – as near as possible.
- It is easy to understand.
- It is likely to benefit smaller parties.
- It does not necessarily lead to the disproportionate influence of small parties, because safeguards such as thresholds can be built in.
- By-elections are not necessary if an MP dies or resigns.
- It may lead to coalition government.

Against
- It breaks the close link of individual MP to one constituency.
- There is no allowance for voter choice of candidate.
- It gives the parties considerable power to determine the placing of candidates on the list.
- It produces 'weak, coalition' governments.
- There may still be some disproportionality, if thresholds are used.

Open party lists (as used in Finland and Sweden: Luxembourg and Switzerland operate especially open and flexible methods)

Each party submits a list of its candidates to the electorate. The voter may have several votes and use them across different party lists. Seats are allotted to those candidates with the most personal votes.

For (some similar points to closed lists)
- It allows voter choice of candidate.
- It usually yields a proportionate result.
- It is easy to understand.
- It is likely to benefit small parties.
- It can have safeguards, such as a threshold.
- By-elections are not necessary.
- Coalition governments may be the outcome.

Against (some similar points to closed lists)
- It breaks the close link between MPs and their constituencies.
- It produces 'weak, coalition governments'.
- It still produces disproportionality, if thresholds are used.
- It usually results in coalition governments and therefore can produce problems regarding party manifesto promises and mandates from the electorate for particular policies.

The single transferable vote (STV)

This system is used in Eire, in Northern Ireland for elections to the European Parliament and to the National Assembly, and in Malta. It operates multi-member constituencies. Parties may submit as many candidates as there are seats to be contested in each constituency. Voters may list all candidates in order of preference, just some, or just vote for one.

For each constituency, a formula known as the Droop Quota is used to calculate the number of votes needed by a candidate in order to be elected. The formula for the Quota is:

$$Q = \left(\frac{\text{total votes cast}}{\text{number of seats} + 1} \right) + 1$$

In a 5-member constituency in which 360,000 electors cast their votes the quota would be 60,001.

In the first phase of the count any candidate gaining 60,001 or more first preferences would be elected. Usually, at least one candidate will be elected at this stage. He or she will almost certainly have gained more votes than were needed to achieve the quota. These 'surplus' votes are not wasted, but redistributed proportionately among the other candidates on the basis of the second preferences (no. 2 positions on the ballot papers). This process may lead to the election of another candidate. The next stage is the elimination of the bottom candidate and the redistribution of his second preferences. Elimination from the bottom and redistribution continue until all the five vacancies have been filled.

For
- It retains the link between MP and constituents, although in the setting of a multi-member constituency; it therefore gives voters a choice of MPs from whom to seek help.
- It ensures a broadly proportional result.
- It provides voter choice, both of candidates and parties.
- It produces coalition government.

Against
- The link of the MP to a particular constituency is limited in multi-member constituencies.
- The creation of multi-member constituencies reduces the proportionality of the result.
- Parties still retain much power to choose candidates.
- It is seen as a very complex system and procedure – difficult for voters to fully understand.
- It creates 'weak, coalition government'.
- There are problems re the mandate, if a coalition is formed.

Hybrid

Additional member system (AMS)

This is a mixed system combining the elements of simple plurality and proportional representation. It is sometimes called the two-vote system. One vote is cast for the choice of constituency candidate in a single-member constituency. This is the simple plurality element. The second vote, cast at the same time as the first, is for a party, which provides the proportional element. Each party has a list of candidates, i.e. potential non-constituency members, or Additional Members; the lists are drawn up on a national or regional basis.

From the first vote, in each constituency a candidate is elected by a simple majority (SMSP). This part of the election is counted and completed first. The second votes are then totalled for each party on a national or regional basis. It is this second vote that is designed to produce a proportional result overall. The proportion of the vote won by each party on this second vote is compared with their share of seats won in the constituency elections. Where, for example, a party has gained few constituency seats but has faired better on the second vote, a 'topping-up' of additional members takes place.

Germany is usually held up as the model for this system. It has been used since 1949 in West Germany and in the re-unified Germany since 1990. For elections to the Bundestag, half of the members are elected from the 336 constituencies. The other half – the additional members – are elected from the lists on a proportional system based on each *Land* or state (e.g. Bavaria). The German model operates a threshold for the 'topping-up' process. To qualify, a party must win either 5 per cent of the second vote or at least 3 constituency seats on the first vote.

For
- The voter has some choice – two votes.
- It retains MP–constituency link.
- It comprises simple plurality and proportionality.
- It has worked well in Germany since 1949.
- It prevents gross over-representation of parties in the assembly.
- It (according to some commentators) offers a sensible compromise for reform in the UK system.
- It is likely to produce a coalition government.

Against
- Additional members have no constituency and so are not immediately accountable to the voters who elected them.
- It creates two different types of MP
- Candidates in the first vote may still be elected with less than 50 per cent of the votes cast in the constituency.
- Parties retain considerable power over the choice of candidates, especially for the additional members.
- It requires large constituencies so diminishing the MP–constituency link.
- It is likely to produce coalition government.

Alternative vote plus (or top-up) system

This system was recommended by the Jenkins inquiry which reported in late 1998. It combines the alternative vote with the additional member system, as follows:

1 The first vote is to elect an MP for the constituency. This is done on an AV basis providing voter choice. (In AMS, a simple plurality is used.) Most MPs are elected this way.
2 The voter then has a second, separate and single vote for a party on a regional basis. This is the plus or top-up element. The purpose here is to elect a number of additional MPs in proportion to the votes cast for the parties in the region. Between 10 per cent and possibly 25 per cent of MPs would be elected in this way.

For

Similar points to AMS but also:

- The additional or 'top-up' members would provide representation for a 'wider constituency'.
- It would be less likely than the German system to produce a coalition government. Strong and stable single-party government might be maintained.

Against

There are similar objections to AMS, but also some see it as a threat to single-party government. This was the line taken by the Conservative Party.

The Jenkins proposal (main points)

- **Single-member constituencies**: Boundaries across the UK to be re-drawn to create between 530 and 560 constituencies. Between 80 and 85 per cent of the MPs would be elected to the House of Commons in this way. AV. system of voting to be used.
- **'Top-up' seats**: These would make up the additional 15–20 per cent of the MPs to be elected to the Commons. This would be done via regional lists, as in the additional member system. There would be between 1 and 3 of these per area. Voting would be by a semi-open list system; voters would either choose a candidate from the party list or choose one party.
- **The 'Top-up' areas** would be based on the counties and cities in England, and in the electoral areas for AMS in Scotland and Wales. Northern Ireland would have AV plus also.

In The Times on 31 August 2000, Lord Jenkins conceded for the first time that his electoral reform proposals would be abandoned by Labour. He recognised that the party's national policy forum had effectively ruled out adopting the 'AV plus' system. The report speculated that Labour would hold the promised referendum on electoral reform for Westminster elections, but that it would be the non-proportional Australian-style 'AV' system that would be voted on (see Chapter 17 on electoral reform).

FURTHER READING

C. Robinson, *Voting Behaviour and Electoral Systems*, Hodder & Stoughton Access to Politics series, 1998.
D. Watts, *British Electoral Systems: Achieving a Sense of Proportion*, Politics Association/SHU Press, 2000.

USEFUL WEB SITES

Charter 88 **www.charter88.org.uk**

Electoral Reform Society **www.electoral-reform.org.uk**

SAMPLE QUESTIONS

1 The following list gives possible requirements taken from a wide range of different views. Please note that some of these requirements are therefore conflicting and may even be incompatible. No one system can fulfil all of these requirements.

Complete the questionnaire *before* you study electoral systems. Respond to each with 'Yes', 'Unsure' or 'No'.

An electoral system should:

(a)   be understood by the voter;

(b)   be easily and efficiently operated;

(c)   provide voters with a choice of candidates and parties;

(d)   ensure a close relationship between representatives and their constituents;

(e)   ensure representatives are accountable to their constituents;

(f)   reduce the number of wasted votes;

(g)   provide voters with more than one vote;

(h)   enhance the role of the individual voter and promote public confidence in the political process;

(i)   produce an elected assembly representative of the views of the electorate;

(j)   produce strong and stable government;

(k)   produce a government that is fairly representative of the views of the electorate;

(l)   ensure that the major parties gain fair representation but not over representation;

(m) ensure smaller parties gain fair representation;

(n)   have safeguards to ensure that parties with no support gain no representation;

(o)   provide a clear mandate for the elected government;

(p)   ensure a fair system for all.

2 (a)   What are the main features of the Alternative Vote system?

(b)   In Britain, what has been the impact of the simple plurality system on representation?

(c)   Describe and explain why new electoral systems have been established in some parts of the United Kingdom, but not for elections to the House of Commons.

Part III

REPRESENTATION

Pressure groups

6

AIMS OF THIS CHAPTER

➤ To outline the variety, number and categories of pressure groups.

➤ To distinguish between pressure groups and political parties.

➤ To consider the ways in which pressure groups campaign.

➤ To assess the factors that determine pressure group success or otherwise.

➤ To evaluate their contribution to democracy.

General elections produce a government and this sets the basic context for decision making over the next few years. Election pledges are notoriously simplified. The formation of policies in government is complex, requiring consultation between ministers, civil servants and representatives of those interests that are likely to be affected. The latter are leaders of **pressure groups**.

Pressure groups are not a new phenomenon. The nineteenth century witnessed the strong growth and development of such groups. For example, the Anti-Corn Law League, established in 1839, aimed to persuade governments to repeal laws which kept the price of corn, and therefore bread at artificially high prices for the benefit of landowners.

> **pressure groups**
> Organisations formed by people who wish to protect or further a common interest. They may campaign widely like political parties but they aim to influence government only on certain policy issues, and are not attempting to form a government.

In 1866, the Howard League for Penal Reform was established to campaign for more humane conditions in prisons. In the twentieth century, particularly after 1945, many groups developed to defend and promote interests that were likely to be affected by government policies. The specialist input of such groups in the creation of policy, was also helpful to successive governments.

Variety and number

It is probable that over half the population of Britain belongs to a pressure group. In the box below, we see an illustration of a person who belongs to several different groups.

Michael Topps

1 Teacher: Member of the Association of Teachers and Lecturers (ATL);
2 Car driver: Member of the Automobile Association (AA);
3 Interest in Victorian period: Member of Victorian Society;
4 Politics teacher: Member of the Politics Association;
5 Beer drinker: Member of CAMRA.

Many people belong to what amounts to a pressure group. Mr Topps belongs to the ATL and the AA for the protection that it gives to him as a teacher and a car driver. Although he has not been involved directly in conservation projects undertaken by the Victorian Society, he attends events. He is actively involved in the Politics Association and CAMRA. Many other adults have membership of a variety of organisations, without actually realising that they are members of a pressure group! The groups to which Mr Topps belongs, have been established for several years. However, some groups are short-lived. In 1992, the Directory of British Associations listed in excess of 7,000 groups with national recognition. This figure is a very conservative estimate for the country as a whole, for short-lived groups and strictly local groups would not have been included.

The preoccupations of pressure groups are hugely diverse. Some are large, powerful and permanent and instantly recognisable: for example, the British Medical Association (BMA), Confederation of British Industry (CBI), and Trades Union Congress (TUC). They have considerable resources, employ hundreds of people, and have membership lists in tens of thousands.

At the other end of the spectrum are far more specialised groups – e.g. The Tall Persons Club of Great Britain and the English Collective of Prostitutes.[1] Small groups may operate at a very local level, as in the case of a village, where a landowner planned to develop part of his estate. This would have involved demolishing over 10 houses that he rented out. The tenants would have been re-housed, but they did not want to be. They formed a pressure group, gained local media attention and won. Such local groups are sporadic; they succeed or fail, and then disband.

Some pressure groups operate globally. Amnesty International, formed in Britain in 1961, campaigns for the release of people imprisoned without trial throughout the world. In 2002, the New York-based pressure group Human Rights Watch made the news when it published a report on human rights in 66 countries, arguing that the USA's response to the September 2001 terrorist attacks had encouraged many of these countries to introduce repressive measures. The immediate concern was for the Al-Qa'eda prisoners taken by the USA to Camp X-Ray in Cuba. Members of the Red Cross were subsequently sent to Cuba to investigate and report back.

Pressure groups and political parties

Pressure groups are sometimes referred to as 'protest groups', lobby groups or 'interest groups'. For some, the word 'pressure' implies the use of coercion but this does not usually happen. Others are uneasy about 'interest' as a term to describe groups seeking to promote a cause of no personal gain to themselves.

The definition of groups given in the box on p. 90 provides a starting point but cannot accommodate both a large organisation like the TUC and the tiny local group in the village hall trying to protest against the demolition of their homes. Below are some definitions of pressure groups by leading writers on the subject:

> A pressure group is an organisation which seeks to influence the details of a comparatively small range of public policies and which is not a faction of a recognised political party. (R. Baggott)[2]

> In general, pressure groups are social aggregates with some level of cohesion and shared aims which attempt to influence the political decision-making process. (A. Ball and F. Millard)[3]

> ... any group attempting to bring about political change whether through government activity or not, and which is not a political party in the sense of being represented at that time in the legislative body. (F. Castles)[4]

The definitions by Bagott and Castles focus on the apparently clear distinction between pressure groups and political parties. Pressure groups do not try to win general elections, although some have fielded candidates at by-elections to gain publicity. At the 1997 general election, the Referendum Party fielded 547 candidates. It called itself a political party, but it was a pressure group, because it campaigned on one issue only, Britain's membership of the European Union (EU). It wanted a referendum, hoping that the British public would vote to pull out of the EU. Political parties, because they want to form a government, have a set of policies on most major issues. Even if a political party is unlikely to win the general election, like the Liberal Democrats in 2001, it is essential to have policies on major issues because forming a government is its eventual objective.

Generally then, pressure groups do not fight elections. Although the powerful British Medical Association does not field candidates at elections, it attempts to influence government policy on the health service which involves a variety of issues from waiting list times to staff shortages and their implications. Other groups may be more specific; Action on Smoking and Health (ASH) has campaigned vigorously to reduce the popularity of cigarette smoking. While political parties usually have broad interests, pressure-group activity is narrow and highly specific. Nevertheless, while the BMA and ASH are continually involved in pressure-group activity, other groups tend to operate in defence of their interests. This has been traditionally the case with the British Field Sports

Society that has only concerned itself with hunting and attempts to stop it. In recent years, the proposed legislation against 'hunting with dogs' along with other 'countryside' issues has made it more active and it has become involved with the Countryside Alliance. Other pressure groups – by their very nature – have a wide range of policy interests, for example the CBI and the TUC.

Distinctions between political parties and pressure groups are not always clear-cut. Historically the Labour Party has had a very close relationship with the trade union movement, whereas the Conservative party has had close links with business. In each case, funding from the pressure group to the party has been an important element in the relationship. In more recent years both parties have distanced themselves from these interests. This has particularly been the case with New Labour since 1994 under Tony Blair's leadership.

Pressure groups of a type exist within political parties. These are **party factions**. The main political parties claim to be 'broad churches' in that they accommodate and represent a wide variety of opinion. The Labour party does not now have the proliferation of factions that it had in the 1960s and 1970s; the Campaign Group and Tribune Group are current examples. Examples within the Conservative Party are the Tory Reform Group and the Charter Movement.

> **party factions**
> Tendencies, sections or groups within parties that focus on particular areas of policy, while supporting the aims of the party as a whole.

PRESSURE GROUPS AND PARTIES: A SUMMARY

Pressure groups

1 Represent one particular issue/interest or relatively narrow set of issues/interests
2 Focus on a single or relatively narrow set of issues.
3 Occasionally field candidates at elections but only for publicity
4 Aim to influence government policy

Political parties

1 Accommodate a broad coalition of interests within one organisation
2 Have policies for most major issues
3 Field candidates at elections to gain representation in Parliament.
4 Aim to form a government

Social movements

Movements are closely related to pressure groups. A social movement consists of a large body of people united around a central idea or issue with the aim of changing attitudes and institutions along with policies. Their activities often begin at grass-roots level and develop into national crusades. Their organisation is often loose, flexible and has no hierarchy. Examples that fall within this definition include the protest movements of the 1960s in the USA. These were the black civil-rights campaigners, women's liberation and student movements that combined to form a powerful lobby whose unifying idea was for the USA to end the war in Vietnam. Examples of movements focusing on a single issue in Britain have been the animal rights campaigners who have taken up a range of causes on animal welfare.

More recently an environmental movement composed of a wide range of groups as well as a number of Green political parties has developed in Western Europe including Britain. The environmental movement consists of:

Traditional nature conservation movements

Examples include: The Royal Society for the Protection of Birds (RSPB), The National Trust and The Victorian Society. The main thrust of these groups is conservation. This may be to protect species in danger of extinction (e.g. the RSPB) or to protect buildings in danger of demolition (e.g. the Victorian Society).

'New Left' movements[5]

Examples include: Greenpeace, Friends of the Earth and Earth First. These groups have a more radical agenda. They aim to place ecological and social needs above economic policy and economic growth as the top priorities of government and society. They may use direct action.

There are considerable differences between old and the new social movements. An old social movement was the labour movement of the nineteenth century. It comprised many individuals and groups who pressed governments for change to improve harsh industrial conditions of work. New social movements, be they the women's movement or the environmental movement, are new

> 'in the sense that they challenge a new set of dominant ideas and constellations of power ... Like the preceding social movements, they have a radical edge and visions of a world transformed by their demands ... [They] are characterised by their informal modes of organization: their attachment to changing values as a

Table 6.1 Old and new social movements

Old social movements	New social movements
Usually concerned with economic issues	'Post-materialist' issues – e.g. environment
Often supported by working class	Much support from middle classes
Possessed an organisational structure	Built around informal networks
Relied more on representation	Rely more on participation
Attempt to influence via political process	Use of direct action – symbolic protests
Example: labour movement in the nineteenth century	*Example*: environmental movement

central part of their political challenge: their commitment to open and ultra-democratic, participating modes of organization . . . and their willingness to engage in direct action to stop outcomes which they see as harmful.[6]

Types of pressure group

The diversity and number of pressure groups has made generalisation and categorisation difficult for political scientists. One of the earliest attempts was made by J. D. Stewart[7] who distinguished between sectional and cause groups:

Sectional

These groups seek to protect and represent the common interests of their membership. Membership is restricted to those with a shared background or carrying out a common socio-economic function. As they primarily work to protect the self-interest of their members, as defined by the group, they are also known as 'protective' or 'interest' groups. Confusingly some writers use the term 'interest groups' to refer to all pressure groups.

Members of these groups are directly concerned with the work done on their behalf because they stand to gain from it both professionally and financially. Employers' associations, professional bodies and trade unions are all sectional groups. Examples include the Society of Motor Manufacturers and Traders, the Law Society and the National Union of Mineworkers.

Cause

These groups primarily operate to further the interests of others or the public interest as defined by the group. Membership is open to those who support the cause. Unlike sectional groups, their aims are not necessarily of direct benefit to their membership. They are also referred to as promotional groups. Examples of the many cause groups are: Shelter (homelessness), Age Concern (the elderly), and Campaign for Nuclear Disarmament.

Wyn Grant[8] has subdivided cause groups into three types:
- **Sectional cause** groups, which aim to protect and improve the interests of a particular section of society e.g. Age Concern (the interests of the elderly) and the Child Poverty Action Group (interests of children in poverty).
- **Attitude cause** groups, which aim to inform, educate and change people's attitudes to particular issues. The environment groups are prime examples of this.
- **Political cause** groups, which campaign for change to the political system. Charter 88, since 1988, has campaigned for a written constitution, reform of the House of Lords, a Bill of Rights and reform of the electoral system to the House of Commons.

Difficulties with the sectional/cause distinction

1 **Some groups in both categories**. Professional bodies aim to protect the interests of their members but may also campaign on what seem to be 'Cause' group issues. For example, the British Medical Association has pressed the government for tougher measures to deter smoking. The Association of Teachers and Lecturers (ATL) has recently linked up with the Commission of British Muslims and Islamophobia in an effort to reduce prejudices following the terrorist attacks on 11 September 2001.

2 **Some sectional groups support causes or establish cause groups**. The British Dental Association is a sectional group that protects its members but supports pro-water fluoridation groups. The Royal College of Physicians set up Action on Smoking and Health (ASH) in 1971 to campaign against smoking.

3 **Which is more influential?** The assumption frequently made with this classification, that sectional groups are more influential than cause groups is not necessarily the case. Many sectional groups are very powerful, but others are nothing like as influential as they would like to be – for example, those representing pensioners. Moreover, since the early 1970s, there has been a significant growth in cause-group activity, particularly in the environmental sphere (see Table 6.3). Media publicity and the growth of direct action have given them a much higher profile. In addition, many cause groups have used sophisticated marketing strategies to increase membership using mail-order methods. They are basically in the protest business. Many people have begun to support cause groups like Amnesty International because they are not party political. There are also psychological and social explanations for the growth of cause groups. The growth in the material standard of living of an increasing

Table 6.2 **The growth in membership of leading British environmental groups since 1970**

	1971	1981	1989	1995
National Trust	280,000	1,050,000	2,100,000	2,300,000
Wildlife Trust[a]	64,000	140,000	250,000	260,000
Royal Society for the Protection of Birds	100,000	440,000	850,000	890,000
World Wide Fund for Nature	12,000	60,000	200,000	210,000
Woodland Trust	–	20,000	150,000	150,000 (1993)
Greenpeace	–	30,000	320,000	410,000 (1993)
Friends of the Earth	1,000	18,000	120,000	230,000 (1993)
Council for the Protection of Rural England	21,000	24,000	45,000	45,000
Ramblers Association	22,000	37,000	87,000	94,000

Source: Adapted from D. Toke, 'Power and environmental pressure groups', *Talking Politics*, vol. 9: 17, 1996.

[a] Formerly the Royal Society for Nature Conservation.

proportion of the populations of the developed world has led to the development of post-material values. Basically, more of the public are shifting their attention away from economic, financial and security concerns to the non-economic and quality of life values of a post-industrial society.

Insider and outsider groups

Wyn Grant[9] has made a different distinction, that between 'insider' and 'outsider' groups. He focuses on their relationship to central decision makers, more than on their status and strategies.

Insider groups

Groups may want the status of being 'on the inside', but only governments may grant it. It confers access to decision makers in government. These groups abide by 'the rules of the game'. Grant classifies insider groups into three categories:

1 **Prisoner groups** dependent on government assistance or support – e.g. English Heritage (a government-appointed body which conserves buildings/places of historic interest). Such groups are regularly consulted over matters relevant to them.

2 **Low-profile insider groups** which work mainly behind the scenes. The CBI was an example of this group, but the BMA now provides a better one. These have regular contact with government on a range of relevant issues.

3 **High-profile insider groups** which seek prominence in the media in order to gain public support to strengthen their exchanges with government; the CBI has shifted to this strategy in recent years. The National Farmers Union (NFU) has assumed this status following the BSE crisis and the foot and mouth outbreak in 2001.

Outsider groups

These groups either prefer not to come into regular contact with government or are attempting to gain insider status and have as yet failed to do so. Again, Grant subdivides them into:

1 **Potential insiders** which have the capacity to gain insider status, but may need to adopt a more responsible strategy in order to gain the attention of government. They may need a change in the political climate related to their concerns or a change of government. This was the case with the Institute for Public Policy Research which was an outsider group before 1997. After the general election they gained insider status. Potential insider groups often work with opposition parties.

2 **Outsiders by necessity** which lack the necessary knowledge and skills required for success in gaining meaningful access to government officials. Sometimes these groups make demands that undermine their credibility.

3 **Ideological outsider groups** which reject the existing political system, believe that their radical aims can only be achieved by operating as outsiders and often prefer to use direct action. Earth First is an example.

Difficulties with the insider/outsider distinction

1 **Achieving insider status is not difficult**. Jordan *et al.*[10] argue that Grant's model overestimated the difficulty of achieving insider status. This was because it did not distinguish between a group's strategy and status. Page[11] found that 44 per cent of his respondents were of insider status. It is worth noting, however, that many groups with insider status may only be on a consultation list and have little impact on policy formulation. For example, there are approximately 200 groups that are consulted automatically on matters to do with motor bikes; their views are not all regarded as having equal importance.

2 **Strategy choices are limited**. Grant's model assumed that groups have a degree of choice about adopting an insider or outsider strategy. Jordan argued that most groups do not have a real choice. The group's objectives, resources, finance and history are the key determinants.

3 **The simultaneous pursuit of insider and outsider strategies**. Page argued that groups sometimes pursue a 'good cop/bad cop' strategy. For example, a group with 'insider' status might leave its leaders in discussion with government officials whilst organising public demonstrations, letter-writing campaigns or even direct action (all three are outsider tactics). In the mid-1970s, the leaders of farmers' unions who had access to government became anxious when demonstrations by their members about Irish beef imports escalated into physical action with railway lines being ripped out of the ground. Greenpeace, famous for its non-violent direct action methods worldwide, has gradually shifted more towards a dialogue with business and governments. Yet it retains an outsider image, while recruiting high level political and business advisers. This outsider image is sustained by successes like defeating Shell over its plan to dump the Brent Spa oil platform at sea. However, the 'lounge suits' have gradually begun to replace the 'rubber suits'.

4 **The 'new politics' argument**. Some argue that Grant's model was relevant when it was first developed but is no longer applicable now that politics is a 'multi-level, multi-area game'.[12] Table 6.4 indicates the changes in pressure group activity since the 1950s. After the Second World War, most pressure groups were organised around one of the great 'Estates' that represented the key elements of society, the professions, business and labour. There were also a limited number of cause groups. In 2003, society is far more fragmented and

the huge increase in the number and range of pressure groups mirrors this fragmentation. Whereas personal identity was at one time rooted in a professional grouping or a social class, now there are far more possibilities. Support for a particular pressure group can often be a lifelong choice.

In 2003, political activity takes place on a variety of levels, but this does not of itself invalidate Grant's distinction. In many cases, pressure-group activity still seems to continue in a familiar way with insider and outsider strategies and with the powerful groups remaining powerful, like the CBI and the NFU.

Table 6.3 Post-war changes in pressure-group activity

Period	Participants in policy making	Types of pressure-group group activity
1950s	Sectional groups some cause groups	Focused on the executive usually by informal links
1970s	Tripartism. CBI and TUC the main players Number of pressure groups increasing Environmental groups emerging	Focused on the executive but importance of Parliament, courts and media was increasing
1990s	Declining importance of CBI and TUC Numbers of pressure groups increased over a wide range of fields	Use of many areas: Executive, Parliament, courts, media, direct action

Source: Adapted from W. Grant, 'Pressure groups', in *Developments in Politics: An Annual Review*, Vol. 10, Chapter 2, Causeway Press Ltd, 1999.

Pluralism and the case for pressure groups

What is pluralism? Heywood[13] has defined pluralism in this way:

Pluralism can be broadly defined as a belief in, or commitment to, diversity or multiplicity . . . it implies that diversity is healthy and desirable in itself, usually because it safeguards individual freedom and promotes debate, argument and understanding . . . Pluralism, however, is used more narrowly as a theory of distribution of political power. Classical pluralism holds that power is widely and evenly dispersed in society, rather than concentrated in the hands of an elite . . . In this form, pluralism is usually seen as a theory of group politics, in which individuals are largely represented through their membership of organised groups, and in all such groups have access to the policy process.

The democratic deficit

The pluralist view of politics sees pressure groups reducing the democratic deficit. General elections are usually only held every four or five years.

Between elections, pressure groups provide a form of political participation, a means of influencing government, and a means of representation especially for minorities who lack the support of the elected decision makers. There has been a huge growth in the number and variety of groups in recent decades and they allow many people to get involved in political issues who would not otherwise participate.

Group activity has other advantages:

1 In representative democracies, it is usually the majority view that predominates so pressure groups provide the vital function of defending and promoting the rights of minorities.
2 There are many groups competing with one another for influence over policy. These groups have differing views and decision makers are forced to arbitrate. Competition between groups pressuring government often results in a dispersal of power away from the centre.
3 In their relationship with government, pressure groups:
   • provide a link between government and governed;
   • provide expertise in the formulation of policy and assistance with its implementation;
   • hold government to account through the media;
   • gain knowledge of the government's position over the groups concerns and make better informed decisions, e.g. about strategy of their own.
4 Pressure groups raise issues that parties may not have considered, or demand that an issue be given greater consideration. They may also attach themselves more to one party than another on the basis of such pressure.

Criticisms of group activity

Although many commentators would agree that pressure groups have their uses, there are many criticisms of the pluralist model.

Formation

Pluralists assume that forming a pressure group is an easy task and that there are few obstacles in the way. Olsen[14] portrayed 'lobbying' as a public good but recognised that groups that were diffused throughout society, such as consumers, often had to offer 'selective incentives' to ensure sufficient support and sustainable strength. This might mean that many joined not to support the particular interest but were persuaded by the 'special incentives' (see National Trust, p. 101).

Resources

Pluralists also assume that even though the economic strength of groups is variable, all groups can have some access/influence on the policy process. But the large, powerful and well-resourced groups have an advantage. Money is important, but so too are permanent offices and staff; simple activities such as producing leaflets or organising a protest march are expensive, financing a media campaign even more so. Some groups have substantial financial resources via annual membership subscriptions – e.g. trade unions (sectional group) and the Royal Society for the Protection of Birds (cause group). Some of the sick and all of the unemployed lack an organised, well-resourced group.

Lack of internal democracy

Superficially, it may be assumed that pressure groups respond to public opinion and represent the opinions of their membership appropriately. Many groups have no elections for the leadership, and often there is little dialogue between officials and members. Some cause groups are deliberately undemocratic, highly bureaucratic and authoritarian in structure. For example, Rucht[15] points out that Greenpeace is controlled at the international and national levels by a small group. Many groups have a large 'membership' who join for the 'special incentives' like the 2 million members of the National Trust who gain access to many historic sites while merely supporting financially an environmental pressure group; this is 'support', not active membership and participation.

Undemocratic

Pressure groups often represent special interests who campaign against developments that may be in the public interest at large. Briefly, this may mean that the majority is defeated by the minority. Professional associations and trade unions are often criticised for their resistance to change. For example, the BMA fiercely resisted both the foundation of the National Health Service, 1948, and its radical transformation through the Health Service Reform Act, 1990. The teaching unions too had many objections to the Education Act, 1988, which allowed schools to 'opt out' of Local Authority control and introduced the national curriculum.

Similarly, some pressure groups appear to stand in the way of economic and social progress for the majority in order to protect their own minority interests. An example was the ministerial plan to extend the M3 motorway across Twyford Down, an area of scientific interest and natural beauty. Other campaigns have occurred when nuclear power plants or factories have been planned.

Under this criticism too, it is relevant to include the NIMBY (not in my back yard) groups. These have grown in number especially in recent years and are linked with the growth of environmental and conservation movements. For example, the Twyford Down campaigners included many local people who may have joined the group for both sets of motives.

NB. This particular criticism of pressure groups is much open to question. In a democracy, the preservation of minority interests, whether professional or local, is in theory vital. Moreover, although professional associations may appear to stand in the way of reforms, their views may turn out to be correct; there have been examples of insufficient consultation or unwillingness to listen by government. Finally, definitions of what constitutes progress depend on a value judgement, for example, is a motorway or the environment more important?

Pressure group power is largely an illusion?

Marxists are highly critical of the pluralist view. Governments have their own agenda, and are determined to preserve capitalism and the power of the ruling class; they do not act as an 'honest broker' between competing groups. Marxists also argue that a few elite pressure groups, presumably with 'insider' status, connive with government by supporting it to further their own interests. Pressure groups give the illusion of meaningful political participation and so betray their membership.

Pressure-group campaigning

Pressure groups aim to influence policy through their involvement in the political process. Baggott[16] points to three ways in which they do this.

1 They attempt to influence the policy makers, e.g. amend legislation, re-allocate resources.
2 They attempt to influence the government's agenda i.e. have their concerns addressed over particular policies.
3 They attempt to influence public opinion and gain support.

The contexts in which they operate are both within and outside the political system.

Group activities within the political system:

The executive

This includes the whole of the core executive (see Chapter 12) including the Prime Minister, Cabinet Ministers, government departments, civil servants and executive agencies. In creating policy, ministers and civil servants consult interested parties. These contacts may be formal, or informal bilateral/trilateral meetings. At this very early stage, a pressure group may be able to exert considerable influence. When a government Green Paper is issued, further soundings are taken. Once a White Paper is published, then the possibility of influence is low. The final stage is the passage of an Act of Parliament followed by its implementation via the appropriate government department. Pressure groups may well draw attention to any shortcomings of the legislation as it is implemented.

For example, the teaching unions and others drew the government's attention to the difficulties of teaching the whole of the national curriculum in schools after the Education Act, 1988. As a result of representations made, it was very much reduced in size. Access at this level, with senior decision makers is evidence supporting Grant's insider/outsider distinction discussed earlier. There are many other forms of consultation such as advisory committees, Committees of Inquiry and the larger-scale Royal Commissions.

Government ministers and civil servants consult with pressure groups for a number of reasons:
- Consultation is part of the democratic process.
- The specialist knowledge, expertise and sometimes research undertaken by pressure groups can be extremely helpful.
- The cooperation of pressure groups in implementing a policy may be vital – e.g. the BMA and NHS reforms.

Parliament

Baggott's research[17] indicated frequent contact between MPs and pressure groups. Approximately 33 per cent of the groups surveyed made contact every week, and 60 per cent once per month. There are a number of avenues open to pressure groups within Parliament.

- **Private Members Bills** Members of Parliament who win a high place in the ballot for a Private Member's Bill (see Chapter 14) are often approached by pressure groups to introduce a Bill supporting their cause.

- **Select committees** Many groups find themselves on the circulation lists of departmental select committees; some may be asked to give evidence.

- **Political parties** Some pressure groups have traditionally had close links with one political party. Labour has had close links with the trade unions, while the Conservatives have linked themselves to business interests. During the period of Conservative Party dominance from 1979–97, an increasing number of groups, companies and New Right **think tanks** felt encouraged to establish closer links than ever before.

> **think tanks**
> These are organisations set up to research and formulate public policy ideas and press government to adopt them. They range right across the political spectrum and are usually connected to one political party, concerned with all policy areas and have a clear ideological stance.

Other avenues within the political system include the House of Lords, local government and the devolved assemblies in Scotland and Wales, and the courts. The courts have become a more important target of group activity in recent years. Most large pressure groups have legal representatives. In Britain, pressure groups are increasingly likely to use the courts to contest government policy decisions. This growing trend has been encouraged by the primacy of European law and the European Court of Justice. Environmental groups like the World Wide Fund for Nature, have used the courts in order to secure better implementation of international environmental policies. As we shall see, Europe has played an increasingly important part in national pressure group activity in recent decades.

Europe

Lobbying of the European Union has expanded since the early days of British membership of the then European Community, for several reasons:

- the growth of influence of EU institutions over British domestic policy. Lobbying in Europe became essential when the Community was able to extend its policy making to areas previously the sole preserve of national governments, as in the case of the environment;

- measures passed by the EC/EU which have extended that influence, notably the Single European Act (1987), the Maastricht Treaty (1992) and the Amsterdam Treaty (1997);

- the openness of EU institutions by contrast with Whitehall;

- the tendency of pressure groups with common interests from EU countries to create Eurogroups (federations of national pressure groups) or to act together or lobby from a position of strength.

Pressure groups lobby the European Union in three ways. They may put pressure on the national government, hoping that a minister will make a firm stand in the Council of Ministers. They may, as we have seen, act via a eurogroup. Or they may lobby the three main EU institutions involved in the policy-making process, directly. The complex division of responsibility between EU institutions has been conveniently summarised by Simpson,[18] though his simplified version fails to do justice to the growing power of Parliament in the EU machinery. In outline, the Commission proposes, the Parliament discusses and the Council of Ministers implements policy.

Direct lobbying of EU machinery may involve a visit to the Commission, a meeting with one of the British commissioners, a meeting with the local MEP or even attending a meeting of Parliament or one of its committees. In some cases, lobbying is conducted via an office established in Brussels, as with the Law Society and the CBI. Groups also employ the European Court of Justice which interprets European law, to further their campaigns. Rather than lobby it directly, they use it as an arena in which to mount legal challenges. As a result of one such challenge, the Court overruled the British government in

1997 over the Working Time Directive, on grounds of health and safety in the workplace.

The fate of the attempts to abolish fox-hunting

In May 1997, the Labour MP Michael Foster, came first in the ballot for Private Members Bills. A number of anti-hunting pressure groups not only approached him but subsequently helped him to draw up its main proposals. The result was the Wild Animals (Hunting with Dogs) Bill which was introduced in November 1997. The Bill was not passed but in 2002 it was likely to be introduced as a government measure. The pressure groups supporting Foster included the Royal Society for the Prevention of Cruelty to Animals (RSPCA), the League Against Cruel Sports and the International Fund for Animal Welfare. The latter financed a MORI poll in Worcester to test opinion in Foster's constituency and 70 per cent supported the Bill. Michael Foster was returned at the 2001 election with only a 1.5 per cent reduction in his share of the vote.

The Bill was opposed initially by the British Field Sports Society. However, opponents of the Bill became part of a wider opposition to the government's handling of rural issues generally such as the plight of farmers, the right to roam, insufficient public transport and petrol prices. This became known as the Countryside Alliance, an amalgamation of the BFSS, the Countryside Business Group and the Countryside Movement. The strength of the Alliance was reported to have startled ministers when it campaigned in London.

Group activity outside the political system

Pressure groups need the support of public opinion. They may gain public support when they work within the political system if they attract media attention. When working outside the political system they are much more media conscious. Groups have become increasingly aware of how appropriate use of the media may raise public awareness and support. Many of the largest groups now employ professionals to manage their relations with the media.

Groups appeal to the public through the media directly, through marches/demonstrations which gain media attention, or through direct action.

Group campaigns are of two types: long-term, background campaigns, aiming to change public opinion gradually; or short-term, 'fire-brigade' campaigns, aiming to bring an immediate issue to the public's attention. Outsider groups are more likely to operate in this way than insider groups although this is not an 'iron law'.

The main limitation in using the press and broadcasting is the difficulty of sustaining a media campaign for more than a few days. The Snowdrop Campaign to ban the private ownership of handguns after the Dunblane tragedy in 1996 was an exception.

Direct Action

(See Table 6.4 for typology.) 'Direct action' is seen as part of the 'new politics' of a new 'Protest Culture',[19] cutting across a number of issues like animal rights, road building and civil liberties. Garner[20] points out that (direct action) covers a huge variety of actions and should not be thought of as synonymous with illegality. Such action may:
- be outside the formal political process;
- range from legal and non-violent to illegal and violent;
- not be focused on government but on an organisation or company while trying to persuade government through media attention.

Direct action has increased because many people believe that:
- they cannot be heard through conventional channels;
- those in power will never listen;
- Parliament and its MPs cannot be trusted to act on their behalf.

Methods adopted include:
- protest marches – e.g. Countryside Alliance 1998;
- boycotts – e.g. motorists in Germany not buying Shell petrol when Shell was planning to sink the Brent Spar oil platform at sea;
- stunts – less used today, but they can provide useful media attention;
- blockades – e.g. September 2000 when drivers of petrol tankers and lorries including farmers blockaded fuel depots and oil refineries. They were protesting about the high level of tax on petrol at a time when prices were rising rapidly;
- destruction of property – e.g. destruction of genetically engineered crops by the 'Lincolnshire Lollards' in 1998;
- violence against the individual - e.g. demonstrators from the Animal Liberation Front (ALF) have been involved in targeting the Huntingdon Life Sciences Laboratory.

Factors determining the success of pressure group activity

So many factors affect pressure-group success that it is extremely difficult to establish their individual contribution. Victory is not always achieved as a result of their lengthy engagement in lobbying. In November 1998, a ban on the testing of cosmetic ingredients on animals in Britain was introduced. The British Union for the Abolition of Vivisection and the National Anti-Vivisection Society both stated that it was consumers turning to products not created in this way that had more influence than their long-term campaigners. But some specific factors may affect whether a group is believed to be successful or not.

Resources: membership and money

The quantity and quality of membership is important. A large membership provides both strong finances, evidence of strong support and perhaps the ability to engage wider support. Membership of sectional groups, like the NFU and CBI, remains steady from year to year but long-term trends may differ. The

Table 6.4 A typology of direct action

Form of action	Legality	Main objectives
Protest marches	Usually legal	To demonstrate to decision makers the scale of support and concern on an issue
Boycotts	Legal	To inflict commercial punishment on a firm
Stunts	May be illegal	To focus attention on an issue through publicity
Blockades, occupations and other disruptions	Open to civil action and increasingly criminalised	To exert direct pressure or to inhibit or prevent activities
Destruction of property	Illegal	Bringing an activity to an end
Violence against individuals	Criminal	Punish those seen as responsible for 'immoral' acts

Source: Adapted from Wyn Grant, *Developments in Politics: An Annual Review Vol. 10*, Causeway Press, 1999.

NFU has about 150,000 members and an annual income of £20,000,000. For sectional groups, membership density is important. Most doctors are members of the BMA, but teachers are divided across a number of trade unions, with the result that they have often been divided by inter-union competition and thus unable to achieve their objectives.

Yearly membership of cause groups is variable and subscriptions lapse, resulting in a continuous campaign for new members. The World Wide Fund for Nature's income dropped by £3 million between 1989 and 1992 as a result of a 10 per cent loss in membership. The difference in resources between cause groups and sectional groups is often very significant. Good quality membership for cause groups – continuous and active – is often better than large numbers. Grant[21] argues that groups whose membership is drawn from a disadvantaged section of society, are less likely to be effective than a group based on middle-class membership. The latter provide the stronger resources of organisational ability and educational background.

Both sectional and cause groups with huge memberships, like the CBI and Greenpeace respectively, often find themselves divided internally over strategy, issues and methods. Big is not always best.

Big may not always be best, but an adequate income to buy office space and employ professional staff is vital. The CBI has a strong reputation for hiring staff who have produced authoritative documents on business issues or macro-economic policy, and are capable of lobbying decision makers effectively. However, it would be wrong to assume that a pressure group automatically employs full-time staff. Part-time staff and volunteers, especially for the smaller cause groups is often the case. Financial uncertainties, even for the larger cause groups, (like WWF), cause uncertainties about the employment of permanent staff.

Access

We have already referred to group contacts on pp. 102 and 103). Remember that pressure groups build up contacts with individual MPs and may use professional lobbyists to do this work for them.

The case of the Elgin Marbles

Between 1803 and 1812, Lord Elgin the British Ambassador to Greece bought and removed a large series of sculptures from the Parthenon in Athens. They became known as the Elgin Marbles. They are 2,400 years old and have been one of the great treasures of the British Museum since 1816. From 1830, when Greece gained its independence from Turkey, there has been a standing request by the Greek government for their return.

In mid-January 2002, a pressure group was formed to campaign for the return of the marbles to the Parthenon in time for the Olympic Games due to take place in Athens in 2004. The group, called Parthenon 2004, is based in Britain and consists of over 90 MPs – including Richard Allen (a Liberal Democrat), several actors and actresses (including Vanessa Redgrave) and a number of public figures. The MPs signed an Early Day Motion in favour of restitution and calling on the government to begin discussions with Greece.

Robert Anderson, the director of the British Museum argued that he and the other trustees of the Museum had no power to surrender the marbles or any of its treasures, even if they wanted to. All the treasures of the museum are safeguarded by rules laid down by the trustees against any attempt to dispose of them.

Richard Allen appeared on the television news, as did Robert Anderson on the same day. Anderson also put his case in an article in *The Times* on 14 January 2002. It remains to be seen what the outcome will be.

Sanctions

Several methods can be employed, such as **non-cooperation with government**. This can take place either in the consultation process prior to legislation, or in the administration of legislation. For example, in 1993, the teachers' unions boycotted the government-imposed assessment tests in schools. The Anti-Poll Tax Federation in the late 1980s and early 1990s organised a non-payment of the tax. Along with the widespread unpopularity of the poll tax, this helped secure its repeal.

Economic measures can also be taken, such as industrial action by trade unions. Another is the campaign by anti-apartheid groups who tried to persuade consumers to boycott South African products until its racist policies ended. Companies may withdraw or threaten to withdraw investment from a particular part of Britain.

The economic and political environment

The period from 1979 to 1997 when the Thatcher and later the Major govern-ments tried to roll back the state and abandon interventionism, saw a reduction in the influence and status of trade unions, public-sector profes-sionals like doctors and teachers, and the CBI. Margaret Thatcher disliked

---

Pressure groups and democracy: a summary

A positive contribution
1 They provide functional representation in relation to occupation and belief.
2 They provide a means of political participation for individuals.
3 They ensure that minority groups and interests have a means of participation and repre-sentation in the political system.
4 They provide an outlet for longstanding concerns and grievances.
5 They provide a check on the excessive powers of government and also a method of public scrutiny of government policies.
6 They supply ideas, advice and expertise that governments may find helpful.

A negative contribution
1 They provide representation for narrow 'vested interests' whose only concerns are for the group and not society as a whole. Governments are elected to represent the public good.
2 They may lack an internal democratic structure. A number of problems follow from this, in particular: the view of the leadership may be unrepresentative; members may not be truly participating – many 'members' of a group are just 'supporters'.
3 Groups with strong financial resources may wield a disproportionate influence on governments.
4 Insider status provides opportunities for powerful groups to gain influence informally and secretly. Outsider groups are denied such continuous access.
5 Pressure groups protecting their sectional interests undermine the free market by causing inflation, unemployment and raising public expenditure. By obstructing market forces they slow down economic growth.
6 Pluralists argue that competition between a number and diversity of groups produces equal competition which is healthy for democracy, but most of the time the competition is very unequal and certainly not healthy.

the **corporatism** and consensus politics of earlier years. She believed that close cooperation between government and pressure groups was undemocratic as it gave too much influence to narrow interests and undermined the efficient operation of market forces. During her premiership, advisory committees declined in number, though contact between individual ministries and groups was not abandoned. Many groups, like the doctors and the teachers, were excluded from the early stages of policy formulation only for the government to find them uncooperative or non-cooperative with the eventual implementation.

corporatism

In its broadest sense, it means incorporating organised interests into the processes of government. In pre-Thatcherite Britain, it 'refers to what Heywood[22] calls 'the tendency found in mature liberal democracies for organised interests to be granted privileged and institutionalised access to policy formulation'.

REFERENCES AND FURTHER READING

1 R. Baggott, *Pressure Groups and the Policy Process*, SHU Press/Politics Association, 2000.
2 As note 1 above.
3 A. Ball and F. Millard, *Pressure Politics in Industrial Societies*, Macmillan, 1986.
4 F. Castles, *Pressure Groups and Political Culture*, Routledge, 1967.
5 D. Watts, *The Environment and British Politics*, Hodder and Stoughton, 1999.
6 T. Doyle and D. McEachern, *Environment and Politics*, Routledge, 1998.
7 J. D. Stewart, *British Pressure Groups*, Oxford University Press, 1958.
8 W. Grant, *Pressure Groups, Politics and Democracy in Britain*, Harvester Wheatsheaf, 1995.
9 W. Grant, *Insider Groups, Outsider Groups and Interest Group Strategies in Britain*, University of Warwick, 1978.
10 G. Jordan, J. Maloney and A. McLaughlin, Insiders and Outsiders and Political Access, British Interest Group Project Working Paper No. 3, Aberdeen University, 1992.
11 E Page, *Consultation on Public Policy – Who is Left Out?*, University of Hull, 1998.
12 G. Dudley and J. Richardson, *Political Studies*, Vol. 46, 1998, pp. 727–47.
13 A. Heywood, *Politics*, Macmillan, 1997.
14 M. Olson, *The Logic of Collective Action*, Harvard University Press, 1965.
15 D. Rucht, 'Think globally, act locally', in D. Liefferink, *European Integration and Environmental Policy*, Belhaven, 1993.
16 As note 1 above.
17 R. Baggott, 'The management of change in pressure group politics', in *Talking Politics*, Vol. 5:1, 1992.
18 D. Simpson, *Pressure Groups*, Hodder & Stoughton, 1999.
19 E. Brass and S. Koziell, 'Gathering Force', in *The Big Issue*, 1997.
20 R. Garner, *Environmental Politics*, Harvester Wheatsheaf, 1996.

21 W. Grant, 'Pressure Groups', in *Developments in Politics: An Annual Review* Vol. 10, Causeway Press, 1999.

22 A. Heywood, as note 13 above.

R. Baggott, *Pressure Groups and the Policy Process*, Politics Association/SHU Press, 2000.

D. Simpson, *Pressure Groups*, Access to Politics Series, Hodder & Stoughton, 1999.

USEFUL WEB SITES

Main list of UK pressure groups **www.ukpoliticsbrief.co.uk** This includes the broad categories of pressure groups. It also contains the rules for lobbying of national parliaments.

SAMPLE QUESTIONS

1 Distinguish between the different categories of pressure group and give examples

2 What factors influence pressure group success?

3 Outline the case **for** and the case **against** the view that pressure groups support democracy.

7

Political parties and the party system

AIMS OF THIS CHAPTER

➤ To outline the functions of the political parties.

➤ To examine the issues of funding and membership of the parties.

➤ To outline the organisation and structure of the parties, focusing especially on the leader.

➤ To outline four types of party system, and assess Britain's party system.

The functions of the parties

Political recruitment

Tony Wright[1] recognises the importance of parties in the political system in his reference to them as 'the gatekeepers to political office'. **Political parties** perform the key role of recruiting members, training potential candidates, selecting candidates for election to Parliament, and electing a leader who, along with the other leading members of the party, may ultimately form a government. Similar functions apply at local government level.

> **political party**
> A political party is an organisation of people who share basically the same ideological position and series of preferences. As a group, it seeks to gain political office, usually through elections, and to form a government.

Political careers have a variety of origins, but it is through the party that advancement lies. Some, such as William Hague and Jack Straw, started their careers in student politics. Others, while working in full-time jobs as lawyers, company directors, teachers/lecturers etc, may become active in politics on a part-time basis but this again takes place via the parties. Rarely does an MP get elected without a party label. An exception was Martin Bell, the former BBC television reporter, who won the seat of Tatton in 1997, defeating the Conservative incumbent Neil Hamilton. But Bell would not have won on his 'anti-sleaze' ticket if the Labour and Liberal Democrat candidates had not pulled out of the contest.

Having entered the House as a party politician, a person of ability and appeal may obtain the leadership if circumstances work out well for him, or her. Having become leader, if the party is successful at the polls, then the premiership beckons. Tony Blair was initially selected as the candidate for Sedgefield by the local party constituency association, and won the seat in the 1983 general election. He became leader of the party in 1994, following the death of the leader, John Smith, and Prime Minister when New Labour won the general election in May 1997.

Aggregating groups and opinions

The three main political parties attempt to draw together into a coherent whole, the demands of a wide variety of groups, and variations of opinion within society. Parties may therefore attempt to represent the interests of particular groups within society, among them the poor, those wanting a better welfare system and/or high-income groups wanting lower taxation. They may also attempt to respond to, and represent, broad variations of ideology, values and beliefs that prevail in society as a whole, including the desires for greater equality of opportunity, a better health service or environmental reforms. The parties attempt to respond to the demands of particular sections of society, and to the broad concerns of society as a whole.

Even this basic summary reveals some of the fundamental difficulties of the major parties:

1 the representation of often difficult and competing interests in society (e.g., a better welfare system for the poor might require higher taxation for higher earners);
2 the need to be inclusive, and appeal to as broad a spectrum of public opinion as possible;
3 the need to have a basis of core beliefs, values and interests of their own;
4 the need to be responsive and also persuasive, to shape public opinion as well as respond to it;
5 the need to secure majority support in a general election, and form a government.

This leads naturally on to the next function.

Package deals

The parties provide a political 'package deal' for the electorate which embraces every key policy issue for the country. This 'package deal' is contained within the party's general election manifesto. The creation of this large programme involves 'aggregating' (i.e., assembling as a whole), the demands of groups within society and ensuring that the result is pleasing to all of them and gels with the national interest. This outcome is achieved by a process of negotiation and compromise.

As there are only a small number of major parties in the UK, inevitably this means that the package deals are broad in scope. Nevertheless, the 'package deal' contained in the party election manifesto includes a set of 'promises' to be kept, should that party form a government. An election victory on the basis of the manifesto is described as a **mandate** to implement the contents of the document. This link between manifesto and mandate is a vital element in British party politics. Manifestos have become increasingly detailed, provide a basis for debate between the parties during the general election campaign, and are used by opposition parties to examine the extent to which the party – once in power – is fulfilling its manifesto commitments.

In a sense, a party that wins a general election, forms a government, and wins a mandate from the electorate, may be seen to have established a contract to fulfil its manifesto pledges. The problem with this notion is that a mandate is not a strict contract for the following reasons:

1 The general election result only tells us which manifesto has been approved, and those which have been rejected.
2 Those voting for the 'winning' manifesto may disapprove of parts of the package.
3 Unexpected events may force a government to retreat from a manifesto pledge.
4 Once in power, a party may wish to initiate a policy that was not in its manifesto.

Overall, then, the 'package deal' that is the manifesto is a useful guide for the electorate at the time of a general election campaign. It tells them what the party's policies are at that time, and what its intentions are. But the mandate that the winning party receives is essentially a mandate to govern.

Party membership

Like other parties, the Conservatives have a problem with membership. The days of the mass party are over. In the early 1950s, the party had 2.5 million members. Since then, there has been a steady decline, with occasional and limited revivals. Precise figures for membership have always been difficult to acquire. In 1999, a leaked figure from the party headquarters put the number at 335,000, almost certainly a higher total than that today.

Even more than Labour and the Liberal Democrats, the Conservatives have a problem with the age of their members. Their average age is increasing, with over half aged more than 66; at the bottom end, there are too few young adults willing to join. The age factor also accounts for limited party activism.

In 1953, Labour membership was estimated at 1 million. By 2002, having experienced a revival in the early days of the Blair leadership, it had slipped

---

The political parties and democracy: a summary

How parties help promote democracy

- They provide an opportunity for participation in politics, either on a part-time or full-time basis.
- They provide information and policy options on all areas of concern.
- They play a part in all of our major political institutions, from local and devolved government to Parliament and central government. Without party activity, these institutions would not be sustainable.
- They support parliamentary democracy, and the use of legal and peaceful methods.
- They are accountable to the electorate in many ways, including through their manifestos and through the work of their MPs in the constituencies.
- At elections, they provide voters with a choice of possible Prime Ministers and ministers, as well as a choice of possible MPs for the constituency.

How parties undermine democracy

- The range of policies they put forward is often quite narrow.
- Issues are often over-simplified by the parties; they may be distorted by an excessively adversarial approach.
- Much of the election campaigning is negative, so that in 2001 many commentators complained that the parties failed to engage with the public on the streets in a positive discussion of their policies.
- They have a small membership base, and there is often a gap between the views of a small number of activists and the population at large.
- Money, or the lack of it, means that the parties are vulnerable to the accusation that they accept large donations in return for granting 'favours'.

---

from 400,000 in 1997 to 280,000 in 2002. In a survey conducted after the 1997 election, Whiteley and Seyd[2] found that Labour party members:

- were predominantly middle class;
- had an average age of 51, just below that for the other two main parties;
- often came from a university background (34 per cent);
- were largely male (61:39 per cent);
- were more likely to be active if they were Old Labour members than New Labour ones.

The Liberal Democrats have approximately 80,000 members. Whiteley and Seyd[3] found that:

- they had an average age of 55, with over half being 56 or over;
- they were overwhelmingly middle class;
- nearly half (42 per cent) were university educated, the highest figure for one of the three main parties;
- activism was strong, with nearly 50 per cent making some form of contribution every month;
- members tended to be far more critical of Hague and Conservatism, than Blair and New Labour.

Party funding

Table 7.1 General election spending (£m)

Year	Labour	Conservatives	Lib Dems
1997	25.7	28.3	2.3
2001	17.0–18.0	14.0	3.5

Source: Adapted from the *Guardian*, 14 October 98 and D. Butler and D. Kavanagh, *The British General Election of 2001*, Palgrave 2002.

The new rules from the Neill Committee limited national spending by any party with 600 or more candidates to £20 million. What with the costs of running their national organisation, it is no surprise that with declining memberships the parties now rely heavily on personal donations, especially prior to general elections. There is some variation, however:

- Conservatives are heavily reliant on personal donations.
- Labour receives 20 per cent from 'large' donors; 40 per cent from membership subscriptions; 30 per cent from trade unions; and 10 per cent from commercial activity.
- Lib Dems. In 1992–97 members' subscriptions accounted for 30–66 per cent of the party's income

All parties have initiated commercial approaches to fund-raising – Labour set up the 1000 Club where members pledge £1000 per year. All parties have traditionally used fund-raising events and raise money on conferences and sales of books, souvenirs and memorabilia.

State funding of political parties

For several years, there has been a debate over whether or not there should be state funding of political parties. Discussion has recently been provoked by concern over large donations such as that made by Bernie Ecclestone to Labour in 1997. He had given £1 million to the party and critics felt that this contribution may have helped determine government policy on allowing tobacco advertising to continue in Formula One motor racing, over which he has a major influence.

Other factors in the debate are the recognition of the importance of parties to a healthy democracy and the need to create a more level playing field in which all parties have a chance to compete on an equal basis at election time.

Arguments against state funding

- Funding for the parties would come from taxation which would be unpopular.
- The parties would become part of the state and lose their status as free institutions.

- It might produce complacency, reduce activism even more and reduce fund-raising activities.
- It could widen the gap even more between the three main parties and the minor ones, depending on the system used to implement it.

Arguments for state funding

- 'Sleaze' is one reason for the public's growing indifference and distrust of politics and politicians. State funding would 'clean up' politics, as Neill discovered to be the case in Canada and Germany.
- The parties would operate more effectively and efficiently to produce a healthier democracy in which they would be able to re-engage with the public.
- The present financial position of the parties is insecure with declining membership and spiralling costs. One Labour MP, giving evidence to the Neill Committee, suggested that these trends could lead to a slum democracy, with parties poorly staffed and ill-equipped for government.

Party organisation

The Conservatives

Until 1998, the Conservative party consisted of three entities which were legally separate, the parliamentary party, Central Office (CCO) and the National Union of Conservative and Unionist Associations. Following reforms initiated by William Hague as leader, the three elements were united in a party structure which has a written constitution and national membership scheme.

The Annual Conference is the time when leading Conservative activists from around the country meet up. It is essentially a gathering of the party faithful, rather than a policy-making body. Debates do take place, votes are occasionally taken, but the leadership does not feel bound by the outcome. In effect, Conference is a public relations exercise to show unity, boost morale of members and establish communication between the leadership and local activists. It is also a showcase for the leader.

The Conservative leader

The leader of the party has traditionally exercised enormous power. The position is subject to few formal restraints which is why some writers have suggested that he or she is the most powerful political leader in the democratic world. Among the powers of the leader are:

- exclusive responsibility for writing the election manifesto and formulating policy;
- the right to choose the Cabinet (or Shadow Cabinet in Opposition);
- not having to report to conference on Parliamentary progress throughout

the year, nor attend meetings of the 1922 Committee, the committee of Conservative backbench MPs;

- control over Conservative Central Office, including the right to appoint (or dismiss) the party chairman and vice-chairman.

This is an important array of powers. Only since 1974 has the leader been subject to annual re-election and the possibility of a leadership challenge. Generally, the Conservatives have not stressed internal democracy as much as Labour, and have devised a form of organisation designed to serve the leader's inclinations. It embraces the idea of strong leadership, seeing authority important in any organisation. However, it is leadership 'by consent', for although there are seemingly so few restraints on the leader's freedom, there is ample precedent for power melting away and that consent being withdrawn. This is particularly the case when the Conservatives are in opposition, but even in office things can go wrong. The experience of Margaret Thatcher in 1989–1990 and of John Major in 1993–95 show that a Prime Minister is not necessarily as secure as a formal reading of the leader's powers would lead one to assume.

Election of the leader

The Conservatives have elected their leader since 1965. This was traditionally done by the party's MPs alone, but in 1997 this proved to be a small electorate as the party only had 165 members when it chose William Hague on the third ballot. Some Conservatives were concerned at the lack of democracy in the arrangements which provided for only informal consultations with ordinary members of the party. The rank-and-file wanted to be involved. As a result of the discontent, new rules were devised by William Hague. Among the provisions are that:

1 The party leader can be removed by a 51 per cent vote of 'no confidence' by the Conservative MPs. He or she may of course resign.
2 In choosing a new leader, there are to be a series of ballots in which only Conservative MPs may stand and only the parliamentary party may vote.

In 2001, when Hague stood down following the landslide election defeat, the result of the third ballot of MPs was:

> Kenneth Clarke   59
> Iain Duncan Smith 54
> Michael Portillo   53

As a consequence, the third-placed candidate dropped out (as had two others in the second ballot), because only two names could go forward. This time, it was to be the ordinary members of the party at large who would vote, by postal ballot. Iain Duncan Smith won on a comfortable 2:1 margin.

Labour

Labour was originally formed from a variety of organisations outside Parliament who came together to get more working-class people elected to the House. These included representatives of socialist societies and trade unionists. When the constitution was drawn up in 1918, it made provision for the control of the party by its extra-parliamentary elements; in other words, the party in Parliament was made responsible to the party outside. Traditionally, the party attempted to avoid the focus on the figure of the leader, and several organisational positions were powerful, such as the Treasurer who was elected by the Annual Conference.

Conference was allocated the function of directing and controlling the affairs of the party. It was given responsibility for party policy, so that decisions taken by a two thirds majority were supposed to be regarded as sacrosanct. For years, the exact role and significance of Conference was a matter of debate, and strong leaders – even in Opposition – tended to override its decisions if they had the backing of the party's National Executive Committee (NEC). Given the modernisation of party organisation in recent years, Conference now has a much-diminished role, as alternative sources of power and influence have been created. Many party stalwarts have been highly critical of the downgrading of Conference in the Blairite era. Often, there now seems to be a degree of stage-management of the occasion, similar to that at which the Conservatives excelled in the 1980s. Rarely are there opportunities for supporters to rock the boat in front of the television cameras. The hard choices of policy are made elsewhere, and Conference is an opportunity for the party to sell its wares to the electorate, via the media.

The NEC is the body supposed to prepare the Conference agenda, propose policy, advise Conference and act as the guardian of Conference decisions. It is the administrative authority of the party, working in close association with party headquarters. The extent of its influence had varied in particular periods, depending on the attitude of the leader and the composition of its membership. Neil Kinnock found that an NEC dominated by his supporters or sympathisers could be an asset in foisting his centralising and modernising policies on a somewhat doubtful party. Much of the policy work associated in the past with Conference and the NEC is now carried out by the National Policy Forum (NPF). Created to streamline policy making, it appoints commissions for particular areas of policy, each chaired by a frontbench MP. They produce reports for the NEC and for Conference's approval. The effect of these and other changes has been to make the leadership far less likely to be embarrassed by conference votes for policies that the leader does not want.

The Labour leader

Originally the Labour Party had a chairman rather than a leader. The job frequently changed hands, and there was often little effective coordination of parliamentary activity. Today, the leader is either Prime Minister or a potential Prime Minister, and Labour has accepted the need for its leader to have stronger powers than it once envisaged.

The Constitution (1918) imposed several restrictions on the leader, in an effort to ensure his subservience to the party in Parliament and in the country. It provided for:
- periodic re-election;
- the leader to attend meetings of the backbenchers in the House and in opposition, to preside over them;
- the leader to attend Conference and give an annual report of the work of the Parliamentary Labour Party (PLP);
- no personal control over the party organisation.

There has long been a gulf between the leader's powers in opposition and office, and successive Labour Prime Ministers felt able to ignore Conference decisions. Since Neil Kinnock's era, there has been a major centralisation of the party and an attempt to crush internal dissent. In the Blair era, the iron grip of the leadership has been maintained or even increased. The trends of recent years – weeding out dissident voices, loosening the ties with the unions and concentrating power in the leader's hands – have all been given renewed impetus. Starved of election success for so many years, Labour was willing to allow its leader and then Prime Minister a remarkably free hand. But there is unease within the party about the way in which it is led. Some members feel that there is a danger in concentrating power in too few hands and recall that Tony Blair has been allowed to arrogate more power than was ever intended by those who created the party's organisational machinery.

Election of the leader

Until the early 1980s, the leader and deputy were elected by Labour MPs, but the party then decided to establish an electoral college in which the majority influence would be given to the trade unions, and equal rating given to the constituency Labour parties and the PLP, on a ratio of 40:30:30. There was criticism of the unequal weighting, in particular the influence accorded to the trade unions whose methods of determining their favoured candidate were sometimes of questionable democracy. Some unions balloted their members, but even then their entire or 'block' vote went to one candidate.

Under John Smith's leadership (1992–94), the weighting was equalised, at 33.33 per cent for each element in the Labour Party. The block vote was scrapped, in favour of 'one man, one vote' (OMOV). There are still some oddities about the system. For instance, it allows plural voting, by which a party member who is also a trade unionist might get two votes. In 1994, Neil Kinnock qualified for seven!

The system was used in 1994 to elect Tony Blair and John Prescott as his deputy. In these elections, nearly one million votes were cast and the process worked smoothly. Blair was the clear winner in all three elements of the party and there was general praise among commentators for an election which was widely seen as the biggest democratic exercise in European politics. Supporters of the new leader proclaimed his 'million vote mandate'.

Party systems

Sartori[4] defines a party system as 'the system of interactions resulting from inter-party competition'. Heywood[5] puts it more straightforwardly: 'a relatively stable network of relationships between political parties that is structured by their number, size and ideological orientation'. There are four main categories of party systems: single-party, multi-party, two-party, and dominant party.

Single-party systems

The word 'system' here is misleading. If only one party is legal and all the others are banned then Sartori's definition involving 'interactions (and) inter-party competitions' does not occur, because one party cannot produce a system. Nevertheless, identifying single-party systems provides a starting point from which other systems may be identified. Single-party systems are undemocratic and **totalitarian**, with one ruling party having complete power. Nazi Germany (1933–45) and China (1948–2003) are examples of such regimes. They are often justified by their defenders as a necessity to overcome a national emergency (Hitler) or as a transitional stage in preparation for a new and better society (Lenin).

> **totalitarian**
> 'Total rule' by one party, usually with an all-powerful leader. There is usually one strict ideology to be followed without question and rule is ensured by the open use of brutality and terror.

Multi-party systems

The main characteristics of a multi-party system are that:
- more than two parties compete on a reasonably equal basis;
- it is unlikely that any one party will gain an overall majority and so be able to govern alone;
- power may alternate between the leading parties;
- coalition governments are usually formed. This is where formal agreements between two or more parties are made concerning policies and the distribution of ministerial posts.

Italy is a good example. Until 1993, it had a multi-party system but an unstable government. In 1993, it changed the voting system from proportional representation to simple plurality, in the hope that this would produce strong

government. Weak and unstable government is often associated with multi-partyism, but defenders might point out that:
- they provide a fairer and more representative spread of public opinion especially for minority parties than do two party systems;
- they produce a consensus for negotiation between parties, as opposed to the more adversarial and confrontational approach which critics dislike in British politics.

Two-party system

The characteristics of a two-party system are that:
- two parties compete on a reasonably equal basis, to gain an overall majority of seats;
- one of these two parties is likely to win. Other parties may win some seats, but exercise little power against this two-party dominance;
- the winning party forms the entire government and governs alone;
- the two dominant parties alternate in power.

The USA has a two-party system with the Democrats and the Republicans. Whether Britain has a two-party system follows later. The strengths and weaknesses of this system are set out in Table 7.2.

Table 7.2 Two-party systems

Strengths	Weaknesses
Clear choice for voters.	Insufficient choice for voters.
Doctrine of manifesto and mandate operates clearly.	Doctrine of manifesto and mandate is not clear because, in Britain, parties gain power with less than 50 per cent of the votes cast.
Usually produces stable and strong government.	Weak governments do occur, e.g. Labour (1964–66, 1974–79) and Conservative (1992–97).
Adversarial politics sustains the choice of government party or opposition party.	Adversarial politics is negative and destructive. The manner of this is unpopular with the electorate. The truth is hard to find.
Her Majesty's Opposition, is a ready made alternative if the government should fail.	House of Commons is undermined by the ease with which governments can push through their legislation.
At general elections, accountability is clear.	The two parties are opposed on many issues. If they alternate in power, there are reversals of policy and no continuity.

Dominant party systems

In a dominant-party system, many parties compete for power and put up candidates for election. However, only one party tends to win power either on its own or as the leading member of a coalition. It is very different from a single-party system; other parties are legal, and democratic elections are regular but the electorate continue to vote for the dominant party.

The characteristics of a dominant-party system are that:
- one party consistently wins more seats to the legislature than its opponents – i.e. it gains power regularly;
- it is able to govern as it is returned to power regularly;
- it is able to govern for a long period without a break;
- it has a dominant ideology and a set of policies that, when in government, it is able to implement.

The Liberal Democrats in Japan, between 1955 and 1993, were the dominant party being returned to the lower chamber of the legislature with more seats than their opponents. Such a situation has the advantage of producing strong and stable government, but critics might point out that:
- the dominant party's ideological and policy stance may well have to be assimilated by opposing parties;
- its leaders may gather 'excessive' powers for themselves, as they are frequently re-elected;
- opposition parties are weak and ineffective in Parliament and at general elections, where they do not offer a credible alternative;
- the dominant party may be perceived by the electorate as the 'natural party of government'.

Britain's party system

1945–74

From 1945 to the present day, either the Conservative or Labour parties have formed a government. However, the two general elections in 1974 are often regarded as a turning point. Before then, there was a 'classical' two-party system at work, in which:
- one of the two parties won a sufficient parliamentary majority to form a government, even though Labour won in 1951 and 1964 with very small majorities;
- after each general election, the winning party governed alone;
- power rotated four times – in 1945, 1951, 1964 and 1970;
- most of the votes were cast for either Labour or the Conservatives – on average 91 per cent over eight general elections;
- strong class and partisan alignment was evident (see Chapter 4);
- no other party could realistically compete for power.

1974–2001: a multi-party system?

The two general election results of 1974 marked a significant change in the party system, in that:
- the combined vote for the two main parties fell from a previous average of 91 per cent to approximately 75 per cent at each election;
- the vote for the Liberal Party rose from 7.5 per cent in 1970 to 18.3 per cent in 2001;
- the imposition of direct-rule led to the Northern Ireland parties adopting separate identities and distancing themselves from the Conservative, Labour and Liberal parties;
- the Scottish National Party gained 11 seats in October 1974;
- subsequently, the Labour government lost its tiny majority of 3 in 1976.

Although the Conservative Party won four successive general elections between 1979 and 1992 and stayed in office for eighteen years, there was growing evidence of a decline in the two-party system and the beginnings of a multi-party system.
- The combined vote of the two main parties, including the 2001 general election, has remained under 80 per cent since 1979.
- Labour's share of the vote dropped to only 27.6 per cent in 1983 whilst the Conservative vote dropped to 30 per cent in 1997.
- From 1974, more and more parties contested seats at general elections.
- There was much talk in the 1980s of a multi-party system. In the mid-1980s, the Liberal–SDP Alliance came close to Labour's percentage of votes, but did not gain the proportionate number of seats. Tony Wright MP[6] explains why: 'In short, the two-party system had been saved by the electoral system. Its high "breakthrough" threshold meant that it was difficult for competitors to get in.'

The increased electoral success of the Liberal Democrats is evidence perhaps of a 'two-and-half-party system', although it remains the case that in recent elections only two main parties have competed for political power with a meaningful chance of outright victory.

What type of party system do we have today?

In the 2001 general election, twelve parties contested seats in Northern Ireland, and 64 in the rest of Britain. There are four parties with representatives in the Scottish Assembly and the same number in the Welsh Assembly. Yet the two-party system still dominates Parliament and national government, even if the allocation of seats is no fair reflection of the wishes of the electorate.
- In 2001, Labour and Conservatives gained a combined total of 72.7 per cent of the votes cast and 87 per cent of the seats, 578 seats out of 659.

1979–97: A dominant party system?

At first sight, using the criteria that define a dominant-party system, the Conservatives would appear to have achieved this between 1979 and 1997, appearing to be 'the natural party of government'.

- They regularly won more seats at elections than their opponents.
- They won four successive general elections.
- They governed continuously for eighteen years.
- Their New Right ideology became dominant, their pubilc policies were radical and influenced the thinking of other political parties.

Simpson[7] has questioned the extent of Conservative dominance. The following are just a few key points:

- In their four election victories, the Conservatives never gained more than 43 per cent of the votes cast.
- The Conservative government of 1992–97 was by no means dominant. It started with a majority of 21; the party was torn by divisions over Europe, was smeared by 'sleaze' and had virtually no majority by 1997.
- Support in Scotland for the Conservatives was not dominant. It was in decline.
- The Liberal Democrats not only did well in the 1997 general election but throughout the period increased its representation on local councils.
- The Labour Party, although very weak in 1983, retained its seats in inner cities and in the north.
- The degree to which the Conservatives changed the state and society is questionable. In the 1990s many people still supported such policies as the NHS and social security.

Yet in spite of such considerations, there was in these eighteen years a sense of Conservative dominance within the party system, But the application of such labels (which was common among political writers before 1997) is dangerous, for one different election outcome can shatter the theory. Labour was gradually improving its position in the elections after 1983 and in 1997 any suggestion of a two-party system but one-party Conservative dominance proved to be ill-founded.

- There are only 9 nationalist MPs from Wales and Scotland, and 52 Liberal Democrats.

There are other elements of continuity from the days when the classical two-party system operated most effectively:
- Only the two main parties form governments.
- The two main parties dominate the political and policy agenda.
- Adversarial government versus opposition politics continues to be dominated by the two main parties.

Norris[8] provides a balanced summary: 'Britain has not become a multi-party or predominant system. Rather Britain has evolved from a *dominant* two-party system to a *declining* two-party system during the last fifty years.' In effect, we have a two-party system, but three (or in Scotland and Wales four) party politics.

REFERENCES AND FURTHER READING

1 T. Wright, *British Political Processes*, Routledge, 2000.
2 P. Whiteley and P. Seyd, *New Labour – New Grassroots Party?*, University of Sheffield, 1998.
3 P. Seyd and P. Whiteley, *Liberal Democrats at the Grassroots. Who are They?*, University of Sheffield, 1999.
4 G. Sartori, *Parties and Party Systems. A Framework for Analysis*, Cambridge University Press, 1976.
5 As note 1 above.
6 A. Heywood, *Politics*, Macmillan, 1997.
7 D. Simpson, *UK Government and Politics in Context*, Hodder & Stoughton, 1998.
8 P. Norris, *Electoral Change Since 1945*, Blackwell, 1997.

D. Simpson, *Political Parties*, Access to Politics series, Hodder & Stoughton, 1999.

SAMPLE QUESTIONS

1 Outline the functions of political parties in a democracy.

2 Why are some people critical of Britain's two party system?

3 Describe and explain the trends in Britain's party system in the last three decades.

Political parties: ideologies, policies and approaches

AIMS OF THIS CHAPTER

➤ To establish the concept of a political ideology.

➤ To consider two methods of classification.

➤ To outline developments in Liberalism, Conservatism and Socialism down to the present day.

Components of ideology

Human nature

If our basic view of human nature is optimistic, then we see our fellow human beings positively. If we are pessimistic about human nature, then we see our fellow human beings negatively. Our view of human nature influences our views on many political issues. If we believe the best about people, we might think that those claiming unemployment benefit are in genuine need and cannot find or cope with work. If we are doubtful about the fundamental decency of some of our fellow men and women, we might think that they just do not want to work.

> **ideology**
> A belief system consisting of social, economic and political assumptions, values and ideas that provides a basis for organised political action.

The individual and identity

As individuals, the extent to which we identify ourselves solely as individuals or as members of a group according to, say, social class or race, or with a wider community, is an indicator of our personal **ideology**. It is also a guideline for our political ideology. For example, when a political decision is made, should the individual or community be the main consideration?

The past, present and future

Our interpretation of the past informs our view of the present and our vision of the future. If we believe that gradual change has produced a satisfactory present, then we are likely to believe that gradual change will produce an even better future. However, if we believe that gradual change has produced an unsatisfactory present, then we may want to use radical methods or adopt far-reaching changes to produce a better future.

The state

The role of the state is very significant in any ideology. Essentially, the issue is about what the state should or should not do. Do we want the state to perform a minimum number of functions such as preserving law and order, and defending the nation from external attack? Or do we want an enlarged number of functions such as providing a National Health Service and an educational system in which there is opportunity for everyone? If we favour the latter, then we must recognise that the price will have to be paid in the form of higher taxation.

Although the ideologies that follow later in this chapter are directly associated with particular parties, it is important to remember that there is an element of consensus or agreement between them.

Classification

Linear model

This model (see Figure 8.1) attempts to locate the full range of ideologies on a linear political spectrum between the two extremes of Far Left and Far Right. Originally, this model was used to denote the extent to which a person or group wanted change in a forward or reverse direction. The following terms are usually employed:
- **Centre** – those who support the present state of affairs.
- **Right wing** – those who either want change in a backward direction or to preserve the status quo (keep things as they are) as much as is possible.
- **Left wing** – those who in varying degrees want change in order to create a better, more fair and just society.

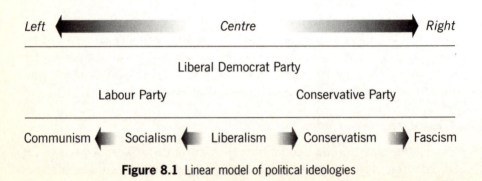

Figure 8.1 Linear model of political ideologies

Circular/horseshoe model

NB: Fascism is anti-Marxist and anti-democratic. Its central concept is that of an organically unified national community which is the embodiment of strength through unity. The individual's identity must be entirely absorbed and subservient to the community. Fascist regimes have been typified by strong leaders such as Mussolini and Hitler, and an intense nationalism.

Communism is revolutionary socialism. One of communism's central concepts is the overthrow of capitalism and the state supporting it, the introduction of an economic and political system in which the common ownership of property is established and in which the state eventually 'withers away'.

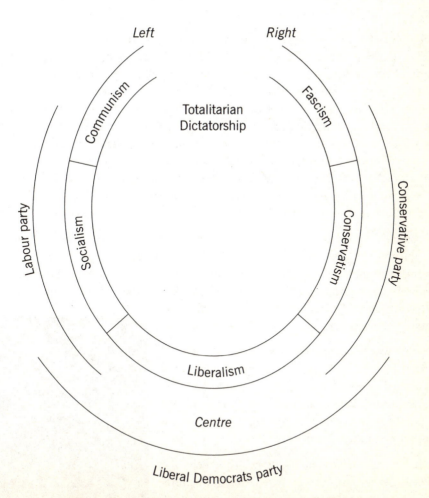

Figure 8.2 Circular/horseshoe model of political ideologies

Liberalism

'It has been said that Socialism is about equality. If you ask for an equivalent short-hand description of liberalism I should say that it is about freedom and participation' (Jo Grimond, leader of the Liberal Party 1956–67).[1]

Basic elements

Liberals see human beings as self-seeking, self-reliant, rational and capable of self-improvement. Traditionally, liberals are guardedly optimistic about human nature. As rational beings, liberals

> **altruistic**
> Being 'unselfish' or concerned for the interests of others.

believe that individuals are best capable of judging their own self-interest. Classical (or early) liberalism focused on this self-seeking aspect, while New and Modern liberalism took a more optimistic view believing that human nature could also be **altruistic**.

Liberals believe in the central importance of the individual over and above any other social group or collective body. Thus, in the creation of society, the individual's needs and interests are the starting point. In particular, society should be so constructed that the individual has the greatest possible opportunity to satisfy his or her interests and fulfil their potential. They also believe in the need to ensure that such freedom is consistent with a similar degree of freedom for everyone else. Classical liberals supported negative freedom, that is the absence of external constraints on opportunities and choice; in short, non-interference. New and Modern liberalism advocate positive freedoms. These are freedom from social evils such as poverty and ignorance in order to ensure the greatest opportunity for individual development and fulfilment.

Classical liberalism emphasised rationality in human nature which, in turn, supported the case for freedom. Central to the **Enlightenment** of the seventeenth and eighteenth centuries was the belief that humankind needed to be freed from the past and the present which were characterised by ignorance, superstition and paternalism. Reason, not force, should be used to resolve conflict and bloodshed.

In the words of Andrew Heywood, the liberal view of justice is 'about giving each person what he or she is 'due'.[2] It is interchangeable with the concept of Equality. Liberals support the ideas of equality of worth and of opportunity, but do not support equality of outcome.

> **the Enlightenment**
> A broad European intellectual movement that reached its peak in the eighteenth century. Enlightenment thinkers were critical of existing society, hostile to religion, and believed in the liberating possibilities of rational thought and the concept of social progress. Such principles were seen as justification for the French Revolution of 1789.

Liberals also believe in tolerance. They echo the words of Voltaire, the French writer and philosopher of the eighteenth century who declared: 'I disapprove of what you say, but I will defend to the death your right to say it.' Liberalism not only tolerates diversity and pluralism, but positively celebrates them whether they be political, moral or cultural. Voltaire's famous quotation underpins this toleration in that liberal democracy supports basic freedoms and guarantees the rights of the individual to disagree.

Classical and New Liberalism

Liberalism has been subject to considerable change and adaptation. In its **classical** form, it emphasised:
- government by consent;
- limited government;
- representation;
- laissez-faire economics (non-interference by government in the workings of the economy) and free trade.

These ideas were supported in the nineteenth century by both Liberal and Conservative governments. Liberalism actively supported and celebrated the rise of individual capitalism. Liberals were not particularly concerned with the inequalities created by laissez-faire economics. Some argued that laissez-faire economics would produce a 'trickle down' effect whereby, long term, the living standards of the working class would improve. Liberals subscribed to the Victorian values summed up in the title of the book by Samuel Smiles, *Self-Help* (1859). Provided that individuals adhered to these values, there were more than enough opportunities for them to prosper.

New Liberalism was a response to the problems associated with classical liberalism. Classical liberalism supported free-market capitalism and a very limited role for the state. While many benefited from this system, many more lived in deprivation. Two associated problems were identified:
- increasing poverty caused by capitalism and an inactive state;
- the disadvantaged circumstances in which some people began life, so that their opportunities to prosper were unequal. Those born into poverty died in poverty despite their best efforts.

'New Liberal' thinking

T.H. Green (1836–82), professor of moral philosophy at Oxford University provided a clear break with Classical Liberal thought. His ideas were to influence a generation of New Liberal thinkers. He believed that human beings were not just self-seeking, but socially responsible as well; they were capable of altruism. He challenged the classical liberal concept of negative freedom and argued that meaningful freedom involved freedom from such social evils as poverty and unemployment.

The pinnacle of New Liberalism's achievement lay in the social reforms of the Liberal governments from 1906 to 1914; old-age pensions, national insurance in the case of ill-health or unemployment, and trade boards to set minimum wages were just some examples. Some argue that the Liberals laid the foundations of the welfare state with these reforms. Others might disagree but most believe that they at least prepared the way for the creation of the welfare state after the Second World War.

Modern Liberalism: post-1945

Modern liberal thinking has extended the ideas of New Liberalism. It has been influenced by the work and influence of two progressive liberals, John Maynard Keynes (1886–1946) and William Beveridge (1879–1963). Keynes wrote his most famous work *General Theory of Employment, Interest and Money*, in response to the widespread unemployment caused by the Depression of the 1930s.

As the leading economist of his day, Keynes argued that further state intervention was essential to advance the positive freedom of the individual. Free-market capitalism was subject to cycles of boom and slump; all individuals, employers, workers and consumers, would benefit from a stable economy. When a slump occurred and demand for goods fell, the government could stimulate demand for example by lowering taxation to encourage private investment or by spending public money to invest in new economic activity. These methods would be used in an attempt to reverse a downward economic spiral as in the depression of the 1930s. **Keynesian** economic policies were to be pursued by both Labour and Conservative governments from 1945 to the mid-1970s.

> **Keynesianism**
> Keynes envisaged a **mixed economy** that would ensure greater stability, reduce hardship and create opportunities. However he did not call for a redistribution of wealth unlike socialist economists.

> **mixed economy**
> This was an economy that included state ownership of industries and services, as well as private enterprise.

William Beveridge was a leading civil servant and Liberal. 'The Beveridge Report' produced in 1942 became a blueprint for the welfare state which was set up by the post-war Labour government. His report claimed that there were five giant evils to be overcome: 'want, disease, ignorance, squalour and idleness'. According to his thinking, the government should set up schemes for health service, secondary education, national insurance, housing and child allowances. Indeed, Beveridge outlined a system of social security 'from cradle to grave'.

In line with its traditions of constitutionalism, modern liberalism has been characterised by its long-term support – since 1945 – for constitutional reform.

A set of issues have consistently set it apart from the Labour and Conservative parties. These have included:

- reform of the voting system – the introduction of Proportional Representation;
- a 'Bill of Rights';
- reform of the House of Lords;
- decentralisation of Government;
- devolution for Scotland and Wales.

The ideas of Beveridge and Keynes formed the basis of the post-war consensus from 1945 to the mid-1970s (see p. 143). Much, but not all, of modern liberalism's programme for constitutional reform was implemented by the New Labour government of 1997–2001.

Modern liberal thought has had a profound influence on government policies since 1945 on both Labour, Conservative and New Labour governments. However, as will be shown, Margaret Thatcher's Conservative governments were profoundly influenced by a return to classical liberalism.

Conservatism

Basic elements

Conservatives are more pessimistic about human nature. They believe that humanity has the potential to do wrong, is morally corruptible, is dependent and insecure, and possesses few powers to rationalise. Compared with the other ideologies, Conservatism lacks idealism and focuses on the imperfectability of human beings.

Conservatives stress the importance of authority and the rule of law. Authority is vested in the nature of society, from the teacher in the school to the government. This Conservative concept of authority has traditionally been manifest in its paternalist style of government, with government as father and the population at large its children. Widespread acceptance of authority and support for the rule of law is necessary to prevent anarchy.

Conservatives believe private **property** is fundamental to order and harmony in society. It provides a sense of identity, security, an incentive to work and respect for the property of others.

property
Simply put, in this context it includes land, buildings, savings and shares.

They also emphasise the importance of tradition, and have a high regard for traditional institutions such as the Crown and the House of Lords. Formal institutions such as Parliament and informal ones like the family, bind society together and prevent disorder. Any change in society must be gradual and in accordance with past developments.

For Conservatives, the preservation of freedom is the main purpose of government and politics. Individuals need as much freedom as possible to make the most of their lives, provided that they do not reduce the freedom of others. They support capitalism, seeing free enterprise as the basis of economic success and as a safeguard of freedom. They do not believe in equality of outcome, seeing inequality in society as inevitable – given people's diverse abilities and efforts. They do support equality of opportunity.

From the above, it is apparent that Conservatives believe that the maintenance of social and political harmony is important. The functions of government should be limited, although they accept that in the twenty-first century some governmental intervention in economic and social life is inevitable and necessary. They certainly want to limit the role of government, seeing 'big government' as a threat to freedom. Traditionally, they have favoured pragmatic (practical), undogmatic policies. They have portrayed socialism as a rigid ideological creed which does not gel with human nature. They dislike plans and blue-prints, and prefer policies that are realistic and practical rather than ones tied to abstract theories and ideals.

Traditional Conservatism

'Tory' is a term widely used today as a synonym for Conservative, mostly by political opponents of the Conservative party. After the passage of the 1832 Reform Act, the Tories were more usually called 'Conservatives'. This name was used for much of the twentieth century, though some individuals still like to use 'Tory'.

Traditional Conservatism contains all of the basic elements of Conservatism. In addition, two ingredients became increasingly important in the late nineteenth and twentieth centuries. **Paternalism** concerned the obligation of the nobility (the rulers) to the lower orders of society who in turn were to stay loyal to their 'betters'. Humanitarian reform, especially to improve living and working conditions for the working classes, was closely linked with this idea, especially during the time of Disraeli's premiership (1874–80). This was later referred to as Tory democracy or, post-1945, as 'One Nation Conservatism'. Between the 1950s and 1970s, One Nation Conservatism was much in vogue and Conservative governments pursued policies which were pragmatic and of broad appeal. The party accepted the welfare state and even most of the nationalisation which the post-war Labour government introduced. There was no attempt to reverse the tide. These were the years of so-called consensus politics (see p. 142).

paternalism

This concept refers to the relationship between the 'ruler' and the 'ruled'. The rulers, given their wealth and power, have obligations to the ruled. For the ruler it is the price of privilege. In return, the 'ruled' are obliged to be loyal to the ruler. The idea derives from the role of the father in relation to his children.

Authoritarian and libertarian Conservatism

There have always been some Conservatives – mainly the right of the party – who hold authoritarian views. They tend to take a particularly tough stance on law and order, wanting longer sentences and maybe the death penalty as well. They usually favour censorship, and oppose 'progressive' ideas on matters such as educational policy and sexuality. This 'tough' approach is often also associated with a restrictive policy on immigration and an emphasis on British nationalism. Authoritarians are sympathetic to governmental control over the lives of individuals, believing that it is necessary to lay down and enforce many rules.

In contrast, **libertarianism**, another strand in Conservatism, has much in common with classical liberalism. They recognise the need for a strong state to maintain traditional values, but also emphasise personal freedom in the economy and a minimum of governmental regulation. They believe that the laws of the free market should be allowed to operate with as little state interference as possible. This strand of Conservatism was little in evidence in the post-war period until New Right thinking began to make its impact in the mid 1970s.

> **libertarianism**
> This concept gives precedence to freedom over all other values. For example, unlike classical liberalism, it gives precedence to freedom over order.

The New Right

The term New Right includes a variety of views, but its two key components are the free market and the strong state. This means that it has much in common with Libertarian Conservatism, sometimes known as Liberal Conservatism. The liberal aspects of New Right thinking draw on classical liberalism, with its emphasis on negative freedom, a free market and a minimal state. Friedrich Hayek, an Austrian economist and philosopher, and Milton Friedman, an American economist and adviser to President Reagan, revived the classical economics of Adam Smith, the political economist and author of *The Wealth of Nations*, and challenged post-war Keynesian economics. They championed the free market and opposed state intervention. If free enterprise was pursued, prosperity would eventually be enjoyed by all. They emphasised the need for 'sound money' and were advocates of **monetarism**.

> **monetarism**
> An economic doctrine that focuses on the causes and control of inflation. The root cause of **inflation** is too much money and credit circulating in the economy. Control of inflation, not full employment, should be the first aim of government economic policy.

The New Right also revived the classical liberal concept of negative freedom. This required the removal of external restraints on the individual.

> **inflation**
> Increases in the amount of money circulating in the economy produce rising prices and a reduction in the value of money. So, in the UK, increasing inflation means that the £ will buy less and less.

In its view, the welfare state had tended to reduce individual self-motivation, the ethics of hard work and the profit motive.

In addition, the New Right recognised the importance of a strong state which they saw as vital to preserving social order. The collapse of authority, decline of 'family values' and permissiveness which began in the 'swinging sixties' had combined to produce more juvenile delinquency and rising crime, to name but just two issues. A strong state would reassert traditional values and encourage self-help.

> **capitalism**
> This is the economic system in which property and the means of production, distribution and exchange are privately owned rather than owned by the state. It is a system driven by the profit-motive and relies on private investment. It relies on minimal state intervention and is closely associated with liberal democracies.

New Right ideas have had a significant effect on party thinking since the mid-1970s. They were much associated with Sir Keith Joseph, an MP and former minister. He introduced them to the new leader, Margaret Thatcher, who assumed the leadership in 1975. Thatcherism appealed strongly to all elements on the Right, be they libertarians or authoritarians. Its impact was felt not just within the Conservative Party but it affected its political opponents and British society at large.

Socialism

Socialism has been described by Heywood as 'an ideology that is defined by its opposition to **capitalism** and its attempt to provide a more humane and socially worthwhile alternative'.[3]

In Latin, the word 'social' means to combine, or share. However, modern socialism developed as a critique of the dire social and economic conditions experienced by the **working classes** that arose from the growth of industrial capitalism in the nineteenth century.

The critique of capitalism was based on several key points:

> **social class**
> A social class (e.g. working, middle and upper class) is a group of people who share a similar social and economic position. Marx defined 'class' in relation to the means of production; bourgeois and proletariat. Non-Marxist definitions are based on income and status difference between occupational groups.

- **Exploitation**. In a capitalist system the means of production, distribution and exchange were in the hands of private owners, the capitalists. The working classes were 'employed' by these capitalists who profited from the 'fruits' of the labour of their workers, by paying minimum wages. In this way, the mass of working people are dehumanised by lives deprived of both material and spiritual necessities.

- **Inequalities and social injustice**. Society was characterised by great inequalities of wealth between the capitalists who were very rich but few in number, and working people who were very poor but many in number. The capitalist system perpetuated these inequalities from one generation to the next.

- **Impact on the state**. Leading capitalists dominate the institutions of the state. The capitalist ethos intrudes into all walks of life and governments govern in the interests of the few, not the many.

- **Inefficiency**. Finally, the capitalist system was inefficient. It was subject to cyclical variations, boom and slump. In a boom, capitalists gained much and working people little. In a slump, the capitalists safeguarded themselves and their interests, and the 'casualties' were the working people.

  Marx and Engels in *The Communist Manifesto* (1848) argued that the growing antagonism between the two classes – bourgeois (capitalists) and the proletariat (working class) – would lead to the overthrow of the bourgeoisie and the state that supported them. A socialist society would follow.

Basic principles

The socialist view of human nature is optimistic. They believe people to be basically good. In their view, our behaviour is shaped more by **nurture** than **nature**. We are fundamentally social creatures. In a favourable environment, cooperation is possible and beneficial for both the individual and for society as a whole. It is the highly competitive and selfish nature of the capitalist system that creates flaws and denies the essential goodness of human beings to develop fully. In developing his definition of socialism, Heywood goes on to refer to it as an 'ideology characterised by a particular cluster of ideas, values and theories', which are:

nature

In this context, the individual characteristics – or genes – passed on to us by our parents.

nurture

This means the individual characteristics produced by our 'experiences', e.g. in our environment, interaction with others and education.

collectivism

This is basically the belief that human endeavour is of greater practical and moral value than individual self-seeking.

fraternity

The belief in brotherhood i.e. the ability and potential of human beings to live and work together in mutual harmony.

individualism

This is the belief in the supreme importance of the individual over any social group or collective body to any political theory (see 'New Right' p. 135).

- **Community**. As social creatures, it is sensible for human beings to draw upon the power of the community by working **collectively**, rather than individually, to overcome similar problems. Socialists believe that the community should be **fraternal**, characterised by cooperation rather than **individualism**.

- **Cooperation**. A socialist system promotes harmony, whereas capitalism fosters division.

- **Equality**. Heywood sees equality as 'the central and some would say defining value of socialism'. Socialists do not believe that all individuals are born equal in terms of abilities and skills, but they do believe that the most significant forms of human inequality are produced by divisive and unjust structures in society, such as class divisions. Socialists demand social equality for all so that individuals, not just the privileged, are able to develop themselves to their full potential. Social equality both strengthens the community and expands individual freedoms.

- **The satisfaction of need**. Socialists demand a fair distribution of material benefits in society. In the capitalist system, the workers create the wealth, but the capitalists profit by paying them low wages.

- **Common ownership**. Socialists argue that the institution of **private property**, the means of producing wealth or 'capital', is unjust as it leads to worker exploitation by capitalists. Widening social divisions ensue. Socialists have argued for the common ownership of 'capital' or that a balance be achieved between property rights and the needs of the community.

> **private property**
> In this context, it refers to the means of producing wealth or 'capital', not personal belongings.

- **Ethical basis**. Socialism is portrayed as having a morality that is superior to capitalism, in that human beings, as essentially social creatures, are ethical creatures 'joined' to each other by mutual concern.

By the beginning of the twentieth century there was great controversy among socialists about **means** – how might socialism be achieved? There was much discussion also of **ends** – what was to be the ultimate goal and form of the socialist project?

Means

Revolutionary socialists saw the complete overthrow of the capitalist system and the political and social structures that supported it, as essential. In short, they wanted a revolution, and were prepared to use violent and mass action to achieve it. This was the position taken by Lenin and the Bolsheviks prior to the Russian revolution of 1917. The Bolsheviks were later to be known as Communists. They wished to abolish capitalism and introduce an economic and political system in which the common ownership of property and equality are key elements, and in which – following the establishment of the dictatorship of the proletariat – the state 'withers away'.

Reformist socialists supported the creation of socialist parties that worked within the democratic system, gained representation legally and eventually formed a socialist government. They believed that change should come about as a result of passing legislation by a democratically elected assembly. This was the path chosen by the British Labour Party, formed in 1900. However, two broad traditions have co-existed in the Labour Party. These are democratic socialism and social democracy. Here, the division is to do with ends.

Ends

As we have seen, **revolutionary socialists** favour the abolition of capitalism and the state to which it is so closely linked, and replace it with a socialist society characterised by the basic principles outlined above. Many would still describe themselves as Marxists.

Reformists fall into the two groups mentioned above. These two types of reformist socialism have provided the basis of political thinking and the basis of discord within the British Labour Party since the Second World War. The creation of New Labour under Tony Blair's leadership since 1994 has involved a new basis of thought which, at this stage, may be simply described as 'The Third Way'.

Democratic socialism was the unifying belief of the British Labour Party from its beginnings in 1900. Since the Second World War, it has been characterised by:
- a belief in collectivism, redistribution of wealth and equality of outcome (a much more equal distribution of rewards);
- support for the National Health Service and a universal system of social security and welfare benefits;
- cooperation with the trade union movement;
- support for Clause Four of the party's 1918 Constitution, which used to read: 'To secure for the workers by hand or by brain the full fruits of their industry and the most equitable distribution thereof that may be possible upon the basis of the common ownership of the means of production, distribution and exchange, and the best obtainable system of popular administration and control of each industry or service.'
- a belief in the value of nationalisation (state ownership) of key industries and utilities, as envisaged in Clause Four. As a result of the programme of post-war nationalisation by the 1945–50 Labour government, some 20 per cent of industry was under state control, 80 per cent in private hands. The result was a 'mixed' economy.

Social democracy developed in the 1950s. Some Labour intellectuals, including the leader Hugh Gaitskell (1955–63) looked for a new direction. Particularly influential among them was Anthony Crosland who wrote *The Future of Socialism* in 1956. He developed the concept of social democracy which was a revised version of socialism for the Labour party. This 'revisionism' was never accepted by the Left of the party who saw it as a dilution of their ideology; they remained committed to democratic socialism.

Crosland believed that socialism was essentially about equality. In the same way as Tony Blair attempted to modernise the thinking of the Labour Party in the 1990s, so Crosland from the 1950s also attempted to modernise the post-war thinking of the party. He felt that the achievements of the Labour governments from 1945 to 1951 had been substantial. However, Crosland believed that Labour should focus on ends rather than means. The ends were values like equality, cooperation and community. He felt that it was unnecessary to create any more nationalised industries. In his words, 'the ownership of the means of production has ceased to be the key factor which imparts to society its essential character'. Revisionism, therefore, included support of a mixed economy as it stood in the mid-1950s.

While more traditional socialists focused on collectivism, social democrats placed far greater emphasis on individualism, arguing that the main and only purpose of collectivism was to create opportunities and choices for individuals. Closely allied to this was the concern of social democrats about the impact of collectivism on individual freedom, especially in relation to such issues as excessive compulsory taxation.

Social democrats share the view of all socialists that humans are born equal, their lives being of equal moral value; they also agree that the legal and political status of the individual in society should be one of 'equality before the law'. Their point of departure from democratic socialists is their belief in equality of opportunity. Social democrats accept that there are inequalities between individuals in terms of abilities, motivation and other personal qualities, but believe strongly that they should all have equal life chances. They do not favour equality of outcome, which they see as a concept whose application penalises individual freedoms.

Social democrats support a welfare state, funded by progressive taxation, as a means of assisting those who are especially vulnerable and redistributing income to a degree. For those who are unable to provide for themselves, the state should step in and give support, but the means to return to work should also be in place. 'New Labour' has a similar idea of social justice. It too favours the welfare state and increased public expenditure especially in areas such as education, where it is most needed.

REFERENCES

1 J. Grimond, *The Liberal Challenge*, Hollis and Carter, 1963.
2 A. Heywood, *Political Ideologies: An Introduction*, Macmillan, 1998.
3 As note 2 above.

USEFUL WEB SITES

Conservative Party **www.conservatives.com** This includes 'Welcome to the Conservative Party' web site which contains news, campaigns, recent speeches, conferences, etc.

Labour Party **www.labour.org.uk** This contains current policies, latest news, campaigns and an interactive section.

Liberal Democrats **www.libdems.org.uk** This, too, contains up-to-date information on policies, beliefs, etc.

In addition to the above, many MPs have their own individual website, e.g.

Conservative Party – Ann Widdecombe **www.annwiddecombemp.com**;

Labour Party – Frank Field **www.frankfieldmp.com**;

Liberal Democrat Party – Charles Kennedy **www.charleskennedy.org.uk**

It would also be useful for students to log on to the website of their own constituency MP.

Groups with links to the major parties attempt to influence their thinking and policies. Some may be found on the internet: Fabian Society **www.fabian-society.org.uk** This is a left-of-centre think tank founded in 1884; Tory Reform Group **www.toryreformgroup.tory.org.uk** This is a small group of MPs who are committed to liberal, 'one-nation' Tory policies. During the Thatcher years they were known as 'wets'.

SAMPLE QUESTIONS

Questions are likely to focus on: The similarities and differences of ideas between the parties; The ideas of a particular party now (e.g. how socialist is New Labour?, how Thatcherite is the Conservative Party today?); The importance of political ideas generally for a political party.

Political parties 1945–2002: post-war trends

AIMS OF THIS CHAPTER

➤ To consider the post-war consensus 1945–79.

➤ To outline the developments in ideas and policies of the Conservative, Labour and Liberal Democrat parties 1979–2002.

➤ To describe the rise and fall of the Social Democrats.

The post-war consensus 1945–79

There is a strong case for arguing that there was a **consensus** over a number of key policy areas between successive Conservative and Labour governments from the late 1940s until the mid-1970s (see Figure 9.1, ideological fluctuations). Not only was there a consensus between the two major parties about how politics should be conducted and wide acceptance of parliamentary democracy in an essentially two-party system, but also a consensus about the aims of

> **consensus**
> General agreement between potentially opposing groups.

government policies and the nature of the post-war economy and society that they were to protect and develop. Even though there were differences of emphasis between the two parties when either formed a government – something that the party forming Her Majesty's Opposition was always likely to focus on – the consensus between them provided continuity.

On the other hand, there is evidence that denies a post-war consensus between governments over this 25-year period. In particular, some argue that in this period politicians did not recognise it and that it is a retrospective historical interpretation that was made in the 1980s.

The period reviewed

The Labour governments between 1945 and 1951 created a mixed economy, strongly influenced by Keynesian orthodoxy, and the welfare state, inspired by the Beveridge Report. The Conservative party provided opposition but by the late 1940s had accepted that in the 'New Jerusalem' as it was sometimes

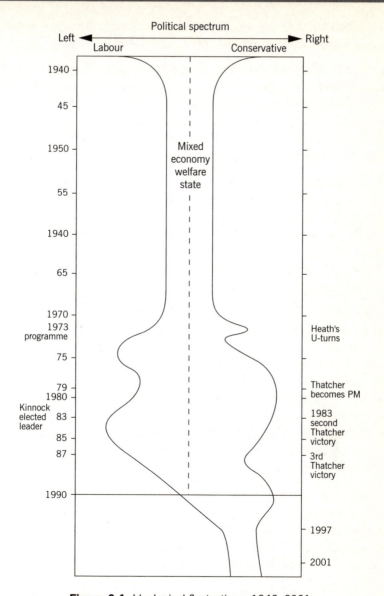

Figure 9.1 Ideological fluctuations, 1940–2001

Source: Adapted from Bill Jones and Dennis Kavanagh,
British Politics Today, 6th edn, Manchester University Press, 1998.

called, there was much with which they could agree. Traditional Conservatism, with its paternalistic thinking, and typified by Harold Macmillan's *The Middle Way* (1938), could accommodate and accept the welfare state, broadly accept nationalisation and still stress the importance of a vigorous private sector. Quintin Hogg (later Lord Hailsham), a Tory reformer like Macmillan pressed the Conservative Party 'to lead and dominate revolution by superior statesmanship instead of to oppose it, to by-pass the progressives by stepping in front of current controversy instead of engaging in it'.[1]

The popularity of the reforms and the scale of the party's defeat at the 1945 general election were also key motivations. The Labour Chancellor of the Exchequer, Hugh Gaitskell (1950–51) and his Conservative successor R.A. Butler (1951–55) each in part gave their name to this consensus, which is sometimes referred to as the 'Butskellite consensus'. Social democracy and a renewed 'One Nation Conservatism' could agree on many issues of policy.

During the 1950s and until the later 1960s, successive governments aimed to achieve full employment, rising living standards and the expansion of welfare-state provision. As Harold Macmillan said, soon after becoming Prime Minister in 1957: 'Let us be frank about it; most of our people *have never had it so good*. Go around the country . . . and you'll see a state of prosperity such as we have never had in my lifetime . . . What is beginning to worry some of us is, is it too good to be true? Or perhaps I should say, is it too good to last?'

The 'never had it so good' phrase overshadowed the later uncomfortable questions. Macmillan's concerns for the future were well founded as the British economy failed to keep up with its competitors. Recurring balance of payment problems, low investment and productivity coupled with poor indus-trial relations necessitated government economic stop–go policies. Economic growth was not smooth as a consequence. The consensus was therefore eventually questioned because economic decline could not support both rising living standards and improved welfare provision. This was certainly the case by 1970 when the Conservatives were returned to power after a six-year absence from government.

The Heath government aimed to maintain the welfare state but hoped to improve economic performance and escape from the stop–go trap by reducing controls on the private sector, entering the European Economic Community in 1973, reducing government expenditure and taxation and ending costly government interventions in the economy, such as saving 'lame-duck' indus-tries. The powers of the trade unions were to be reduced by statute law. Subse-quent investment in industry did not improve, inflation rose rapidly and balance of payments deficits increased. Unemployment rose to one million and opposition to the Industrial Relations Act of 1971 resulted in the loss of nearly 24 million working days through strikes in 1972. This resulted in a sharp U-turn by Heath leading to a policy of holding wages down (leading to more industrial unrest) and the reimposition of controls on the private sector. The overnight increases in oil prices by OPEC (the organisation of Petroleum Exporting Countries) following the **Yom Kippur War** added to the difficulties. This U-turn proved to be so damaging to Heath within the Conservative Party that he lost the leadership election to Margaret Thatcher in 1975.

Labour was in office from 1974 to 1979, but the governments returned in the two general elections of 1974, suffered from three major difficulties: a narrow overall majority in the Commons, trade union wage demands and an inflation rate that reached 24 per cent in 1975. A combination of rising inflation and unemployment led to a financial crisis in 1976 in which international confidence in the pound fell badly, resulting in a request for a loan from the International Monetary Fund (IMF) by Denis Healey the then Chancellor of the Exchequer. The loan was granted, but at a price; Labour had to make massive cuts in government spending, curb wage demands and accept rapidly rising unemployment. The government's new major priority was to be the reduction of inflation.

Yom Kippur War

6 October 1973. This was essentially between Israel and Egypt (with Syrian support). For Jewish people, Yom Kippur is the Day of Atonement, i.e. a day of fasting, penitence and cleansing. As a result, Israeli forces were taken by surprise. Egyptian forces crossed the Suez Canal. The war ended after three weeks with the USSR supporting the Arab nations and the USA supporting Israel. Tension persisted in this region which was and remains strategically sensitive for world oil production.

Analysts see this crisis period in 1976 as the point where Keynesian economics were abandoned. In this period of enforced policies, some also see the forerunner of the monetarist policies of the 1980s. Following what became known as the 'Winter of Discontent' in 1978–79 during which public sector workers struck for higher wages, Labour was defeated at the polls and Margaret Thatcher became Prime Minister in May 1979.

The managed economy, based on Keynesian orthodoxy, was central to the post-war consensus. A series of factors brought about the demise of Keynesianism as the dominant theory of government policy. The critical factor had been 'stagflation' (i.e. growing unemployment accompanied by growing inflation); 'demand-side' management of the economy – pumping in money to stimulate demand and reduce unemployment – had ultimately not worked. Increased expenditure not only fuelled inflation but did not reduce unemployment. As early as October 1976, this was signalled by Prime Minister Callaghan in his speech to the Labour Party Conference:

> We used to think that you could spend your way out of recession and increase employment by cutting taxes and boosting government spending. I tell you in all candour that that option no longer exists, and that in so far as it ever did exist, it only worked on each occasion . . . by injecting a bigger dose of inflation into the economy, followed by a higher level of unemployment as the next step.

Margaret Thatcher and the New Right believed they had a clear and consistent theory to underpin a new economic strategy.

There appears to be more evidence for a consensus than against. Perhaps there are two other critical elements to this debate. Firstly, there was a continuity of policy making from one government to the next, irrespective of party; it was politicians from the centre like Macmillan and Wilson who dominated their

Was there a consensus?

- Historians like Ben Pimlott have argued that the consensus was a myth, a retrospective interpretation of post-war Britain created in the 1980s. Certainly the word 'consensus' does not appear to have been used by many politicians or members of the public in the period itself.

- Until the early 1970s, politics was locked in a rigid two-party system – Labour and Conservative – which seemed highly adversarial. Bitter debates took place and polarised positions were often taken over many issues such as the Suez crisis in 1956, industrial disputes, especially those leading to the three-day week in 1974, entry into the European Community which cut across party lines, immigration and race relations, defence spending and Britain's nuclear deterrent, and the introduction of comprehensive education.

- There were differences in emphasis taken by the two major parties, especially when in opposition, over economic policy. The Conservatives focused on the importance of free enterprise and the reduction of taxation while Labour concentrated on economic planning and the interests of working people.

- General election campaigns highlighted the differences between the two parties competing for government, while ignoring the areas of agreement between them.

parties. Secondly, the lack of consensus in the ideas, values and policies of the two major parties became so marked for much of the 1980s that it was easier to perceive that a post-war consensus actually had existed.

The main policy areas of the postwar consensus

- managed economy
- a mixed economy;
- full employment;
- the importance of trade unions, employers and government working in harmony;
- the welfare state;
- the reduction of inequalities;
- defence and foreign affairs;

Thatcherite Conservatism in practice 1979–90

The Thatcher years 1979–90 are frequently referred to as the 'Thatcher revolution', because during this period she set aside the post-war consensus. Her New Right ideology was radical and at variance with the policies of post-war governments of either party. Nevertheless despite this radicalism she was pragmatic about how and when to introduce the changes she desired.

In her view, there were many things wrong with the state of Britain at the time of her take-over.

- Keynesian policies, implemented by successive post-war governments, had partly caused Britain's continuing economic decline.
- The trade unions had enjoyed too close a relationship with government (corporatism) and union power was undermining the authority of governments.
- The welfare state was too expensive, a drain on the taxpayer; and it also eroded self-reliance and created a culture of dependency.
- Britain's status on the world stage had been reduced and this process had to be reversed.

What was Thatcherism?

Based on New Right principles and policies, Thatcherism was not a prescription prepared completely in advance and in detail. Some aspects were introduced in response to events. However, from the beginning there were certain key elements:

- The replacement of Keynesianism by monetarism, and an emphasis on defeating inflation.
- Privatisation of industries and utilities.
- A reduction of trade union power: the defeat of the miners in the 1984 to 1985 strike served to show the government's approach to union militancy.
- The rolling back of the state to encourage individual freedom and an enterprise economy. In reality, Thatcherism involved the creation of a strong state but one which was directly concerned with such issues as law and order, not economic issues.
- Strong leadership, as exhibited during the Falklands War of 1982. As she appointed more Thatcherite ministers (dries) to the Cabinet and sacked more traditional Conservatives (wets), this impression was enhanced (see her premiership, p. 200).
- An emphasis on Victorian virtues of hard work, enterprise, thrift and self-reliance.
- Opposition to any trends towards integration in what was then the European Community.
- An electoral phenomenon – the Prime Minister won three elections in a row, making her the most successful party leader at the polls, in the twentieth century.

Majorite Conservatism: Thatcherism with a human face?

When John Major succeeded Mrs Thatcher as leader of the Conservative Party and therefore became Prime Minister, it was with her blessing. She believed him to be the best person to carry on her policies. He led the Conservatives to a further general election victory in 1992, and to defeat in 1997.

His government's economic policy involved managing an inherited depression – Black Wednesday, an enforced exit from the exchange rate mechanism (ERM) and a gradual recovery. Privatisation of coal mining was prepared for closing thirty-one pits despite much initial protest. The privatisation of British Railways went ahead and the privatisation of the London Underground and the Post Office were subsequently discussed. In 1991 Major put forward the 'Citizen's Charter' which was a commitment to improve public services. He negotiated the Maastricht Treaty in 1991 which committed Britain to greater integration in Europe. He also negotiated an opt-out from the Social Chapter which involved numerous regulations designed to protect people from exploitation at work. Major believed that acceptance of the Social Chapter would be to allow socialism to creep in by the back door. However, the Thatcherites saw Maastricht as too pro-Europe.

At the annual conference in 1993, Major called upon the party 'to go back to basics . . . .(we want) our public service to give the best . . . respect for the family and the law . . . ' He intended his words to be taken as a moral crusade for better standards in public life, but tabloid journalists saw an opportunity to hunt down sleaze in every corner of the Conservative party. As a man who supported family values and sought to improve the tone of society, he was nevertheless unprepared for the revelations about sexual and financial misconduct which often dominated the headlines.

To an extent, Major pursued Thatcherite policies with some privatisation and trade union reform. On the other hand he abandoned the poll tax and signed the Maastricht Treaty. Overall, his government found it difficult to be pro-active especially after Black Wednesday.

William Hague 1997–2001

Early indications that there would be a return to a more pragmatic and compassionate Conservatism did not really emerge in the policy document, *The Common Sense Revolution*, which was published for the annual conference in 1999. The party then and through to the 2001 election was strongly Euro-sceptic and fiercely opposed to the Euro, tough on law and order and committed to tax cuts.

During the 1980s, the Conservatives had divided between wets and dries on economic policy and in the 1990s between supporters and opponents of greater European integration. The first issue had declined, but what emerged were differences over society's changing values. *The Times* characterised the two groups as 'mods' and 'rockers'. The mods (modernisers) wanted the party to relax, be more inclusive and tolerant of different lifestyles, especially those of the young. The rockers represented a much more traditional and authoritarian stance. Ann Widdecombe articulated the viewpoint of this group, usually supported by Iain Duncan Smith. The Rockers opposed repeal of Section 28, and followed a tough line on asylum seekers and drug use. Michael Portillo led the Mods who pressed for more socially liberal views. Those who supported this more tolerant outlook included Francis Maude and David Willetts. Hague appeared to have a foot in both camps. Nevertheless, whether he intended it or not, his conference speech in 1999, and his spring conference speech in March 2001, suggested intolerance: 'Come with me and I will give you back your country.' He warned that the return of the Labour government would turn Britain into 'a foreign land'.

After the party defeats in 1945 and 1966, the Conservatives had instituted wide-ranging reviews of policy. Following the Second World War, R.A. Butler and Harold Macmillan forced colleagues to 'bite the bullet', accept Labour's post-war reforms and assure the public that – if returned to office – they would not seek to reverse them. Nothing on this scale took place between 1997 and 2001. At the general election, the Conservatives campaigned on too few issues. In particular, they neglected education, health and transport, which were matters of great concern to the electorate. But they were on difficult territory, for the party was perceived as having been vulnerable on these issues prior to the 1997 election. It was difficult – too soon – to renounce the record of the previous Conservative governments by adopting new approaches.

Labour 1979–2002

1979–83: from social democracy to democratic socialism

Labour's defeat in the 1979 general election produced a bitter internal battle between the democratic socialists (the left) and the social democrats (centre and right). The left argued that social democracy and Keynesian economics had failed in the 1970s and were furious that public expenditure had to be drastically cut in return for a huge loan from the IMF. Led by Tony Benn, supporters aimed to give the extra-parliamentary elements of the party more power. The voting system for the leader and deputy leader was changed, MPs would face mandatory reselection before every general election; this would enable left-wing activists to deselect right-wing MPs. They failed to gain control of the manifesto from the National Executive Committee. In this period too, many constituency parties and Labour councils were controlled by the old left. The Trotskyite Militant Tendency infiltrated many of these organisations. The left took over the party. Democratic socialism replaced social democracy. For party enthusiasts, the changing approach was welcome, but on the Right there was much disillusion, to the extent that three ex-Cabinet ministers – Bill Rogers, David Owen and Shirley Williams – left the party to join Roy Jenkins (also an ex-Cabinet Minister) to form the Social Democrat Party. Over the ensuing months some twenty to thirty centre-right Labour MPs joined them.

Michael Foot became leader in 1980 and presided over the lurch to the left. In 1983, Labour's manifesto was significantly left-wing. The monetarism of the Conservative government and the old consensus politics were rejected. The party was committed to state ownership of assets recently privatised, to taking a public stake in electronics, pharmaceuticals and other industries, to supporting the steel, aerospace and shipbuilding industry and to policies to further full employment. Import controls would be used to protect British industries. A close partnership with the miners and other key trade unionists was to be established to achieve these goals. Public spending would be increased to improve the NHS and state education. Britain would withdraw from the EEC and NATO and was committed to unilateral nuclear disarmament. They also planned to abolish the House of Lords.

Labour and the Conservatives were now further apart than they had been since 1945. There was no longer talk of consensus. Labour was defeated heavily at the general election.

1983–94: from democratic socialism to social democracy

Neil Kinnock was elected leader after Michael Foot stepped down and Roy Hattersley became deputy leader. From this point, the influence of the left declined. By 1994, it could be argued that the party had reverted to the revisionist social democracy associated with the post-war consensus. On the other hand, others say that they had caught up with the agenda of the Thatcher governments and had broadly accepted them.

At the 1985 annual conference, Kinnock famously denounced Militant Tendency. Subsequently, this group was expelled from the party, including MPs associated with it. By the 1987 general election, an ideological transformation had begun. There was to be no major extensions of public ownership, no withdrawal from the EEC, no abolition of the Lords and no withdrawal from NATO. Unilateralism remained but conventional defence spending would be increased. The party also improved its election campaigning and image but it still lost in 1987.

It was from this point that Labour's transformation was particularly significant. A two-year policy review culminated in the publication of 'Meet the challenge, make the change' in 1989 and this formed the basis of the 1992 manifesto. There was only a vague commitment to nationalisation and the public initiatives that had been privatised would only be returned to public ownership if 'circumstances allowed'. The Conservative trade union reforms were largely accepted. Overall, the party supported the mixed economy, and acknowledged the benefits of free markets and the need for competition. A more positive stance on the EEC was adopted and unilateralism was at last abandoned. The left were highly critical of this drift to the right, worried about the apparent abandonment of full employment as the main aim of economic policy and the linking of public spending to economic growth. Kinnock, a left-winger originally, was heavily criticised by Tony Benn. The party now even seemed to put freedom above equality. In spite of all this, Labour lost again, Kinnock resigned and was succeeded by John Smith.

Labour had gained 34.4 per cent of the vote in the general election, returning 271 MPs to the Commons. So near yet still so far. The direction of party policy back to the centre, the perception that John Smith would prove a 'safe pair of hands' if he became Prime Minister, and that time was healing the damage done in the early 1980s all suggested that Labour should win the next general election. This was known as the 'one more heave' view. Under Smith, more internal reforms took place notably the introduction of OMOV which involved the abolition of the block vote. In 1994, John Smith died, dealing the party a terrible blow. However, long before this, a group of 'modernisers' including Tony Blair, Gordon Brown and Peter Mandelson were anxious to consider further policy review and further changes to its election 'machine'.

1994–2002; Blairism in practice

The extent to which the Labour party has ever been a socialist party is debatable. It was formed in 1900 to represent the interests of Labour in Parliament. The word 'socialist' did not appear in its 1900 constitution, it has never been Marxist, and its leadership has mostly been moderate and pragmatic. The party that fought the 1983 election was the exception. Yet many in the party clung to the socialist idea. This was symbolised by Clause IV of the 1918 constitution, committing the party to socialist ideas and to

> secure for the producers by hand and by brain the full fruits of their industry, and the most equitable distribution thereof that may be possible, upon the basis of the common ownership of the means of production, distribution and exchange and the best obtainable system of popular administration and control of each industry and service.

For Tony Blair, Clause IV symbolised outdated ideas that were now unachievable and even undesirable, notably nationalisation (common ownership). It was also a weakness, a piece of ideological baggage that was vulnerable to attack from other parties. Blair, at his first party conference in 1994, called for reform of the constitution which was code for reform of Clause IV. Adams sums up Blair's position effectively: 'It could be said that after 1983, what Labour leaderships essentially did was to pick among the wreckage of British post-war socialism attempting to assemble from bits of the embers an electorally pleasing pattern. But Blair was something new . . . Blair wanted to abandon the wreckage.'[2]

Despite fears of a party split, Clause IV was revised by the spring of 1995, and contains the following:

1 The Labour Party . . . believes that by the strength of our common endeavour we achieve more than we achieve alone, so as to create for each of us the means to realise our true potential and for all of us a community in which power, wealth and opportunity are in the hands of the many not the few, where the rights we enjoy reflect the duties we owe, and where we have together, freely, in a spirit of solidarity, tolerance and respect.

2 To these ends we work for:
   • a dynamic economy, serving the public interest, in which the enterprise of the market and the rigour of competition are joined with the forces of partnership and cooperation to produce the wealth the nation needs and the opportunity for all to work and prosper, with a thriving private sector and high quality public services;
   • a just society;
   • an open democracy;
   • a healthy environment.

The above is evidence that Tony Blair and 'New Labour' are not socialist when it comes to economics. If pushed, however, Blair might claim that he is a socialist, but he draws upon the long traditions of **ethical** and **Christian socialism**, rather than on the economic heritage. He rarely uses the word socialism.

These two strands influenced Blair to a degree but the Scottish philosopher John Macmurray (1891–1976), was much more influential. He developed his own version of ethical socialism known as communitarianism. In Heywood's words, this is the belief that 'the self or person is constituted through the community, in the sense that individuals are shaped by the communities to which they belong and thus owe them a debt of respect and consideration'.[3]

The implications of this approach are that it takes the radicalism of socialism, stresses traditional communities and institutions like the family and emphasises authority and social responsibility. People have freedom and rights but they must be matched by duties and obligations. The policy implications of this were shown by Blair when he was shadow home secretary: 'I think its important that we are tough on crime and tough on the causes of crime.'

As a committed Christian, Blair has frequently spoken of the strength of his religious beliefs. The

Christian socialism
The view that the Christian virtue of caring for one's fellow man is best expressed in the desire for a better society in which all are treated with decency and respect.

ethical socialism
This encompasses CS but argues that capitalist society, based on competition and greed, is usually deficient and that a better society would be based on cooperation and fellowship.

above shows a toughness on law and order perceived to have been lacking in Labour's previous policies on law and order. Whereas 'Old Labour' attitudes saw people as victims of the capitalist system – the poor, ill-educated or unemployed – Blair and 'New Labour' will have none of this. People must exercise responsibility and help themselves. The government can provide opportunity, as in the 'Welfare to Work' scheme, but will not countenance dependence except from the permanently disadvantaged.

If 'New Labour' was to create a 'New Britain' then constitutional reform, long overdue, must be introduced. These were to include devolution for Scotland and Wales, a continuation of the peace process in Northern Ireland, reform of the House of Lords, a freedom of information act, the incorporation of the European Convention on Human Rights into UK law, and – possibly – electoral reform for the House of Commons (see pp. 304–5).

'New Labour' draws heavily on Liberalism. Blair believes that the opportunity of a left-of-centre progressive consensus, based on cooperation or even merger of the two parties, was lost in 1918 when Labour opted for the narrowness of Clause IV. The Conservative Party and the forces of conservatism dominated British politics as a consequence. The opportunity now is to establish a new broad progressive consensus equipped with ideas and policies to dominate the twenty-first century. Cooperation with the Liberal Democrats, both public and in secret before the 1997 general election, was part of Blair's 'project'. That it was only possible on a limited scale after the election was largely due to 'New Labour's' massive majority.

New Labour ideas and policies were all very well, but getting into power and staying in power were vital. After the 1992 defeat, Labour Party emissaries visited the Bill Clinton election machine in the USA. After the Democrat defeats of the 1980s by Reagan and Bush, Clinton's team had 're-invented' the party to revitalise their appeal. The 'election machine's' function was to communicate this to the electorate. Yet there was more. Labour's people saw a massive system of media monitoring and briefing which was used to counter-attack the Republicans and any media bias against the Democrats. After Blair became leader, a version of this was created at Millbank Tower in London. After New Labour won the 1997 general election, Millbank employees became part of Blair's inner circle – Philip Gould (political strategist), Jonathan Powell (chief of staff), Alastair Campbell (press secretary) and David Miliband (head of policy unit).

At a private dinner in January 1997 with the election approaching, Mrs Thatcher made a speech which included the announcement: 'Tony Blair is a man who won't let Britain down.' This was reported in *The Times* and later revealed by Blair in a newspaper. Her endorsement was not complete because she saw New Labour as a 'boneless wonder'. Nevertheless, Blair had cultivated her support, made clear his admiration for her economic realism, agreed with the need for a dynamic economy to counter increasing globalisation and said that she had got many things right. He also made clear his admiration for her leadership and prime ministerial style. He regretted that Labour had been slow to acknowledge the trade union reforms of the 1980s.

Table 9.1 Some differences between Old and New Labour

Old Labour	New Labour
Particular appeal to working class but to middle classes too	Appeal to all voters
Class politics of the left	Modernising movement of centre left
Mixed economy including nationalisation of key industries (original Clause 4)	Rely on market economy (new Clause 4)
Wealth redistribution from upper and middle to working classes via taxation and public spending	Redistribution via strong economic growth produced by enterprise economy
Corporatism: state dominates over civil society	New democratic state
Trade unions occupy a key role in the party and in the economy	No special treatment for unions. Establish good relations with business
Strong welfare state: 'cradle to grave' care	Social investment state
Some interest in constitutional reform	Constitutional reform to 'modernise' government
Limits on leadership/influence of rank and file in campaigning	Strong leadership/sophisticated communications and public relations machine

Since its creation in 1900, Labour has been associated with equality. A commitment to redistribution was not forthcoming from New Labour before the 1997 election, for such a commitment was believed to be one of the reasons for their 1992 defeat. This partly explains Gordon Brown's commitment to retain Conservative spending plans. New Labour stands accused even by those of the Old Labour right such as Lord Hattersley that the disadvantaged have been badly neglected and that the old goal of equality of outcome has been abandoned. The Chancellor did attempt to redistribute by stealth, but had to be careful not to offend Middle England too much by the use of so-called 'stealth taxes'.

The third way

Tony Blair has embraced the concept of a third way to describe New Labour's ideology. Just as Harold Macmillan adopted a middle way for the Conservative party in the 1930s, so Tony Blair has attempted to carve out a middle way

New Labour in power: key policy areas

- The Bank of England was given the power to control interest rates just days after the election victory.

- Aware that previous Labour governments had been beset with economic difficulties, Gordon Brown as Chancellor kept government spending at the same levels as those planned by the Conservatives, for two years. This helped Labour gain power, helped its reputation as sound economic managers, but did not help Britain's public services, notably health and education.

- Tony Blair had made education a top priority and ministers achieved their aim of ensuring that almost all children of five to seven were taught in classes of less than thirty. Targets in numeracy and literacy in primary schools were close to delivery. The morale of the teaching profession was not raised however and teacher shortages were widespread.

- In health the 1999 Health Act abolished GP fund holding, and the National Health Service (Private Finance Act) 1997 empowered health trusts to enter into private finance initiative deals. Even more than education, the NHS suffered from the early low spending plans that Labour adopted from the Conservatives. By 2001, more investment had gone into the NHS but for many patients there was still very much to be done.

- The government's commitment to raising 'the living standards of the poorest' had a controversial beginning when lone-parent benefit was cut. However, a whole raft of reforms including the National Minimum Wage Act 1998, the Tax Credits Act 1999 which brought tax credits for working families and the Carers and Disabled Childrens Act 2000, providing support for carers of the long-term sick or disabled, had significant outcomes. By April 2001, 1.2 million children and 800,000 adults had been taken out of poverty.

- Comparing 1997 with 2002 most rail and car commuters would say that the situation had deteriorated. The Hatfield rail crash in 2000 revealed serious negligence in the maintenance of the rail network and Railtrack – set up under privatisation during the Major government – was subsequently taken over by government in 2001. The state of the London Underground and road traffic congestion also pointed to the need for large-scale investment.

- On law and order, drugs, asylum seekers and football hooligans, New Labour has taken a tough stance but in March 2002 there was a growing concern about street crime.

- Constitutional reform was more wide-ranging than any twentieth century government (see p. 279).

- Labour is now probably more pro-European than has ever been the case. The creation of a single European currency – the Euro – at the start of 2002 did not include Britain. Gordon Brown has five economic tests to determine when the time is right for Britain to join, but the timing of a referendum probably has as much to do with public opinion as economic convergence.

between left and right, between state socialist planning and free market capitalism. It appeals to centre-left progressives and moderate social democrats. Giddens,[4] the main theorist of the third way, uses the term to refer to social democratic renewal. For renewal was necessary in the late 1990s to adapt to the probably irreversible transformation of Britain by Thatcherism, the revival of free-market capitalism and the realities of globalisation.

Key elements of the third way include:

1 A recognition that human nature is competitive and cooperative, altruistic and self-interested. In this way individuals both depend on the communities in which they live but should also contribute to them. As a result, individual lives and society as a whole are enriched.
2 A definition of equality is inclusion, and inequality as exclusion. Inclusion refers in its broadest sense to citizenship with its civil and political rights, its obligations and its opportunities for self-fulfilment and to make a contribution to society. Measures need to be put in place to reduce the involuntary exclusion of the disadvantaged.
3 The belief that there are no rights without balancing responsibilities. The old social democracy was likely to provide rights unconditionally. Now the rights of citizens are accompanied by reciprocal duties and it is vital that there is mutual responsibility between individuals and institutions.
4 A recognition that there should be no authority without democracy. Constitutional reform is vital for this to be achieved, so is the creation of a more participatory democracy.

'What matters is what works'

This slogan epitomises the third way's approach to policy making. The main consideration is the practical one of delivery for after 1997 Tony Blair had an overriding aim of ensuring a second term so that he could carry out much of his New Labour programme. The long-term goal of the Blair project is to create a left-of-centre coalition that is broad enough to encourage 'progressives' from other parties to enter his 'Big Tent'.

Social Democrats, Liberals and Liberal Democrats

The centre ground of British politics had been occupied by the Labour and Conservative parties until the late 1970s. After her victory at the 1979 general election, Mrs Thatcher began to take her party further to the right. Labour, meanwhile, moved further to the left. The Liberal party, with only 11 MPs, remained in the centre. Nevertheless, what had been created was a huge 'gap' at the centre of British politics between the major parties.

In 1980, Roy Jenkins, a former Labour Cabinet minister and then President of the Common Market Commission, declared that a new party might 'break the mould of British politics'. The left-wing measures passed by the Labour Conference in January 1981 provoked David Owen, William Rodgers and Shirley Williams to leave the party. They were soon joined by Jenkins and became known as the 'Gang of Four', and were the founders of the Social Democrat Party (SDP). By the middle of 1982, there were 30 SDP MPs.

Earlier, in September 1981 an Alliance with the Liberals had been created. Public responses initially were sensationally encouraging although it was unrealistic to believe that it would have been sustained at such a level. The Conservatives regained popularity after the Falklands War and Labour's divisions were 'papered over'. In the 1983 election the Alliance gained 25.4 per cent of the vote compared to Labour's 27.6 per cent. The Liberals gained 17 seats but the SDP gained only 6. The electoral system clearly worked against them. In 1987 the SDP fought the general election with the Alliance again but could only return 5 MPs to the Commons. By this time, Labour had begun to move back towards the centre under Neil Kinnock's leadership, with the main changes in policy still to come in 1988 and 1989.

The SDP and the Liberals attempted to capture the middle ground with a programme that included 'New Right' economics and trade union policies, 1970s Labour defence policies and decentralisation of government. *The Times* in 1981 referred to the SDP's platform as a modernised version of 'Butskellism'. Its main opportunity was probably at the 1983 election, but it proved to be a case of 'so near, yet so far'.

Timescale, Social Democrat and Liberal parties, 1974–87

- **February 1974:** The Liberal party gained 14 seats and 19.3 per cent of the vote, a far better result than any since the Second World War. Edward Heath and his Conservative government did not relinquish power. The Liberals held the balance of power in a 'hung parliament'. Jeremy Thorpe, the Liberal leader negotiated unsuccessfully with Heath. Labour formed a government. This looked like an opportunity lost.
- **October 1974:** The Liberal party gained 13 seats and 18.3 per cent of the vote. David Steel became leader. The Lib–Lab pact (1977–78) in which the Liberals supported Labour's minority government subsequently lost them votes.
- **1979 Election:** 11 seats and 13.8 per cent of the vote.
- **1981:** The Liberal party joined forces with the SDP to form the Alliance.
- **1983:** 17 seats and 13.7 per cent of the votes.
- **1987:** 17 seats and 12.8 per cent of the votes.

In each election, the Liberals did significantly better than the SDP in terms of seats. The SDP then voted to merge with the Liberals.

Timescale, Liberal Democratic Party, 1989–2002

- **1989**: The merged party became know as the Liberal Democrats.

- **1989–92**: Paddy Ashdown was elected leader in 1988 with the party in chaos, due to the merger and financial difficulties as well as a poor showing in the opinion polls. However, a revival began with three by-election victories over the Conservatives and a strong showing in local council elections, culminating in a strong general performance.
- **1992 general election**: 20 seats and 17.8 per cent of the vote.
- **1992–97**: Previously, the party had adopted a policy of 'equidistance' between the other two parties. This was replaced by cooperation with Blair and New Labour over constitutional reform from 1996. However other meetings held in the greatest secrecy (Ashdown Diaries) were also conducted between the two leaders about even closer cooperation over other issues.
- **1997 Election**: 46 seats 16.8 per cent of the votes. The Liberal Democrats joined a Cabinet Committee on constitutional reform which included Ashdown, giving them a taste of power.
- **1999**: Paddy Ashdown resigned and Charles Kennedy was elected leader.
- **2001 general election**: 52 seats 18.3 per cent of the votes.

The Liberal Democrats stand to the left of New Labour. They have been more prepared to raise taxation to increase spending on public services, especially education and health. They worked with New Labour pre-1997 on constitutional reform, much of which has been accomplished. However, elections to the House of Commons are still by the first-past-the-post system. This is a vital policy demand of the Liberal Democrats, as their history since 1979 shows.

They are the most enthusiastic pro-European party in favour of Britain joining the Euro and, long term would favour a federal Europe. On social issues, they lean to the left, to the extent that in March 2002 they voted to legalise the smoking of cannabis. The secret talks between Blair and Ashdown were, in effect, aimed at producing long-term close co-operation between the two parties or maybe, even some type of merger, or in the event of a hung parliament the creation of a Lib-Lab coalition government. When *The Ashdown Diaries* were published (2000), many argued that Ashdown had been 'courted' by Blair as 'insurance' cover for a small New Labour majority. On the other hand, Blair has argued that both parties have the same value systems. Either way, the high peak of Blair–Ashdown cooperation now seems distant history, and the Kennedy leadership has been wary of adopting a position too close to Labour. It is thinking about how it can best court Conservative votes in the future, and proximity to New Labour may be a barrier to attaining this objective.

REFERENCES AND FURTHER READING

1 Q. Hogg, quoted in N. Lowe, *Mastering Modern British History*, Macmillan, 1998.
2 I. Adams, *Ideology and Politics in Britain Today*, Manchester University Press, 1998.
3 A. Heywood, *Key Concepts in Politics*, Macmillan, 2000.
4 A. Giddens, *The Third Way*, Polity, 1998.

D. Simpson, *Political Parties*, Access to Politics series, Hodder & Stoughton, 2000.

USEFUL WEB SITES

Conservative Party **www.conservatives.com**

Labour Party **www.labour.org.uk**

Liberal Democrats **www.libdems.org.uk**

SAMPLE QUESTIONS

1 Outline three areas of broad policy agreement in the post-war consensus.

2 Distinguish between Old Labour and New Labour policies and values.

3 To what extent is the Conservative party still Thatcherite?

Part IV

GOVERNMENT

The British constitution   10

AIMS OF THIS CHAPTER

➤ To outline the various types of constitution.

➤ To examine the sources and main elements of the British constitution.

➤ To consider the issue of civil rights and freedoms under the British constitution.

Definition

A constitution consists of the fundamental rules and principles according to which a state is constituted and governed. These are embodied in the system of laws, customs and **conventions** which define the composition and powers of the organs of state (Parliament, government, the courts) and regulate the relations of these state organs to each other and to the private citizen.

> **conventions**
> These are unwritten rules of the constitution. They are generally agreed practices that have evolved over time within the political system.

Most liberal democracies have a constitution which includes a **bill of rights**, i.e. a legal document that specifies the privileges, rights and freedoms of the individual. Thus, it defines the relationship between the state and the citizen, and establishes the legal extent of civil liberty (see p. 174 for types of bill of rights).

Purpose

The purpose of a constitution is to distribute power and to set limits to the powers of each organ of state. Constitutions are concerned with the process of decision making and the agreed form of rules by which those decisions are made. They usually determine the organisation of the government of a country, the limits to governmental authority and the methods of election and appointment of those who rule. Within this framework, they define the rights and duties of individuals.

Government involves three main functions:
1 the legislative function – the process of making laws;

2 the executive function – implementing the law;

3 the judicial function – law enforcement, deciding if laws have been broken and interpreting the law.

Constitutions usually make clear which people or organs of state have the power to carry out these functions. Some constitutions apply the principle of the separation of these powers in order to prevent a concentration of power into the hands of one person or group. This clarifies the powers of each organ of state, regulates the relations between them and their relations with the private citizen.

Types of constitution

Renwick and Swinburn provide a useful method of classification. They take the following contrasting sets of terms: written/unwritten, flexible/inflexible, and unitary/federal.

In each case, these contrasting terms are ideal types that in reality often do not exist as absolutes.

Written and unwritten constitutions

- **Written**. This type of constitution is found in one single document which outlines the structure of the constitution and the organisation of the state. This is also known as a **codified** constitution. The most obvious example is that produced by the Founding Fathers for America, in 1787.

- **Unwritten**. This type of constitution is not confined to one single document. Much of it may be written down, but in a variety of documents. This is known as an **uncodified** constitution. The most obvious example is the British Constitution which has evolved gradually. (see section on Sources of the British Constitution, p. 164).

Flexible and rigid constitutions

- **Flexible**. This type of constitution is one where changes can take place without a lengthy special procedure. For example, in Great Britain reforms of the House of Lords in 1911, 1949 and 1999 were all accomplished by **statute law** – i.e. Acts of Parliament. Another method of change is by convention like the doctrines of individual and collective ministerial responsibility (see Sources of the British constitution, p. 164).

- **Rigid**. This type of constitution is one where changes can only take place as a result of a special procedure. The following are examples:
  - **USA** requires a two-thirds majority in both houses of Congress and approval by three quarters of the states.

- **Australia** requires approval by both houses of Parliament, then a referendum achieving majority support (a) overall, and (b) in a majority of states.
- **France** requires either approval by (a) both houses of parliament and then referendum, or (b) a three-fifths majority in a joint meeting of both houses.

Unitary and federal constitutions

One of the main problems in creating a constitution is to decide where legitimate power should reside. Basically, there are two options, unitary and federal.

Unitary

In this type of constitution and system of government, ultimate power lies with a central body which is **sovereign**. Theoretically, in Britain, it is Parliament that is sovereign. It has the legal authority to make and repeal laws, to delegate

> **sovereignty**
> This means supreme or ultimate power. In this case, the ultimate authority in a state.

powers to local or regional authorities and to retrieve them (see Chapter 23, Devolution). In reality, this sovereignty of Parliament is not absolute and is limited (see later section on key elements of the constitution for unitary state and sovereignty, p. 168).

Federal

In this type of constitution, legal sovereignty is shared between federal government (at the centre) and the constituent 'states'. The USA is an obvious example. Several states originally joined together for mutual defence; they gave up some of their powers to a federal government in return for its protection. There are therefore two layers of government. The **federal** government takes charge of defence, foreign affairs and immigration – in other words, external affairs, as well as some common domestic functions such as the currency. The **state** governments take charge of functions such as education, law enforcement and public health. In theory, the states can retrieve their powers from the federal government. However, in the USA, when the southern states formed a confederacy and tried to secede (break away) from the Union, a civil war occurred. In 1967, a similar event took place in Nigeria, when Biafra tried to secede from the Nigerian Federation.

Sources of the British constitution

Until the seventeenth century, there was no real separation of powers in the British system of government. Rather, there was an absolute monarchy. The King was sovereign. However, the outcome of the great political upheavals of that century – the civil wars from 1642 to 1652, the execution of Charles 1 in 1649 and the 'Glorious Revolution' of 1688 which included a Bill of Rights to

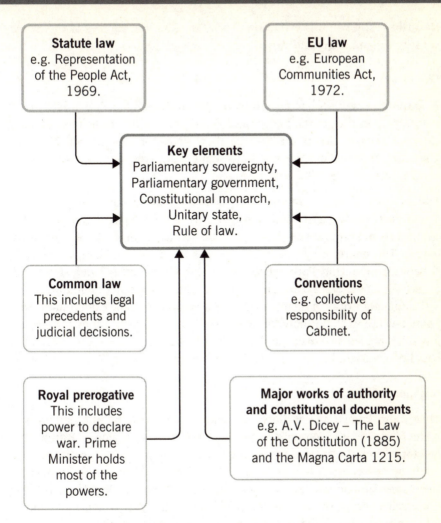

Statute law
e.g. Representation
of the People Act,
1969.

EU law
e.g. European
Communities Act,
1972.

Key elements
Parliamentary sovereignty,
Parliamentary government,
Constitutional monarch,
Unitary state,
Rule of law.

Common law
This includes legal
precedents and
judicial decisions.

Conventions
e.g. collective
responsibility of
Cabinet.

Royal prerogative
This includes
power to declare
war. Prime
Minister holds
most of the
powers.

**Major works of authority
and constitutional documents**
e.g. A.V. Dicey – The Law
of the Constitution (1885)
and the Magna Carta 1215.

Figure 10.1 The sources of the British constitution

Note: Statute law and EU law take precedence over the other four sources.

protect Parliament against royal absolutism – was a **constitutional monarchy**. Since then, the constitution has evolved gradually, but not always peacefully. Changes in the constitution and demands for change have often been accompanied by protest, mostly peaceful, but sometimes accompanied by violence or the threat of violence – e.g. during the Reform Bill crisis of 1830–32 (see Chapter 4 on Elections) and the campaigns of the suffragettes, 1905–14.

constitutional monarchy
In this form of government, the monarch retains considerable power, but also requires the support of Parliament. Britain still has a constitutional monarchy, but now the institution has no political power.

Nevertheless, given this evolution over 300 years, the sources of the British constitution are many and varied.

Statute law

A statute is a written law passed by an Act of Parliament. It is a law that is enforceable in the courts. Many statutes do not embody principles affecting the constitution. Others do because they affect the way in which we are governed, and relationships within the state – e.g., the Representation of the People Acts of 1918, 1928 and 1969.

Statute law is the most important of the sources of the constitution, because of the doctrine of parliamentary sovereignty. For example, it can be used to override common law (see below, p. 166) which is made by judges in the courts. The courts may not strike down such a law as being contrary to the constitution. Only Parliament may do this. On the other hand, statute law is not supreme. Since Parliament passed the European Communities Act, 1972, making Britain a member of the European Economic Community (then known as the EEC, but now known as the EU – European Union), European law takes precedence over the domestic law of member states. In theory, this could be reversed, but only by Parliament repealing the 1972 Act.

Common law

This is also known as 'case law'. Common law is made by judges, and is so named because it is common to every person in every region of Britain. It is law formed on the basis of precedents set in previous cases – i.e. judgements made by one court of law must be followed by other courts in the future if they face a similar case. Such a law is not the product of a legislative process, but a reflection of the accumulated wisdom of the past which binds judges into acceptance of these legal precedents. Most of the original laws concerning civil rights began in this way, such as freedom of speech and freedom of movement.

Constitutional conventions

A convention is a regularly observed practice considered to be appropriate for a given set of circumstances. Constitutional conventions are, therefore, sets of rules established over time by custom and practice, which relate to the exercise of government powers. The concept of precedent is again important, in that these rules/conventions are considered binding on those concerned. However, they are not legally binding, as they are with common law. They apply particularly to the practices of the Crown and Cabinet. Examples include the collective responsibility of the Cabinet, that the Prime Minister should be a member of the Commons, that the monarchy should be 'above politics' and not engage in matters of party controversy, and the impartiality of the Speaker of the House of Commons (see p. 222).

The royal prerogative (see Chapter 16 on the Prime Minister)

The royal prerogative consists of a number of powers or privileges in the past performed by the monarch but now performed by ministers in his or her name. Their authority is derived from the Crown, not Parliament. Examples of these powers and privileges include the rights to:

1 declare war and make treaties;
2 give orders to the armed forces;
3 dissolve Parliament;
4 appoint ministers;
5 dispense honours.

NB: As parliamentary authority is not required to exercise these and other powers, they are in the hands of the executive (in effect, the Prime Minister), so that the legislature (Parliament) is bypassed. Many view this as undemocratic.

Major authoritative political works

Because of the complex nature of the constitution, these works have been produced by certain writers in an attempt to interpret its meaning and produce certain constitutional rules. They have become sources of guidance which are widely recognised and are therefore viewed as authoritative. They often contain the nearest to a written account that we have of the way in which the constitution operates. Examples include:

1 Erskine May, *Treatise on the Law, Privileges, Proceedings and Usage of Parliament* (1844). This is the source for guidance used by the Speaker of the House of Commons, on matters of parliamentary procedure and rights (i.e. 'privileges' of Parliament). Usually referred to as 'Erskine May'.
2 Walter Bagehot, *The English Constitution*, (1867).
3 A.V. Dicey, *An Introduction to the Study of the Law of the Constitution'*, (1885).

Major constitutional documents

A number of documents formed the basis of the constitution because they established important principles. Magna Carta, signed in 1215, established the principle that subjects should be safeguarded from the excessive use of monarchical power. The Bill of Rights, 1689, was an agreement between the new king, William III and Parliament which confirmed parliamentary sovereignty. The Act of Settlement, 1701, strengthened Parliament's position by controlling the succession to the throne.

European Union law

As mentioned in the section on statute law, the laws and treaties of the European Union have become a significant source of the British constitution. Where EU law and UK law conflict, EU law takes precedence. This has been especially important for economic and social legislation (see next section on Parliamentary Sovereignty).

Key elements of the British constitution identified so far

The British constitution is:
- unwritten and therefore *uncodified*;
- flexible and therefore *not rigid or entrenched*;
- unitary and therefore *not federal*;
- To be found in a variety of sources.

However, in spite of its puzzles, it is possible to abstract an order and structure in the British constitution which has evolved over time into a number of key elements.

A unitary state

The British state is unitary. As we have seen, this means that legal sovereignty lies in one place, Parliament, from which central government derives its authority. Local government at a number of levels – district, county and metropolitan – has a long history in Britain. A further level has been created recently, with devolved assemblies for Wales and Scotland (see Chapter 17). Nevertheless, none of this constitutes divided sovereignty. In theory, central government can create and abolish such bodies at will. For example, Edward Heath's Conservative government suspended the Stormont Parliament in Northern Ireland in 1972, and replaced it with direct rule from London. Following the 'Good Friday Agreement', an assembly in Northern Ireland has been recreated, but its position has been under threat as the peace negotiations have faltered. During the 1997 general election campaign, Tony Blair compared a Scottish Parliament to a parish council, asserting very strongly the legal sovereignty of Parliament. In theory, the Scottish Parliament could be abolished or suspended, although it is difficult to imagine this happening now. In a federal system such as the USA, suspension or abolition of a state government such as California by the federal government in Washington, would be nearly impossible.

Parliamentary sovereignty

Parliamentary sovereignty has been described as a cornerstone of the constitution. As the British constitutional expert, A.V. Dicey put it in the late nineteenth century, it is 'the one fundamental law of the constitution'. It stipulates that laws enacted by Parliament are binding and cannot be set aside except by Parliament. This doctrine was established by the Act of Settlement in 1689, binding the monarch and the courts to the laws of Parliament. To fully understand the concept of parliamentary sovereignty in 2003, further explanation is necessary.

Sovereignty refers to the ultimate legal authority in the state, with the exclusive right to wield legitimate power and to make the law within a territory. Sovereignty is said to be indivisible. **Parliamentary sovereignty** therefore means that no other body but Parliament can make the law. In addition to this:

• Parliament can unmake (repeal) a law;
• Parliament can make *any* law within Britain;
• Acts of Parliament are not subject to change via limits set by a higher body or by a written constitution;
• ministers, government departments, local authorities and other agencies apply those laws created by Parliament;
• the courts, in theory, cannot declare these laws unconstitutional, but can only interpret and apply them;
• each new Parliament is not bound by laws made by previous Parliaments.

All of the above emphasises the concentration of legal power in Parliament. However, a number of reservations need to be made.

Political sovereignty and legal sovereignty

The growth of a mass electorate from 4.9 million in 1885 to 44.4 million in 2003 has meant that the House of Commons has become the more important part of Parliament. So where does sovereignty lie? Even Dicey in 1885 perceived the problem. His solution was to distinguish between legal sovereignty, resting with Parliament and political sovereignty, resting with the electorate.

This may seem a sensible distinction, but it undermines the concept of sovereignty being indivisible. Further, Parliament is today by no means a supreme law-making body – as will be considered in the section on parliamentary government. Some also argue that political sovereignty only lies with the electorate on the day of a general election.

This is both trite and true. However, when Dicey distinguished between legal and political sovereignty, he was departing from a traditional doctrine in response to the growth of the electorate. The traditional doctrine – i.e. that ultimate power must reside in one body in the state, had no moral justification because it was rooted in the time when the monarch was sovereign and so he or she dictated what the constitution should be. Dicey argued that of the two types, it was political sovereignty that was morally justifiable. As Kingdom says of Dicey's view:

> the sovereignty of Parliament was derived, not from its inheritance of the absolute powers of the monarch, or from God, but from the people, through the principle of democratic representation. This is the key to the British liberal-democratic constitution. The people do not govern themselves, they elect representatives to Parliament, which governs the country through its committee – the Cabinet. Parliament is legally served by the neutral machinery of the state, comprising institutions such as the judiciary, the civil service and the police force.[4]

The degree to which modern politics in Britain departs from this ideal is one of the key issues in this course (see also chapters on Parliament, Prime Minister and Cabinet, in addition to the following section).

Other considerations regarding parliamentary sovereignty

Legal power but not supreme power

The amount of power that Parliament or government can exercise is subject to limitations. Laws cannot provide for every eventuality or even when severe difficulties occur – such as rising unemployment or a decline in the international value of the £. Laws have their limits. In theory, Parliament has the legal right to introduce many unpopular measures, such as banning rock concerts – but a majority vote would be needed first. Would any MPs vote in favour of this policy?

Referendums

Some argue that the use of referendums has undermined the concept of the sovereignty of Parliament. They were held three times in the 1970s. The Labour government, elected in 1997, held four in 13 months – in Scotland and Wales (September 1997), and in Greater London and Northern Ireland (May 1998). These were confirmations of decisions made in Parliament, such as plans for a devolved assembly for Scotland. Final decisions of this sort can be said to infringe Parliament's authority.

Extra-Parliamentary power

'Extra' – in the sense of outside – pressures placed on Parliament by powerful pressure groups have been able to force revisions to or the repeal of laws, as in the case of the anti-poll tax protests of 1990 (see Chapter 6 on Pressure Groups).

'External' matters (i.e. other than European ones)

Britain has been a member of the North Atlantic Treaty Organisation (NATO) since 1949. Membership has created defence and foreign policy obligations which, to an extent, have taken some degree of absolute control away from Parliament. Parliament could vote to cancel such obligations, but this is unlikely. As one of the founder members of the United Nations in 1945, Britain has also had obligations to fulfil.

These are just two examples of long-standing international agreements that have had an impact on parliamentary sovereignty. Another is membership of the International Monetary Fund (IMF). In 1976, the Labour government – facing a huge financial and economic crisis was forced to negotiate a loan from the IMF. In return, monetarist policies, involving heavy cuts in public spending, had to be introduced. Labour MPs, elected in October 1974, had never contemplated or been elected to support such measures.

Membership of the European Union

Britain's membership of the EU has certainly had an impact. This was highlighted by the Factortame Case (1991–98). In a long episode, it was found that the Merchant Shipping Act, 1988, passed by the British Parliament, contravened the Single European Act, 1986. Factortame Ltd was one of a number of Spanish fishing companies which under the 1988 Act were required to re-register and satisfy additional nationality requirements, in order to continue to operate. It failed to qualify, and was prevented from fishing from 1 April 1989 until the European Court of Justice ruled (1990–91) that the British courts did have the power to suspend acts of Parliament which seemed to breach European law. Factortame Ltd and the other companies were then allowed to recommence fishing. Eventually, they successfully claimed compensation for loss of income during the 18 months when they were prevented from fishing.

The sovereignty of Parliament: key points

1 EU law takes precedence over UK law.
2 UK courts can suspend the provisions of an Act of Parliament.
3 Parliament could, in theory, repeal all legislation connecting Britain with the EU, and so end Britain's membership. This seems very unlikely.

The Single European Act, 1986, and the Maastricht Treaty, 1992, widened the scope and policy areas on which the EU can legislate and with which Britain complies. The Social Chapter, which laid down minimum working conditions for European employees, and was part of the 1992 Treaty was not accepted by John Major's government, but the Blair government 'opted in' soon after its election in 1997.

Parliamentary government (see also p. 20)

Britain has a parliamentary system of government under a constitutional monarchy that was established by the Glorious Revolution. This asserted the supremacy of Parliament over the monarch. By 1800, many argued that the equal balance in the constitution of Monarch, Lords and Commons was to be admired. Thirty years later, the Duke of Wellington was vilified for speaking of the 'perfection' of the constitution prior to the Great Reform Act, 1832. By 1918, with the role of monarchy largely symbolic, a reduced role for the non-elected House of Lords and the creation of near universal suffrage for elections to the House of Commons, it was the latter that had achieved pre-eminence. 'Parliament' came to mean predominantly – if not exclusively – the Commons. By this time also, 'parliamentary government' meant government through Parliament (not by Parliament).

By 1918, the separation of powers, which had been partially true of the constitution in Montesquieu's time had been gradually undermined by fusion. When a political party secures a majority of MPs in the Commons at a general election, the leader of the party is invited by the monarch to form a government. When Blair became Prime Minister again in 2001, he chose most members of his Cabinet and government from his MPs in the Commons. With a separation of powers – legislature, executive and judiciary – the three have powers to limit each other. However, with parliamentary government, it is automatic that the executive has a 'built-in' majority in the legislature. Sustained by an overall majority of about fifty, strong government is assured. Huge majorities like those of 1997 and 2001 simply reinforce the government's domination of the Commons. The powers of the Lords are very limited. All government ministers are bound by the convention of collective responsibility to

> **the rule of law**
> The concept that everyone should be subject to the same laws, even the rulers.

preserve unity. Government may be accountable to Parliament to some extent, but fusion allows for government through Parliament. With a reasonable overall majority, Parliament may be dominated by government (see Chapter 16 on Prime Minister and Cabinet).

The rule of law

A.V. Dicey, again writing in 1885, identified the **rule of law** and parliamentary sovereignty as the twin pillars of the constitution. He also argued that the rule of law was (a) subordinate to, and (b) a check upon parliamentary sovereignty. This seemed logical since in theory Parliament could create a law which could diminish or destroy the rule of law. For Dicey, the rule of law had three key elements:

1 The law was equally applicable to everyone.
2 Everybody charged under the law was entitled to a fair trial and nobody should be punished without due process of law.
3 The general principles of the constitution, such as individual freedom, arise from decisions by an independent judiciary.

However, in 1999, Moyra Grant identified five. Her contention was that: 'Essentially the concept of the Rule of Law seeks to equate law and justice. It seeks to ensure that the law and the legal system are fair and equal. This is an idea which is hard, perhaps impossible, to achieve in practice.'[5]

> **justice**
> This concept has been the subject of infinite debate and many interpretations. Grant's 'fair and equal' is sufficient here.

Her five components of the rule of law were as follows.

1 **Legal equality.** This is the notion that everyone, including those in government, should have equal access to the law and be equally subject to the same laws. Grant maintains that this aim is not achieved. Most people cannot take legal action because it is too expensive. The rich can, of course, and those with little wealth may qualify for legal aid. Members of Parliament have parliamentary privilege which gives them an immunity from prosecution for slander or libel for anything said in Parliament.

2 **The 'just law'.** Implicit in the rule of law is the notion that the law and **justice** are synonymous. If this were so, then there would be no such thing as an unjust law. However, many laws have been viewed as unjust by a majority of people. For example, before the reforms of the penal code between 1823 and 1830, over 200 offences (including minor ones like stealing a loaf) were capital crimes. The community charge or poll tax (1989) was widely believed to be unjust. Grant also points to inconsistencies betweeen judges, in sentencing for the same crime.

3 **Legal certainty.** This is the idea that the law should be absolutely clear and devoid of ambiguity. The problem is that the law frequently relies on interpretation – e.g. what constitutes an 'offensive weapon'? On various occasions, apparently inoffensive articles such as combs and pens have been defined as offensive.

4 **Innocent until proven guilty.** The Criminal Justice Act (1994) diminished the accused's right of silence (see Chapter 17). Media coverage, prior to and during a trial, may well be prejudicial – e.g. the Tony Martin case 2000–01, following his shooting of a burglar who broke into his property.

5 **Independence of the judiciary.** There are many issues here (see Chapter 17). One issue relates to the separation of powers. The Lord Chancellor is a member of all three branches of government – legislature (House of Lords), executive (Cabinet) and judiciary (by virtue of his office). Conflicts of interest are likely as a result.

The protection of freedom in Britain, in the absence of a bill of rights

Heywood distinguishes two types of bills of rights, the **entrenched** and the **statutory**.

> **Key features of the British Constitution: a summary**
>
> 1 Unwritten – uncodified, flexible;
> 2 Unitary – sovereignty lies at the centre;
> 3 Parliamentary government – limited separation of powers;
> 4 Constitutional monarchy;
> 5 Rule of law;
> 6 No bill of rights – to protect individual freedoms.

Entrenched bills of rights have the status of 'higher' constitutional law. Such bills are usually part of a written constitution. Entrenched rights:
- are binding on the legislature;
- may only be introduced, amended or abolished via a complex constitutional process;
- are ultimately upheld by a Supreme Court (as in the USA).

The USA Bill of Rights:
- comprises the first 10 amendments to the constitution;
- specifies the rights and liberties of the individual;
- amendments 14, 15 and 19 were added subsequently.

Statutory bills of rights have the same level of legality as other laws developed and passed by the legislature. As such, they can be changed *without* a complex constitutional process, but by a normal legislative process. They are vulnerable to change. They operate in the absence of (a) a written constitution and (b) a constitutional court.

An example is the Human Rights Act (1998) in the UK (operational for the whole of the UK from 2000), incorporating the European Convention on Human Rights into UK law.

NB: Heywood also notes the case of advisory bills of rights. These oblige governments to consider individual rights and liberties in policy formulation. However, as the term 'advisory' suggests, they are not bound to do so.

Protecting individual rights and freedoms

A constitution should not only regulate the operation of the institutions of government, but should also protect civil rights (i.e. the rights and freedoms of individual citizens). These are guaranteed under the constitution and must not be violated by other citizens or by the state.

In written constitutions, civil rights are included and are guaranteed as positive freedoms. In the US constitution, they are contained in the Bill of Rights which includes freedom of speech, religion, association, and of the person and property. In Britain, they are granted as negative freedoms. Civil rights are protected by the ordinary laws of the land (see Sources of the constitution, p. 164), but, as such they are *residual* – i.e. they are not positively conferred by the constitution; they are simply not withheld. So it is possible for a government to pass statute laws which reduce civil rights severely. It is this concern especially that motivated critics of Britain's constitution to demand a bill of rights. This led, eventually, to the Human Rights Act 1998 (see Chapter 17).

There are a number of fundamental freedoms which now need to be examined within the context of the British Constitution.

Freedom of expression (e.g. freedom of speech, freedom of the press)

The freedom to express a political opinion is an essential element in a democracy. Its absence is evidence of an oppressive state. In Britain, it operates on the principle that anything which is not prohibited is permitted (see negative freedom). However, it is subject to restrictions. The individual citizen is protected from defamation of character, untrue or malicious reports by: slander (the above, in the spoken word) and libel (the above, in the written word).

However, liberals have been most concerned by the restrictions on this freedom imposed by agencies of the state. For example, the civil servant Sarah Tisdall broke Section 2 of the Official Secrets Act, 1911, by releasing information to the *Guardian* newspaper that cruise missiles were being brought to Britain. Section 2 was a very broad definition of an official secret. The liberal concern here was that an old, outdated law could be invoked for political reasons. Tisdall was sentenced to six months' imprisonment.

This freedom and attempted restrictions on it by government have also been extended to the media. Between 1984 and 1994, the actual voices of IRA and Sinn Fein members were not allowed to be broadcast in the media, even though their pictures could be shown on television with their words spoken by actors. On the other hand, the media have attempted to guard their freedom of expression. When in 1988 the government attempted to prevent the television broadcast of *Death on the Rock* (a documentary about the SAS killing of three IRA terrorists in Gibraltar), it was still shown.

Freedom of association

This concerns the freedom to meet, process and protest peacefully. As much of politics is about collective behaviour and the voluntary association of individuals, this is a vital freedom in a democracy. Balancing this freedom with the necessary restrictions to ensure public order, has proved difficult and subject to adjustments and compromises.

In principle, those not allowed this freedom include senior civil servants, the armed service, and the police. However, there are 'grey' areas – e.g. the police have a powerful voice via the Police Federation. Further, the Public Order Act, 1986, and the Criminal Justice and Public Order Act, 1994, gave the police stronger powers to prevent public disorder. Nevertheless, mass protests especially in London have continued to take place. On 18 November 2001, there was a demonstration in Trafalgar Square, which many thousands of people attended to protest against the war in Afghanistan.

Freedom of the person and property

Person

The right of a person to free movement within a country is a well-established element of individual liberty. A court case in 1765 ruled that general warrants for the arrest of unnamed persons was illegal. If a person is wrongfully imprisoned, there are a number of methods of gaining redress. The Act of Habeas Corpus, 1679, specified that no person should be arbitrarily detained in prison, without charge. The issuing of a writ for habeas corpus has been the classic guarantee of individual freedom for other persons too; for instance, setting slaves free. Ultimately, however, the government has the authority to take up powers severely limiting individual freedom – like detention without trial under the 1939 and 1940 Emergency Powers Act, when Britain was at war. Even in peacetime, a state of emergency may be declared under the authority of the 1920 and 1964 Emergency Powers Act. In the case of special measures to deal with terrorism, the Prevention of Terrorism (Temporary Provisions) Act and the Northern Ireland (Emergency Provisions) Act have been enacted and renewed by Parliament annually.

Property

The private ownership of property is perceived as a fundamental freedom in a capitalist society. However, the concept of an Englishman's home being his castle – a place of peace which he may defend at all costs – is only partially applicable today. The Tony Martin case (2000–1) is evidence that the issue is complex. Moreover, when the state is involved, there is little difficulty in entering private property; for example, the police may obtain search warrants.

On a grand scale, Parliament has legislated many times to limit such rights in the 'public interest'. In November 2001, residents near Heathrow Airport were very concerned about proposals to build a fifth terminal, and in the autumn 0f 2002, long-term government proposals to enlarge a number of airports were made public. As with individual freedom, there are legal remedies but there are no definitive solutions, as aspects of both areas may be changed by statute law. In any case, these issues are increasingly being seen within a European context.

NB: For further consideration of the issue of freedoms and rights, see Chapter 17 on the Human Rights Act, 1998, and the European Convention on Human Rights.

Constitutional government

This is government limited by the rules and procedures laid down in the constitution and 'according to the principles of the constitution'. Constitutional government exists therefore where these basic principles, rules and procedures are consistently protected and adhered to by the government as a whole, or by members of the government. Where the government or its members act in a way which breaches these basic principles or attempts to change them to suit their own purpose, then this is *arbitrary government*. In the words of Kingdom,[7] 'the essence of *constitutional government* is *limited government*'.

Limitation may be secured by various means – the law, popular control and other institutions. This is sought in the basic principles and shown in the box which follows. Note how for each principle, one element of 'compromise' has been indicated. There are more.

Unconstitutional action

An action is said to be unconstitutional if it breaks any part of the constitution. Any such breach may range from major to minor. In Britain, an action is unconstitutional if it is in breach of certain principles, procedures or rights. The concept of a constitutional convention, with the examples below, illustrates the difficulty of establishing what is an unconstitutional action in Britain.

In the USA an action is defined as unconstitutional by the Supreme Court if it decides that the action infringes the spirit or letter of the written constitution. While this might at first sight seem a credible alternative, it does have its drawbacks.

Although much of the British constitution is uncertain and even unknowable, there is certainty in some circumstances. For example:
- The suspension of habeas corpus, other than in a state of emergency, would be unconstitutional.
- If a Prime Minister and his government suffered a defeat in the House of Commons on a vote of confidence and attempted to remain in power, this would also be unconstitutional.

Anti-constitutional action

An action is said to be anti-constitutional if its aim is to undermine or destroy the constitution, whether its purpose is to replace it or not. Some groups by their very nature are anti-constitutional in their overall aims:

Constitutional conventions

'A Prime Minister cannot nowadays operate from the House of Lords'.

This became the convention after the departure of Lord Salisbury in 1902. However, Lord Home became the leader of the Conservative Party and Prime Minister following the resignation of Harold Macmillan in 1963. This was possible because (a) a few months previously the Peerage Act had been passed, allowing peers to disclaim their titles and seek election to the Commons, and (b) there was no election for party leader. Home fought and won a by-election and became Prime Minister. This is virtually impossible now, as party leaders are elected.

Some constitutional analysts have argued that this convention should apply to the other three great offices of state – Chancellor of the Exchequer, Home Secretary and Foreign Secretary. In recent times, there have been two foreign secretaries in the Lords, Home 1960–63 and Carrington 1979–82. More recently, in 1998, Tony Blair appointed Gus Macdonald – a Scottish media tycoon – as a junior minister, although at the time he was neither an MP nor a peer. This breached the convention that government ministers should be appointed from within Parliament. He was soon given a life peerage by the Prime Minister, and so gained a seat in the House of Lords.

NB: As constitutional conventions are not legally binding, they may be breached or ignored. Such actions may be viewed as either (a) arbitrary, or (b) evidence of sensible flexibility.

The breaking of constitutional conventions can lead to significant consequences. When in 1909 members of the House of Lords broke the convention that they should not interfere with a 'money bill' by rejecting the People's Budget, this led to a constitutional crisis. The outcome was the passage of the Parliament Act, 1911, which reduced the powers of the Lords by statute law and specifically denied it the right to reject 'money bills'. A crisis of this nature has been a rarity.

- **Anarchists** Anarchy literally means 'without rule'. Anarchists believe that political authority in whatever form is evil and unnecessary. Anarchists would, therefore, not replace a constitution, but leave people free to make their own arrangements unfettered by government.
- **Marxists** Marxists would aim to set up a socialist republic based on workers' control.
- **Irish Republican Army** Traditionally, its aim has been to create a united Ireland with the north set free from British rule, so as to be part of the Irish Republic.

NB: Although these and other groups are anti-constitutional in their aims, their methods may be both illegal and violent (bombings by the Irish Liberation Army) or legal and peaceful (meeting of the Socialist Workers' Party).

Constitutionalism

This is the belief in and practice of limited government. This is ensured by the presence of a constitution. It is one of the key elements of liberal democracy and its importance is based on the constant fear that governments are always prone to arbitrary actions against the individual. Constitutionalism is a vital guarantee of individual freedom. Liberal constitutionalism is usually associated with a written constitution, an entrenched bill of rights, and a system of checks and balances between governmental institutions. The British system of government is usually viewed as constitutional, even though it has traditionally been deficient in these three elements.

REFERENCES

1 A. Renwick and I. Swinburn, *Basic Political Concepts*, Stanley Thornes, 1987.
2 *The Independent*, 3 February 1998.
3 R. Bentley (ed.), A. Dobson, M. Grant, D. Roberts, *British Politics in Focus*, Causeway Press, 1999.
4 J. Kingdom, *Government and Politics in Britain: An Introduction*, Polity Press, 1991.
5 M. Grant, *Talking Politics*, Vol 7i, Journal of the Politics Association 1994.
6 A. Heywood, *Key Concepts in Politics*, Macmillan, 2000.
7 As note 4 above.

USEFUL WEBSITES

The Constitution **www.ucl.ac.uk/constitution-unit** This is the constitution unit home page, including information on constitutional reform and devolution. The constitution unit is the foremost independent research body on constitutional change.

SAMPLE QUESTIONS

1 What are the differences between a unitary constitution and a federal constitution?

2 Describe the sources of the British constitution.

3 What would be the main advantages and disadvantages of having a written constitution?

AIMS OF THIS CHAPTER

➤ To assess Britain's constitutional monarchy.

➤ To consider the debate about the retention or abolition of the monarchy.

Britain's constitutional monarchy: a brief historical background

Before the middle of the seventeenth century, Britain had an absolute monarchy. After the Civil War and Cromwell's Protectorate during 1649–60, the British monarchy became constitutional. Over the next 300 years, the powers of the monarchy were gradually eroded. By 1867, Bagehot could describe it in *The English Constitution* as a 'dignified' rather than an 'efficient' part of the constitution, with symbolic authority but little real power. Except when a constitutional crisis occurs, it is true to say that 'the Queen reigns, but does not rule'.

The royal prerogative

This is the term given to the formal powers of the Crown. They are part of common law. Almost all of these powers, however, have passed to the Prime Minister (see Chapter 12) who exercises them in the name of the Crown. Examples include: declaring war; the opening and dissolving of Parliament; and the choice of the date for the general election, within a five-year limit.

Monarch and Prime Minister

In theory, and by convention, it is the monarch who appoints the Prime Minister. In practice, the monarch invites the leader of the largest party in the Commons to form a government. The Prime Minister resigns on behalf of his government if defeated in a general election or in a vote of no confidence in the Commons. If the result of a general election produces a 'hung Parliament', one in which no party has an overall majority, the rules are unclear. When in the February 1974 election no party gained such a majority, the outgoing

KEY TERMS

Crown

- This is the symbol of all executive authority.
- It is the permanent abstract institution embodying the supreme power of the state.
- It is the *formal head of all three branches of government,* legislature, executive and judiciary.
- All acts of state are done in the *name of the Crown.*

Monarchy

- This literally means 'rule by one person'.
- It is the institution of hereditary, royal rule.
- The monarch or sovereign is the person upon whom the Crown is conferred.

Constitutional monarchy

- In this type of monarchy, as in Britain, sovereignty is vested in another institution of government – i.e. Parliament.
- Such monarchs may fulfil a ceremonial role or carry out a few political functions as the formal head of state.
- The British monarch is impartial and non-party political, 'above politics'.

Absolute monarchy

- In this type of monarchy, the monarch claims a monopoly of political power. The monarch is thus literally sovereign.
- In Britain, before the English civil wars, the justification of absolute monarchy was the belief in the doctrine of divine right – i.e. that monarchs were chosen by God. Thus monarchs ruled with God's authority on earth.

Republic

- This is a form of government without a monarch in which sovereignty is vested in the people and their elected representatives.
- The Latin root *res publica* – i.e. common or collective affairs – suggests public participation and popular rule throughout the nation state. The USA and France are classic contemporary examples.
- Republics usually have an elected president who is head of state.

Conservative Prime Minister, Edward Heath, attempted to form a coalition government with the Liberals. Negotiations failed, Heath resigned and Labour then formed a government. This is the one occasion in recent history where the monarch might have had to play a political role if the parties had been unable to resolve the situation.

In the name of the Crown, the Prime Minister makes many important appointments, giving him huge powers of **patronage**. These include the appointment of ministers, peers, senior Church of England clergy, civil servants, and all honours and titles (e.g. Member of the Order of the British Empire, MBE). Only the Order of the Garter and Order of Merit remain in the personal gift of the monarch.

The Prime Minister meets the Queen once every week for an informal conversation about current political matters.

The Monarch and legislation

The Queen attends the state opening of Parliament at the beginning of each annual session. She reads the Queen's Speech, outlining the government's legislative proposals – written by the government – in the House of Lords, whilst the Prime Minister, the leader of the opposition and other MPs stand in the entrance to the Lords.

Each bill – passed by both Commons and Lords – must be given the Royal Assent (signed by the monarch) before it becomes an Act of Parliament and therefore law.

> **patronage**
> The power to bestow offices, privileges and favours on the basis of personal preference, rather than on the basis of election or expertise.

Religion and the succession

The monarch, since the time of Henry VIII, is 'Defender of the Faith', in effect Head of the Church of England. Succession to the throne is determined by the Act of Succession, 1701, and male heirs take precedence over females. The monarch must not be a Roman Catholic, nor is he or she allowed to marry one. The current heir to the throne is Prince Charles who, as such, has the title of Prince of Wales.

The debate over the future of the monarchy

The case for

> [The Monarchy] . . . offers fixed constitutional landmarks and a degree of institutional continuity in a changing world, so that the costs of change come to appear easier to bear. (V. Bogdanor)[1]

Popularity

Even though the monarchy is less popular in 2003 than it was in the 1950s when it seemed above criticism, the evidence of opinion polls suggests that more people favour its retention than its abolition. For example:

1 National Opinion Poll (August 1994) – 66 per cent supported the indefinite retention of the monarchy.

2 MORI Poll (June 1999) – 66 per cent supported the idea of the monarchy having an important role in Britain's future.

3 Also in the National Opinion Poll August 1994 – Only 26 per cent wanted the monarchy abolished at some point. Only 5 per cent said that the monarchy should end some time after the Queen's death.

Head of state/head of Church of England

The monarchy provides a head of state who is 'above' party politics. The hereditary principle ensures this. As head of the Church of England, the monarch promotes Christian values and family life.

Continuity

The monarchy maintains the continuity of British traditions, linking the past with the present in a changing and uncertain world. The State Opening of Parliament, the annual ceremony of Trooping the Colour and the Remembrance Day Service at the Cenotaph every November are all imbued with symbolic relevance. Other traditions provide a psychological, social and unifying function. The honours system provides recognition not just for 'the great and the good' who are well known, but to those who have given great service – e.g. fire brigade officers, local health workers, nurses and others.

Symbol of national unity and traditional authority

This symbolic role is important both to the outside world and to the people of Britain. The present monarch is a unifying influence as the symbolic head of the commonwealth and of Britain, especially following devolution for Scotland, Wales and Northern Ireland. For the people of Britain, the monarchy is an integrating and unifying influence and a symbol of patriotic loyalty. The monarchy represents Britain abroad, helping to promote good international relations and trade.

Finance

The cost of sustaining the royal family in 1998 was £45 million per year, plus £30 million to pay for security.[2] The cost to the taxpayer of the 'royals' has generated much criticism on various occasions. However, this figure is less than the income created by the monarchy via the tourist trade.

Advice

Monarchs who reign for a considerable number of years accumulate a huge amount of knowledge and experience. Queen Elizabeth II celebrated her fiftieth year on the throne in 2002, so that this has already been an exceptionally long

---

Royal finances: the Way Ahead

In 1995, senior members of the royal family and their private secretaries formed the 'Way Ahead Group' to formulate policy for the future. The outcome was a series of measures including:

- the Queen to pay tax;
- the decommissioning of the royal yacht;
- the opening of Buckingham Palace to the public, to pay for repairs to Windsor Castle, following damage by fire;
- the opening of royal accounts to greater scrutiny by Parliament.

---

reign. As a result, some Prime Ministers have publicly acknowledged her value as an observer and adviser, Harold Wilson, James Callaghan and Tony Blair among them. Heywood puts the point clearly: 'The monarch constitutes a repository of experience and wisdom, especially in relation to constitutional matters, available to elected governments.'[3]

Public service

'It is . . . in the practical employment of its symbolic influence, that the monarchy will find its future' (V. Bogdanor).[4]

The monarchy, while pursuing its role as an institution famous for ceremonial occasions, has increasingly become an institution that can bring practical benefits to society via public service. Royal patronage of institutions and charities (such as the Duke of Edinburgh Award Scheme, the Prince's Youth Business Trust and the Save the Children Fund) is a well-established role for the royal family. This commitment has developed significantly during the present monarch's reign and became more obvious to the public in the 1980s and 1990s, if only because Princess Diana raised its profile. This was more recognised by the public than by political journalists and commentators, as Prochaska illustrates: 'Witness the readers of the *Big Issue*, the voice of the homeless and dispossessed, who elected Prince Charles their 'Hero of the Year' in 1999.'[5]

This recognition was merited. By the year 2000, the Prince's Youth Business Trust had created 39,000 companies and 52,000 jobs. It had proved to be the largest business agency outside government. In a society that has shed its collectivist zeal – following the collapse of the post-war consensus (see p. 142) – the movement towards pluralism in social policy has created scope for royal intervention. The Prince's success with this trust is just one example of a practical contribution owing much to royal influence and initiative.

The case against

The Monarchy is the shiny, glittering mask that conceals, so far successfully, the ugly face of a class system that is based on avarice, social injustice and inequity. (Willie Hamilton former Labour MP and arch-republican), 1975)[6]

[The Crown in Parliament is] . . . rubbing in . . . the fact that we have no rights, properly understood, but rather traditions that depend on the caprice of a political compromise made in 1688. (C. Hitchens, 1990)[7]

Popularity

In the long term, the monarchy's popularity and support appears to be in terminal decline. By the 1990s, in contrast with the 1950s when the monarchy seemed beyond criticism, there was strong evidence to show that respect for the monarchy had declined and that this trend was likely to continue. The National Opinion Poll already quoted showed that while people aged 55 or over supported the monarchy by 3:1, younger people did not: '. . . among the under 35s, 48 per cent respect the monarchy, but 51 per cent don't'.[8] This decline in support with successive generations is related to other social trends like the decline of deference. Each generation sees the monarchy as an anachronism, especially at the start of a new millennium.

From the accession of George VI in 1936 onwards, the monarchy has attempted to set standards of citizenship and family life. Whilst the Queen's dedication is not in doubt, the conduct of other members of the royal family – especially with increased media scrutiny – has seriously and justifiably destroyed the myth that had been sustained for so long. The well-publicised break-up of a number of royal marriages, the extravagance associated with many in the family and other personal scandals have called into question the behaviour of these privileged public figures.

Most damaging of all, was the collapse of the marriage of the Prince and Princess of Wales. In the summer of 1992, Andrew Morton's biography of Diana was serialised in a newspaper. It revealed not only the truth of many rumours about the marriage, but was also highly critical of many of the royal family including Prince Philip and Prince Charles. Until Diana's death in 1997, such stories continued. Since the huge outpourings of grief in the week following her death, and criticism of the monarchy's initial response to it, there has been some recovery in the monarchy's popularity, but the long-term trend over the last five decades is clear.

Head of state/head of the Church of England

The continuation of the hereditary principle embodied in the monarchy violates democratic principles. First, it places birth above merit in deter-mining who should be the head of state. Secondly, it gives the monarch political authority on the basis of the hereditary principle. She is not elected and is not accountable. If, at last, the hereditary principle is to be completely removed from the House of Lords, it seems inconsistent to retain it for the monarchy.

It is also anachronistic and inconsistent to have one established church, with the monarch at its head, in a multi-cultural society.

Unprogressive and divisive

The monarchy symbolises a conservative view of society opposed to progressive change and favouring the status quo. It also epitomises hereditary privilege, a class hierarchy, deference and snobbery. Its presence still typifies the notion of the British people being subjects rather than citizens.

Far from uniting the nation, the privileged position of the monarchy and the royal family in general emphasises and helps perpetuate and justify social divisions.

Finance

The Civil List – the annual grant from Parliament – amounted to £8.9 million in 2000. It pays for the personal incomes and households of leading members of the royal family. However, the costs incurred in travel, maintenance of royal estates, etc., brings the total cost to around £100 million. Without a monarchy, these costs would not fall at the feet of the taxpayer. The tourist trade would not suffer as Britain has many attractions apart from those associated with the monarch, some of which are already open to the public such as Buckingham Palace and Windsor Castle. There would be a cost in having an elected president, but it need not be so expensive. In any case, the royal family is wealthy. The Queen has a huge personal fortune: an official estimate in 1975 put the figure at £50 million, but it is now believed to be several times this figure.

Constitutional reform

The formal powers of the monarch such as the royal assent are meaningless. However, the royal prerogative powers and immunities that have been taken over by the Prime Minister are largely unaccountable and by-pass, and therefore weaken, Parliament. The constitutional reforms of 1997–2001 and the proposals for further reform of the House of Lords have neglected this issue completely. Genuine renewal of the constitution should address the matter by replacing the monarchy with an elected head of state – i.e. a president. The change should be forthcoming as part of a new 'package' of reforms which would reduce the powers of the Prime Minister, reassert the role of Parliament and introduce a written constitution which does away with the compromise of 1688.

There is no reason why the functions of a head of state could not be carried out by a president who could be replaced by popular consent. Most republicans support the idea of a president with limited powers. He or she could be both a figure-head and an 'honest broker'.

REFERENCES

1 V. Bogdanor, *The Monarchy and the Constitution*, Clarendon Press, 1995.
2 *Guardian*, 1 July 1998.
3 A. Heywood, *Key Concepts in Politics*, Macmillan, 2000.
4 As note 1 above.
5 F. Prochaska, *The Republic of Britain*, Penguin, 2000, quoting a MORI poll for *The Big Issue*, Dec. 1999.
6 W. Hamilton, *My Queen and I*, Quartet Books, 1975.
7 C. Hitchens, *The Monarchy*, Chatto & Windus, 1990.
8 *Guardian*, 19 September 1994.

The Cabinet and the Prime Minister

12

AIMS OF THIS CHAPTER

➤ To establish the functions of the Cabinet, Cabinet Office and Cabinet Committees.

➤ To assess the factors influencing Prime Ministers when appointing Cabinet ministers.

➤ To consider the concept of collective Ministerial Responsibility.

➤ To establish the work of the Prime Minister's Office, its powers and its relationship with Cabinet.

➤ To consider the roles of Prime Minister.

➤ To assess the styles of leadership of recent Prime Ministers.

➤ To assess the four theoretical models of government – Cabinet, Prime Ministerial, Presidential and Core Executive.

The Cabinet

The Cabinet is the executive committee of government. It is appointed by, chaired by and answerable to the Prime Minister, and as a whole accountable to the Prime Minister. Four ministers sit in Cabinet as a constitutional necessity:

- Prime Minister;
- leader of the House of Commons;
- leader of the House of Lords;
- The Lord Chancellor.

Traditionally regarded along with the post of Prime Minister as the great offices of state are:

- Chancellor of the Exchequer;
- Home Secretary;
- Foreign Secretary.

Overall there are usually between twenty and twenty-five Cabinet ministers. Broadly there are two types. There are those who head a government department such as the Chancellor of the Exchequer (Treasury). There are those who do not head a department but are the government's political managers. For example, the Chief Secretary to the Treasury plays a significant role in the spending round in which government departments submit their financial estimates for the coming year. The Chief Whip always sits in Cabinet but may not be a full member. The Cabinet Secretary, the head of the Civil Service, also attends to record decisions.

It is the Prime Minister alone who chooses who is in the Cabinet. This is a critical task which involves choosing not only senior ministers like the Home Secretary who will sit in Cabinet automatically, but also selecting a team to lead the government. There are many factors at work in this delicate choice, as explained more fully below. They include the following.

- Finding the right person for the job. In 1997, Gordon Brown previously the shadow Chancellor was an automatic choice to head the Treasury. When John Major appointed his first Cabinet in 1990, he kept Margaret Thatcher's appointee, Douglas Hurd, as Foreign Secretary, for it was 'a role to which . . . he seemed to have been born'

- Recognising the status of senior members of the Party; this factor is also true of the two examples above. Margaret Thatcher's first Cabinet in 1979 included ministers with very different views to hers on many issues; not to have appointed them was unthinkable politically.

- Appointing an ally and confidant: Prime Ministers usually operate within a close inner circle. In 1997 Tony Blair appointed Lord Irvine as Chancellor and Peter Mandelson as Minister without Portfolio at the Cabinet Office, for they were personally close to him.

- Finding room for potential rebels. Prime Ministers have enemies or at least rebels within their parties. Lyndon Johnson, a former president of the USA (1963–68), once said of his decision to appoint an awkward critic: 'I'd rather have him inside the tent pissing out, than outside the tent pissing in.'[2]

- Achieving a balance of party opinion. The two major parties cater for a broad church of opinion. Sometimes Prime Ministers try to reflect this in their appointments to Cabinet. This has the virtue of bringing in leading figures who represent a particular faction in the party. This was one reason why Major appointed Portillo and Lilley in 1992, and Margaret Thatcher appointed so many wets in 1979. Blair's appointment of John Prescott in 1997 as Deputy Prime Minister was a gesture to Old Labour in the New Labour government. Once the Prime Minister has achieved dominance, he or she may be able to drop members who are out of step.

- Seeking out and nurturing able, young talent so that there is a growing pool of experience on which to draw in the future. Some stable, relatively unambitious people who are sound administrators, good in Cabinet and remain in touch with public opinion, are also likely to prove an asset.

The functions of the Cabinet

- Deciding on major policy to be followed at home and abroad. Government policy has often been stated in the election manifesto and reflects prevailing party policy. But when in office, the priorities for action have to be decided and a legislative programme drawn up. Details of policy have to be filled in, in the light of prevailing circumstances such as the financial state of the country and the advice received from key pressure groups.

- Dealing with unforeseen major problems. New problems arise from time to time. In former PM Harold Macmillan's words, the main problem for governments is 'events, dear boy, events'. There may be a crisis in the EU, a sudden invasion of a friendly state, an outbreak of violence in an area of strategic interest, a fuel crisis at home, the discovery of a major human or animal disease (e.g. Aids or BSE) or a hospital bed shortage in a winter outbreak of a vicious variety of influenza. New Labour has faced such problems as a foot-and-mouth outbreak, the fuel protests and blockade and the attacks on New York and Washington in September 2001. The latter necessitated discussion of an emergency measure to counter the threat of terrorism.

- Coordinating the policies of different departments. If government is to function well and policy is to be successfully carried out, there needs to be coordination between government departments. In some cases, disputes may have to be resolved between departmental ministers or policies pulled together to ensure what Tony Blair has called 'joined-up government'. There is a natural tension between Treasury representatives and spending ministers who want more for education, health and transport, etc.

- Planning for the long term. Ideally, this is a key area of policy making, but governments are often preoccupied with the here and now. Moreover, ministers come and go, making it difficult to plan ahead with consistency of purpose. Yet some issues require long-term planning, such as those concerning the environment, defence and pension policy. Often this work is done in Cabinet committees.

The Cabinet Office

Since 1997, the Cabinet Office has consisted of four secretariats, dealing with:
- Economic and Domestic policy;
- Defence and Overseas;
- European Union;
- Constitution.

The Cabinet Secretariat carry out the administrative and secretarial work within the Cabinet system and form a major part of the Cabinet Office. In 1998 there were approximately 1000 staff working for the Cabinet Office. The Head of the Office has traditionally been the Head of the Civil Service. In 1998 this was Sir Richard Wilson. Following his recommendations, further changes were made, so that there is now a **Political head** (Cabinet enforcer) and a **Civil Service head** (Cabinet secretary).

The first Cabinet enforcer was Jack Cunningham, later followed by Mo Mowlam. From 2001 John Prescott has occupied this post. It is a strategic and coordinating role. The purposes of the Cabinet Office and the Cabinet Enforcer are:
- to coordinate policy across Whitehall;
- to coordinate the work of government, and avoid fragmentation and omissions between ministries. This is the notion of joined up government;
- not really to make policy, because this takes place elsewhere especially in ministries and Cabinet Committees.

The Cabinet Office also consists of the Performance and Innovation Unit and Head of Government Information and Communication Services.

This along with other measures centralised the direction of policy both short and long term. It was to provide a more immediate and efficient service to the Prime Minister especially.

Cabinet committees

One reason for the creation of Cabinet committees is the sheer volume of work for the government. Their presence in government goes back to the nineteenth century, but their use at current levels began during the Second World War and continued with the creation of the welfare state and interventionist economic and social policies. There are two types of Cabinet committee:
- **Standing committees** These deal with a specific policy area and are more or less permanent – e.g. Economic affairs, Environment , Northern Ireland.
- **Ad hoc committees** These deal with specific short-term problems and are of short-term duration – e.g. Devolution to Scotland and Wales, and food safety.

The Prime Minister decides which committees are to be set up what their terms of reference are, who should be chairperson and who should sit on them. The extent to which the last three Prime Ministers have used them is as follows:
- Margaret Thatcher used them much less than her predecessors and preferred to use informal meetings. In 1978, for example, 941 Cabinet committee meetings were held, but in 1989 only 340.
- John Major had fewer committees but they met more often.
- Tony Blair had set up only 26 by 1998.

A typical committee

Chair person – PM, Chancellor of the Exchequer/senior minister;

Cabinet ministers – the few involved in the policy, a Treasury minister if public expenditure is involved and the Cabinet Office minister whose job is to coordinate policy;

Junior minister – responsible for the specific committee subject in his or her department;

Senior civil servants – from the relevant departments;

Witnesses – those able to provide opinion from outside.

It was John Major who made public the details of Cabinet committees after he became Prime Minister in 1990. Previously, they were unknown to the general public but known about by political journalists and the Whitehall community.

The case for Cabinet committees

1 They make the government more effective.
2 They prevent 'overload' on the Cabinet.
3 They are not bound to increase Prime Ministerial power. Prime Ministers are unlikely to ignore a committee's policy decision.

The case against

1 They may be used to enhance the power of the Prime Minister who sets them up, determines their terms of reference and appoints the chairperson and other members. The Prime Minister may chair any committee, or may appoint with a desired result in mind.
2 They do not initiate policy, but decide on the form that a policy should take.
3 They present Cabinet with no option but to accept their decisions, thus further reducing the importance of Cabinet meetings.
4 Some may be highly effective and hard working. Others, according to some sources, rarely meet or are very slow moving.

Collective responsibility

This is the convention by which all members of government are bound by collective policy decisions. It applies to all holders of government posts from Cabinet minister level to parliamentary private secretary (PPS) level. This convention is based on the assumption that ministers make decisions collectively, so they should support all government policies in public. It also means that minsters should be accountable for government policies in Parliament and in the media. It gives governments the appearance of unity and strength.

How far down the hierarchy of government a Prime Minister can insist on collective responsibility is questionable. Parliamentary private secretaries are not paid so their dissent might be acceptable to some Prime Ministers, although Callaghan reprimanded PPSs who dared to oppose ministerial defence policy. Above this level there are approximately 100 ministers who are paid. It is likely that 'conform or go' would be applied from this level upwards.

When a minister disagrees very strongly with a government policy, then he may stay silent or speak publicly against it and resign. Many ministers decide that on balance it is better to accept that one decision has gone against them, but as long as they remain in office they have a chance of influencing others. On the other hand, in 1997 Malcolm Chisholm, a Scottish Office minister, resigned over New Labour's proposal to cut the lone-parent supplement to child benefit, as part of a substantial backbench revolt.

There are four important aspects of collective responsibility:
1 Decisions reached by the Cabinet or Cabinet committees are binding on all members of the government.
2 There should be total secrecy about Cabinet discussions so that dissent can be aired, and total secrecy maintained about the decision-making process.
3 As government decisions are taken collectively, defeat on a motion of confidence requires the resignation of all members of the government.
4 A former minister who writes his memoirs, drawing on ministerial discussions, must submit them to the Cabinet Secretary for approval to maintain collective responsibility.

Collective responsibility is not law, but it has operated on some famous occasions since 1979, such as in 1986 when Michael Heseltine resigned over the Westland affair on the grounds that he could not accept responsibility for a decision that was not discussed properly in Cabinet; and in 1990 when Geoffrey Howe, then Deputy Prime Minister, resigned over Europe.

The Eurosceptics, Portillo, Lilley and Redwood, constantly briefed against John Major but he did not force their resignation. This was something of an exception to the convention and is evidence of its weakening.

The Prime Minister

Unlike other Cabinet ministers, the Prime Minister does not have a department to run. Nevertheless, there is a Prime Minister's Office which in itself is an institution with a corporate identity. The Office as a whole employs permanent civil servants, as well as political appointees and advisers; some of the latter may be employed as temporary civil servants. Traditionally, Prime Ministers have been served by a total of approximately 40 people. However, in the past two decades these numbers have increased; by 1998 Tony Blair had approximately 150 staff employed in his office. By contrast, individual ministers or departments in Whitehall employ staff in terms of thousands.

The Prime Minister's Office consists of four identifiable sections although the division of functions is not always absolutely clear cut. They are as follows.

1 **The Prime Minister's private office**. This is run by the Prime Minister's Principal Private Secretary. It is mostly staffed by prominent civil servants drafted in from other departments. It deals with the Prime Minister's official engagements, relations with Parliament and Whitehall, and it acts as a filter for the enormous flow of information that comes to the Prime Minister from all branches of government. In this way, the PM has oversight of all major policy initiatives.

2 **The political office**. This links the PM to his party at all levels. It may assist with writing the PM's speeches, drafting policy documents and with tactical party political issues. It is paid for out of party funds. It often contains young people who later go on to become senior politicians. Nigel Lawson started there and went on to become Margaret Thatcher's Chancellor of the Exchequer.

3 **The policy unit**. A policy unit was first introduced to the PMs office in 1974 by Harold Wilson; it has been used by all subsequent Prime Ministers. Its function is to advise the PM on immediate, medium and long-term matters. Essentially, it provides a strategic view of government policy overall. Sarah Hogg headed this unit for John Major from 1990 to 1995. For Tony Blair, the unit has had considerable significance. He brought in David Miliband to lead it, and has increased the number of advisers from the usual 8 to 13. Under Blair, it has become a 'think tank' and he has encouraged his Cabinet colleagues to link up with their opposite number in the unit. Each person oversees the work of his appropriate department while ensuring that the Minister concerned and the PM are, in effect, following the same policy line on any issue.

4 **The press office**. The press office manages the PMs relations with the media. Such a unit was first set up in 1931. However, the power of television – as well as radio and newspapers – has made Number 10 very concerned about its ability to 'manage' the media and present the Prime Minister and his policies in a way that achieves maximum impact with the public at large. The press office has about six members of staff. The job of Chief Press Secretary has become particularly important. Bernard Ingham accurately reflected Margaret Thatcher's forthright views and style. For Tony Blair, Alastair Campbell – a former tabloid journalist – has become even more significant. He has not only managed the presentation of policy but, as a close confidant to the Prime Minister, has helped write speeches, controlled access to Blair, and influenced his political tactics.

In November 1997, the Strategic Communications Unit was set up, with a staff of six of whom some were civil servants while others were political appointees. The purpose of this unit was to coordinate the government's work (e.g. ministerial announcements) with the media and to integrate the work of the Prime Minister's private office and policy unit. As its title suggests, its overall perspective is strategic and long term.

Prime Ministers have also appointed special advisers to cover specific areas of policy. These special advisers may be from the academic world, business or some other area of expertise, for example, professor Alan Walters who became Margaret Thatcher's special adviser on economic policy. Tony Blair brought in many advisers in his first two years of office to express their views on specific policy areas. He has also created task forces which have included outside advisers to investigate and review particular areas of policy.

The Prime Minister and the Cabinet

The office of Prime Minister is held by the leader of the largest party in the House of Commons. This is a principle of Britain's uncodified constitution. However, an exploration of the role, powers – formal and informal – functions, and authority of the Prime Minister are, to some extent at least, imprecise. For, unlike the office of President of the USA, whose origins lie in a strict constitutional framework, the position of Prime Minister is far less clearly defined.

As a starting point, and in the most simple terms, it is possible to say that the office of Prime Minister does not have a job description! This, of course, does not mean that there is no such job. Rather, it means that attempting to establish what Prime Ministers do is something of a 'moveable feast', i.e., from one PM to the next, there are variables, as well as elements in common.

By the end of the seventeenth century, many powers had been transferred to Parliament, but some were retained by the Crown into the eighteenth and nineteenth centuries. With the extensions of the franchise in the nineteenth century (see Chapter 10), the growth of modern political parties, and the consequent increase in the powers of Parliament and Cabinet within the British system of government, the remaining powers of the Crown were essentially lost by 1914. As Parliament was too large a body to take over these prerogative powers, and cabinets could often be divided, they fell to the office of Prime Minister.

Powers of patronage

The Prime Minister has wide and general powers of patronage. The appointments concerned may be either **Crown:** i.e., derived from the monarch, and acting in the name of the Crown or, **Public:** i.e., those specifically the gift of the Prime Minister. The key point here is that, whatever the origin of these powers, Prime Ministers have considerable and, for some people, controversial, powers of patronage within a democratic system.

THE PRIME MINISTER'S POWERS

Several of these are derived from the Royal prerogative and are therefore based on convention.

1 Power to appoint and dismiss ministers.
2 Power to award peerages and honours.
3 Power to make public appointments and appoint top civil servants.
4 Political Head of the Civil Service.
5 Powers relating to government business, e.g. chair full Cabinet, appointing Cabinet Committees, deciding structure of government.
6 Powers to coordinate government policies/activities.
7 Powers as minister for the Secret Services.
8 Powers as representative of the UK abroad.
9 Taking Prime Minister's Questions weekly in Parliament.
10 Communicating government policy to the monarch at weekly meetings.
11 Power over the UK's nuclear strike capability.
12 Power to decide date of the general election within a five-year term.

The royal prerogative

This refers to powers that are legally those of the Crown. Most of these are now exercised by the Prime Minister, and, to a lesser extent, his ministers. These powers are said to be exercised 'in the name of the Queen'. So now, the Prime Minister exercises these powers 'in the name of', or 'on behalf of the monarch'. Nevertheless, the appearance of monarchical power is to some extent preserved. For example

1 The Prime Minister asks the monarch to dissolve Parliament in order to call for a general election.
2 At the state opening of Parliament, the monarch reads the programme of policies to be put before Parliament by her government in the forthcoming year, i.e., the Queen's Speech.

At the same time, there are constraints on the Prime Minister's exercise of these powers (see for example, Appointments to the Cabinet, p. 189).

The power to appoint and dismiss ministers (see p. 189 on appointments to Cabinet)

Once the result of a general election has been decided, the leader of the winning party is called to Buckingham Palace, to 'kiss the Queen's hand' and so receives 'permission' to form a new government. There are over one hundred ministerial positions to fill, including about 22 cabinet appointments.

This aspect of the Prime Minister's power of **patronage** is very significant indeed. The Prime

patronage
The right to bestow offices or honours, especially to supporters of the government.

Minister may 'sack' or promote a politician, and need not give a reason. Unlike other jobs, the politician has no redress in law if he or she is dismissed from the government, but may, of course, remain as an MP, e.g., Harriet Harman (Secretary of State for Social Security) dismissed by Tony Blair in July 1998. By contrast, John Major was promoted from Chief Secretary to the Treasury to the Office of Foreign Secretary in July 1989 by the Prime Minister Margaret Thatcher. In his autobiography, John Major writes,

> Of all the jobs in government, the Foreign Office was the one . . . for which I was least prepared. Moreover, I enjoyed being Chief Secretary . . .
> Thatcher '. . . I want you to be Foreign Secretary . . . '
> Major 'Aren't there others better qualified? . . . Douglas Hurd? Nigel Lawson . . .?'
> She waved a hand dismissively. No words were necessary.[3]

The power to award honours and create peers

Apart from honours like the Order of Merit, which are totally in the personal gift of the monarch, the Prime Minister has the award of honours and the creation of peers very much in his personal control. An honours list consists of such awards as Knight of the Order of the British Empire (KBE), and Commander of the Order of the British Empire (CBE). These are awarded to British citizens who have distinguished themselves in some way. For example, the 2001 New Year's Honours list included the Olympic rower, Steven Redgrave KBE.

The Honours list may also include the creation of peerages and the bestowing of this honour on particular individuals.

Peerages are also created and bestowed during the course of the year. These are clearly a special category because, as Michael Oakeshott, the philosopher said in conversation to Professor Hennessy in 1992: 'They convert the recipient into a legislator.'[4] In other words, they become members of the House of Lords (see section on the House of Lords p. 253). This power of the Prime Minister is significant in three ways:

1 The possibility of a peerage may ensure loyalty and support for the PM before it is conferred.
2 The Prime Minister may wish to create a majority of peers who are supporters of his party.
3 Once an individual has become a peer, he may well have a sense of obligation to the PM.

During Margaret Thatcher's eleven years as PM, she created 210 peers. Since May, 1997, Tony Blair has created 'peers at the rate of nearly one and a half a week.'

Appointments of senior civil servants

This involves the appointment of the top two grades of civil servant, and according to Hennessy includes approximately 220 jobs. A senior Appointments Selection Committee recommends these names for the post in question. The Prime Minister and minister concerned choose one. The 'politicisation' of the civil service will be covered later (see section on Civil Service p. 211). During Margaret Thatcher's premiership of eleven years, it was well known that she took a much greater

> **quangos**
> Quasi-Autonomous Non-Governmental Organisations. These perform public services, and are financed by the government, although not directly.

interest in these matters than her predecessors; a frequent phrase in such selections was, 'Is he one of us?' She certainly oversaw the appointment of nearly all the 27 top permanent secretaries during her period of office.

In addition to this, nowadays, there are top appointments to the large number of **quangos**.

Other appointments

These include the heads of the Intelligence and Secret Services, senior appointments to the armed forces, senior appointments to the judiciary, top posts in the Anglican Church, and twelve regius professors (eight at Oxford, four at Cambridge). These appointments are all made with advice from various sources, e.g., bishops in the Anglican Church on the advice of the Church's own Crown Appointments Commission. Other highly significant appointments include Governor of the Bank of England, and, especially in an increasingly media-conscious time, the chairmanship of the BBC.

Appointments to the Cabinet

Prime Ministers have to take account of a considerable number of factors in appointing their Cabinet ministers:
- They must be members of either the House of Commons or the House of Lords.
- Most cabinet ministers come from the Commons, but some, e.g. the Lord Chancellor, and the Leader of the House of Lords, are there to represent the Upper House.

There is also one element of difference between the appointment of Conservative and Labour Cabinets:
- Labour shadow Cabinets are elected by the parliamentary party, and so become ministers in a new government, as was the case in 1997. Labour Prime Ministers may go in for Cabinet reshuffles within a reasonable time.
- Conservative leaders are not subject to the same constraint.

Overall the appointment of Cabinet ministers to lead the government is a vitally important task for the Prime Minister, as are Cabinet and government reshuffles. Many considerations need to be made.

- Usually, Prime Ministers are bound, almost, to appoint senior members of the party who have long years of experience and are popular within the party. For example, in 1979, Margaret Thatcher virtually inherited Edward Heath's cabinet; as a consequence, there were a number of ministers who were not like-minded whom she appointed, e.g., James Prior; John Major, in creating his first cabinet, appointed Douglas Hurd and Michael Heseltine, both of whom had competed against him in the Conservative Party leadership election.

- Senior politicians may have a strong following both in the parliamentary party and in the party as a whole. As such, they may be representative of a particular wing of the party within Cabinet. John Major attempted to establish a more consensual Cabinet than his predecessors, and so included both those on the left of the party, like Kenneth Clarke, and those on the Right, like Michael Portillo. In such a case, a balanced Cabinet may be the Prime Minister's aim.

- Other Prime Ministers may gradually bring in, via reshuffles, more and more ministers who are like-minded and are loyal allies, while 'sacking' those who are not. Margaret Thatcher, for example, gradually sacked 'wets' like James Prior and Francis Pym, whilst bringing in 'dries' like Norman Tebbit. The election of John Prescott as Deputy Leader of the Labour Party, and subsequently his role as the Deputy Prime Minister in the present Government, was seen by some as keeping a symbol of 'Old Labour' in an essentially 'New Labour' government.

- Ministers also have to be able to deal with highly public and difficult situations, e.g. Mo Mowlam as Secretary of State for Northern Ireland in Blair's first Cabinet, and Kenneth Clarke as Minister for Health in 1988 as John Moore had not overcome many difficulties in attempting to reform the National Health Service.

- Prime Ministers also 'talent spot' and promote politicians whom they believe will be good managers of their departments, having already worked well in other posts, e.g., Alan Milburn was promoted from Chief Secretary to the Treasury, to Secretary of State for Health in October 1999.

- Prime Ministers often prefer to have potential or actual 'rebels' in Cabinet, rather than have them sniping at government from the back benches. e.g., Tony Benn in Harold Wilson's government (1966–70) and Michael Portillo in John Major's government (1992–97).

- Only occasionally does it happen that Prime Ministers appoint those who have a particular knowledge, experience, or preference to an appropriate post. One exception was John Major's appointment of Michael Heseltine as President of the Board of Trade in April 1992.

Roles of Prime Minister

Party leader

The leader of the party with the largest number of MPs in the House of Commons after an election almost invariably becomes Prime Minister. This is to ensure that the leader and his ruling party have control over the introduction, and eventual passage of legislation through Parliament. In the first instance, the party will have elected their leader with his potential as a future Prime Minister very much in mind.

Once installed as Prime Minister, the party leader often has a difficult balancing act to perform between these two roles. Traditionally, it was the Labour party in the 1960s and 1970s which gave its Prime Ministers, Harold Wilson and James Callaghan, most difficulty. A classic example fell to Callaghan in 1976 when his government, facing a huge economic and financial crisis, sought help from the IMF. The price for this financial assistance was large cuts in government expenditure, e.g. on education and health. The Labour Party, from Cabinet down to its rank-and-file membership, was divided on this. Nevertheless, Callaghan was able to retain party unity and power.

Traditionally, Conservative Prime Ministers have been less troubled by this balancing act. Certainly, party dissent from the Prime Minister's position, was far less public until the late 1980s, and into the 1990s. There was an early problem for Margaret Thatcher, however, when she put her party's dissent in second place to her position as Prime Minister. In November 1980 at the Conservative Party Conference, she refused to abandon her monetarist policies at a time of economic slump, and go in for U-turns as Edward Heath had done in 1971. As she put it: 'You can turn if you like. This lady's not for turning.'

Prime ministerial authority over her party had been accepted, but this was not to be the case in the two years leading up to her enforced resignation in November 1990. On the other hand, John Major's premiership from this time until 1997 was dogged by opposition from within his party, especially over his policies towards Britain's membership of the EU. Traditional Conservative party reticence towards it Prime Ministers was a thing of the past.

Party leaders who become Prime Ministers are aware of such potential difficulties, however. Furthermore, once installed as Prime Minister, with all the authority and influence that accompanies this office, the party leader's role is enhanced. At the same time, the Prime Minister's ties to his party are relaxed so as to fulfil the duties of government leader. If a Prime Minister can deliver further general election victories, as Margaret Thatcher did in 1983 and 1987, then problems as party leader are clearly reduced.

The party leader in government

The Prime Minister is the principal figure in the House of Commons. This is most 'newsworthy' nowadays in the weekly Prime Minister's Question Time. The Prime Minister's performance has considerable effect on party morale, both in Parliament, and on the Party as a whole. This has been particularly the case since televising of the Commons began in 1989.

On the other hand, during the twentieth century, the amount of time spent in the House of Commons has been very much in decline. Statements and debates led by Prime Ministers are now only occasional. However, they do need to address their parliamentary parties. Margaret Thatcher was careful not to make the same mistakes as her predecessor, Edward Heath, for most of her premiership. John Major, with a declining and fragile majority in the Commons for 1992–97, was often required to address the 1922 committee when crises arose. Tony Blair attends the Commons only for Prime Minister's Questions – which he reduced to once weekly – to address Labour MPs, and only occasionally to vote.

A representative of the UK abroad and a national leader

The Prime Minister also represents the nation, particularly at European Union summit meetings, and at meetings with the leaders of other countries. The last three Prime Ministers have established strong working relationships with particular Presidents of the USA: Margaret Thatcher with Ronald Reagan; John Major with George Bush; and Tony Blair with Bill Clinton and George W. Bush.

For a Prime Minister to be viewed as a national leader, however, only seems to occur at times of crisis and is, anyway, a more difficult role to adopt than it is for a directly elected president, say, of the USA. To be viewed as a national leader requires the setting aside of party affiliations in order to speak or act for the United Kingdom as a whole. Margaret Thatcher took on this role during the Falklands War in 1982, and the continuation of the Cold War in the 1980s; John Major during the Gulf War of 1990–91; and Tony Blair during the bombing of Kosovo by NATO in 1999, and the death of Princess Diana in 1997.

Prime Ministers and their treatment of the Cabinet

Prime Ministers vary in the use they make of their Cabinets. Clement Attlee, the post-war Labour Prime Minister, saw his role essentially as chairman of the Cabinet. He led an able team and although he could be assertive, it was meaningful to write of 'Cabinet government' under his leadership. Other PMs have had a different style, some tending to be forceful and dominant, others more content to delegate to those around them. At one extreme are the powerful (Margaret Thatcher, Tony Blair), at the other those content to keep the ship afloat (e.g. 'steady-as-she-goes' James Callaghan).

Margaret Thatcher used the Cabinet less than many of her predecessors, her annual average of meetings being 35 as against Harold Wilson's 59. Neither did she use Cabinet standing committee meetings much, preferring to create ad hoc committees of her chosen membership. These often took important decisions on matters ranging from the American bombing of Libya to the introduction of the community charge. She stated her own views at the beginning of Cabinet meetings and was not a great listener. The longer she was in power, the more she surrounded herself with weak ministers whom she could easily control.

John Major adopted a more collegial style, as he explained in his Autobiography: 'Margaret had often introduced subjects in Cabinet by setting out her favoured solution . . . I, by contrast, preferred to let my views be known in private, see potential dangers ahead of the meeting, encourage discussion, and sum up after it . . . I chose consensus in policy-making, if not always in policy.'[5]

Taking over at a difficult time following the fall of Margaret Thatcher, he saw the need to heal divisions and did so by including representatives of all shades of opinion in the party. His approach was more consensual, his Cabinet meetings more friendly. He used committees less than his predecessor and allowed the Cabinet to meet more regularly. He provided less leadership, preferring to hear the views of others and reach an agreed viewpoint. As one member, William Waldegrave, later remarked: 'It was much more what Cabinet Government is supposed to be like.'

John Major did not insist too strongly on collective responsibility and in his last years his Cabinet was very divided and his performance seemed weak and ineffectual. What had seemed to be a welcome change of style, became associated in the public perception with weakness, dithering and an inability to lead.

Tony Blair uses his Cabinet much less than John Major and often attends its meetings for only a short time. He tends to lay down his preferred policy, as on the Millennium Dome, and expects agreement. Generally, he has had Cabinet backing because the party is relieved to be back in power. There have been divisions, for he has some powerful figures around him, unlike Margaret Thatcher whose position was reinforced by election victories. His inclination seems to be to act decisively and strongly, though he has granted reasonable discretion to ministers to get on with their tasks as long as it is evident that they are in line with agreed policy.

To date, Blair certainly ranks alongside Margaret Thatcher as the strongest peace-time Prime Minister in the last 100 years. Unlike Margaret Thatcher in

1979, however, he was able to assert himself over all policy areas from the outset. An overall Commons majority of 179, indications of a 'Blair effect', providing extra votes in the election, and his consistently high popularity rating in the opinion polls all added to the strong position that most new Prime Ministers hold.

It seems likely, however, that even if New Labour had gained the sort of majority they expected (about 50), the form of Blair's government would have been the same. As Hennessy said in April 1997, 'It's going to be a command premiership.' When he and his inner circle entered Number 10, ready to work as they had done in the Labour party, one sensed, to use a cliché, that they 'hit the ground running'.

In July 1999, Blair's updated version of 'Questions of Procedure for Ministers' laid down clearly that all presentations of policy via the media would have to be cleared with Number 10, either through Blair's private office, or his press office. This established his chain of command in government. Peter Riddell in *The Times* recognised what was happening: 'Goodbye Cabinet Government. Welcome the Blair Presidency. The Ministerial Code . . . is . . . the biggest centralisation of power seen in Whitehall in peacetime . . . The idea that heads of department have an independent standing has been torn up.'[6]

In other words, the power of Number 10 and Blair had been enhanced to the detriment of full Cabinet and individual Cabinet ministers. His consultations with ministers tended to be on a one-to-one basis. Blair has also often worked through his political staff in Number 10 which, as a whole, has been very much increased in size, by making his own political appointments in his private office, the press office, the strategic communications unit, and his policy unit. As with other Prime Ministers, Blair of course has also reshuffled his Cabinet occasionally, promoting like-minded and able politicians, such as Alan Milburn as Secretary of State for Health. In this way, he has been seen as the guardian of New Labour's strategy. He has taken a personal interest in several areas of policy, Europe, Northern Ireland, education and health. Via his office, he has attempted to integrate the work of different departments in order to deal with problems that cut across departmental boundaries, for example, the problems of inner cities require input from such departments as the Home Office, Social Security, Health, Education and Employment, etc. Peter Hennessy writes of the two most powerful words in Whitehall being 'Tony wants'.[7]

Subsequently, Hennessy also talks of the Blair government in terms of circles of influence with the Prime Minister at the centre. On the one hand, this may be regarded as an over-powerful model of premiership, essentially presidential in its form. On the other hand, some see it as being the type of streamlined and efficient leadership required for the twenty-first century. Hennessy also portrays the Blair premiership as being modelled on a court, with the majority of Cabinet ministers on the periphery. His chapter on the Blair era is significantly entitled 'Command and Control'.[8]

One further consequence of this form of leadership has been the neglect of Parliament. Blair's predecessors had become increasingly detached from Parliament (and Cabinet too) by international meetings, e.g. European Union sessions, meetings with the US President elevating the Prime Minister well above senior colleagues, but also taking him or her away from Parliament, and the Commons in particular. Blair spends little time in the Commons, has a very poor voting record there, only appears once a week for 30 minutes for Prime Minister's Questions (it had previously been two sessions, each of 15 minutes) and most of his, and other ministers's major policy announcements are made via the media, and not in the House. Yet it must be remembered that this practice has a long history, prior to 1997.

Finally, the media have found it more convenient to focus on personalities both before and since 1997, so the Blair v Hague/Duncan Smith battle becomes a direct appeal by each for the votes of the electorate. Certainly, more than ever before, Blair has become the most important communicator of the government.

Prime-ministerial or Cabinet government?

The Prime Minister is the most powerful politician in the country. He or she heads a group of powerful figures some of whom have a party or national standing in their own right. The way in which they work together will depend upon the mix of personalities involved.

At the beginning of the twentieth century the Prime Minister was thought to be 'primus inter pares', first among equals. The description **Cabinet government** seemed appropriate, even though some Prime Ministers were stronger than others and were capable of dominating their administration – especially in time of war (e.g. Lloyd George after 1916). Yet for half a century there has been discussion of whether Britain has **Government by Prime Minister** and at times the academic debate on the issue has been lively. It was Richard Crossman, a Labour MP, Cabinet minister and academic, who in the early 1960s wrote of the transformation into **prime-ministerial government** and of the Cabinet becoming one of the 'dignified elements' of the constitution.

Lord Oxford (formerly Liberal Prime Minister Herbert Asquith) judged that: 'The office of Prime Minister is what its holder chooses and is able to make of it.' His emphasis on the ability, character and preference of the incumbent is generally accepted, as is the role of particular circumstances. The trend in the twentieth century was for Prime Ministers to exhibit greater dominance over their colleagues, and many examples can be quoted in which premiers have by-passed the whole Cabinet and taken key decisions in committees, an inner cabinet or bilateral meetings.

Yet not only does prime-ministerial power vary between holders of the office (with sometimes a 'strong' one being followed by a 'weak' one, and then another 'strong' one, as with Thatcher, Major and Blair). Even the same Prime Minister can seem 'weaker' or 'stronger' according to the political circumstances, including the size of the government's majority.

It is difficult to apply one label to the British system. The term prime-ministerial government seems inappropriate as a description of the Major years but more relevant to the experience of life under Tony Blair. An old exam question invites discussion of a quotation: 'The power of the Prime Minister has increased, is increasing and ought to be diminished.' But there has not been a gradual, unbroken trend to prime-ministerial dominance, more of an ebb and flow of power.

Models of government: the balance of power between the Prime Minister and the Cabinet

There are four different models of the form of Britain's government which cover the key relationship of Prime Minister and Cabinet:
1 Cabinet government;
2 Prime-ministerial government;
3 Presidential government;
4 A core executive.

Cabinet government

- The legislative (Parliament) and the executive (PM, Cabinet ministers and the civil service) are fused (joined together) via the Cabinet.
- The Cabinet is at the apex of the executive. It is a collective political executive and so constrains the power of the Prime Minister. The principle of collective responsibility means that the Cabinet makes the most important political decisions.
- Power is distributed among Cabinet members on an equal footing which constrains the power of the Prime Minister while acknowledging that as head of the Cabinet he is *primus inter pares*.

Prime-ministerial government

- The fusion of the executive and the legislature gives the Prime Minister, as leader of the largest party in the Commons and as head of the civil service, direct influence over both.

- The Prime Minister controls the policy process, sets the framework for ministerial policies, dominates executive decision making and may make key decisions with whomsoever he or she chooses, often without reference to the Cabinet.
- The full Cabinet is a sounding board or source of advice for policy making. It may simply ratify a policy decision made elsewhere. It is not a policy maker but a policy coordinator.
- Despite the first two points, the concepts of collective responsibility and accountability are still in operation.

Presidential government

- The Prime Minister has a particular ideological commitment or vision that is separate from the party and government, in other words an ideological detachment.
- Prime Ministers distance themselves politically from their office and the vested interest within government, by developing a wide constituency of support within the party and the public at large; there is the cult of being a political 'outsider'.
- Prime Ministers may – via obsessional media coverage – establish a political leadership that bypasses government, Parliament and Whitehall.
- The media's obsession with personality enhances this model to such an extent that the Prime Minister becomes the personification of national concerns. This further enhances their personal standing and popularity.
- The Cabinet is very much subordinate to the Prime Minister who has a personal and dominating influence on policy. Nevertheless, the concept of collective responsibility is still in operation.

The core executive

- The core executive is a network at the centre of power, consisting of the Prime Minister, Cabinet and the people, organisations and practices that surround them. As such its elements include:
1 the Prime Minister, senior advisers in the Prime Minister's office and the 'Kitchen Cabinet';
2 the Inner Cabinet;
3 Cabinet committees;
4 Cabinet and Cabinet Office;
5 highest-ranking civil servants in vital departments such as the Treasury and Home Office.

Power within the core executive may be perceived as follows:
1 It is in every location within the core, not in any one place; it is not equally distributed in every location.
2 It is fluid rather than static and is more to do with relationships within the core executive than to do with any one part of it.

3 It therefore varies over time and according to the situation at the time.

Tony Blair's presidential style: evidence in support

- Tony Blair's period as Prime Minister since May 1997 has stimulated renewed debate about the location of power within the British executive, the relationship between Prime Minister and Cabinet and the nature of British government as a whole.

- Blair's government appears presidential even though the British system is parliamentary. Other Cabinet ministers stay in the background unless there is a policy initiative or a controversy, as with Stephen Byers, the railway industry and Railtrack. Blair's approach to leadership is consciously modelled on Mrs Thatcher although his management of Cabinet and personal style are less confrontational and abrasive. As one of the founders of New Labour he portrays himself as the ideological conscience of his government, personally dictating overall strategy and direction – much like Margaret Thatcher. This is done in well-publicised public presentations from time to time.

- The stress on the 'Blair project', Blairism, the Third Way and New Labour all give his premiership a presidential character. Further there is a strong sense that New Labour is being imposed on the Labour party as a whole.

- Blair's presidentialism is also reflected in his Cabinet management. The meetings are short, tightly managed and usually focus on disseminating information. Full Cabinet debate is very rare. He relies on Cabinet committees as have previous Prime Ministers, but his reliance on special advisers is unprecedented.

- Prime Ministers are not presidents. Prime Ministers depend on the continued support of their Cabinet and party. US presidents are elected independently and hope for a second election success. Prime Ministers have to work hard to ensure unity in Cabinet and party, and – of course – win general elections. However, it is worth finally focusing on the word 'president'. Andrew Rawnsley has written of Bill Clinton's visit to Tony Blair in 1998:

> At a photo-opportunity with the Cabinet, Clinton expressed . . . a lust for Blair's majority of 179. He might be the leader of the world's only remaining superpower, but there are checks and restraints on an American president which are wholly absent in Britain. Within his own universe, no democratic leader is potentially more powerful than a British Prime Minister with a reliable parliamentary majority and an obedient Cabinet.[9]

Prime Minister and US President: a comparison

For several years, academics and commentators have drawn comparisons between the offices of Prime Minister and US President and attempted to see which is the most powerful. There are several considerations to bear in mind.

President

The President is initially elected by his party (the Democrats or the Republicans) to stand as its presidential candidate. Following the election campaign proper in the autumn, he is chosen via an electoral college, in elections which are separate from those for members of Congress. His mandate comes directly from the American people. He appoints his cabinet who are *not* elected, without having to consider the wishes of his party. His other powers of patronage also include the appointment of approximately 3,300 officials.

He is not dependent on majority support in the legislature. Bills are presented to Congress which in theory they judge on merit. Defeat in Congress may well take place, but the president is not obliged to resign.

As well as being chief executive or head of government, the President is also head of state. As such he can appeal to the people as a whole and bypass his party and Congress. As chief executive, he is the head of a huge bureaucracy with vast resources and expertise for creating, initiating and administering policy. He has immediate access to the media and so is able to address the nation at almost any time.

He is elected for a fixed term of four years. He may only serve two such terms of office, following a constitutional amendment after the Second World War.

Prime Minister

The Prime Minister is, in the first instance, selected by a local constituency association to stand as its candidate to be the constituency's MP in the House of Commons. Eventually, as an MP gaining more responsibility within the party (either in government or opposition), he will have won the election for the leadership of his party. At a general election, he will have led his party to victory, as a result of the party gaining a majority of MPs in the Commons. At this point, he becomes Prime Minister.

As Prime Minister, he is the head of the government and, as an MP, sits in the Commons. He also appoints his Cabinet and other ministers (mostly from the Commons) to form his government.

It is the decision of the Prime Minister – sometimes on advice – to fix the date of the next general election as he sees fit within five years of the previous general election. As a consequence, a Prime Minister who leads his party to further election victories, in theory could remain in power until he and his party are defeated at a general election.

REFERENCES

1 J. Major, *The Autobiography*, HarperCollins, 1999.
2 Quoted in R. Rose, *The Prime Minister in a Shrinking World*, Polity, 2001.
3 As note 1 above.
4 P. Hennessy, *The Prime Minister. The Office and its Holders Since 1945*, Penguin, 2000.
5 As note 1 above.
6 P. Riddell, *The Times*, October 1997.
7 As note 4 above.
8 A. Rawnsley, *Servants of the People*, Penguin, 2001.

USEFUL WEBSITES

www.cabinet-office.gov.uk On this site there is much useful material including the following: Cabinet committee lists – membership and terms of reference; Cabinet ministers – a guide to the members of the Cabinet and their responsibilities; Ministers and departments – an information page.

SAMPLE QUESTIONS

1 (a) What is collective ministerial responsibility?

(b) What factions influence the Prime Minister's appointment of ministers?

(c) How powerful is the Prime Minister?

2 Read the three extracts and then answer the questions which follow.

> I don't claim it's the only way of running a Cabinet but there's a lot to be said for a consensus form of Cabinet in a democratic system. You can run it as a dictator. You can cow your colleagues, make them afraid of you and not give the opportunity of expressing their views. That will come to an end sooner or later. (Lord Callaghan, former PM 1976–1979 in conversation with Michael Cockerell)

> Margaret Thatcher was going to be the leader in her Cabinet. She wasn't going to be an impartial chairman. She knew what she wanted to do and she was not going to have faint hearts in her Cabinet stopping her . . . Nor was it suitable to decide matters by vote in view of the constitutional position. (Nicholas Ridley *My Style of Government*. Quoted in Hennessy, 2000) NB: Nicholas Ridley was a minister in Mrs Thatcher's Cabinet.

'All roads lead to Tony' in the words of one Cabinet Minister. All the power of the British state has drained to the small office in Downing Street in which Mr Blair works. And when the government has found itself in difficulties it is the PM who has to stake his personal authority on the matter. L'etat, c'est Tony (Sion Simon, *Daily Telegraph*, 16 November 1998)

(a) Using Extract 1, explain what is meant by a 'consensus form of Cabinet'.

(b) Using Extract 2 and your own knowledge, explain why Margaret Thatcher was not prepared to be an 'impartial chairman' in her Cabinet.

(c) Using Extract 3 and your own knowledge, explain why many believe that with Tony Blair we now have a British presidency.

AIMS OF THIS CHAPTER

➤ To outline the work of government departments, ministers and the civil service.

➤ To consider the concept of individual ministerial responsibility.

➤ To outline the traditional role of the civil service and the impact of recent reforms.

➤ To consider the issues surrounding political advisers in government departments and the debate about quangos.

Government departments

Most Cabinet ministers are responsible for the work of a government department. They are usually known as Secretaries of State. Each department has coverage of one policy area, although these areas may change at the discretion of the Prime Minister. In 1997, Tony Blair combined responsibility for the environment, transport and the regions into one department. In 2001, the environment was joined to agriculture in a new Department for Rural Affairs, Transport and the Regions. All departments are responsible for preparing legislation, administering that legislation when it becomes law and also administering existing legislation.

Departments vary in size and importance. The Treasury is always the most important, because its remit is the economy and government finance, central policy areas which help to determine the fate of any government. The Foreign and Commonwealth Office and the Home Office are the other two 'great' departments of state.

Departments are large bureaucracies. The minister has a number of junior ministers to assist him. He also has a large workforce of civil servants, two of whom are particularly significant, the Permanent Secretary (the civil service head of the department) and the Private Secretary (the civil servant who coordinates his work with that of other departments). Departments are usually divided into policy sectors, so that in the Department of Education and Skills there is a schools minister, and a further and higher education minister, among others.

Most departments also have responsibility for a number of 'executive agencies' and oversee the work of quangos (see p. 219).

Ministers

Basically, ministers are amateurs who have to grasp the main policy issues of their department while trying to handle them successfully and cope with a punishing daily schedule. At first, having been given responsibility for a department, they are bound to rely enormously on their civil servants. They know that they will probably not be in the job for much more than two to three years. If they wish to gain promotion at that point, they will have had to make an impact quickly.

The job of a minister involves many roles:

1 Most are MPs, though a few may be in the Lords.
2 In the House, they answer questions and steer bills through the law-making procedure.
3 In the Cabinet and the government at large, they represent the department, seeking to secure adequate funding, influence decisions and arrange bilateral meetings with other ministers and – on key topics – the Prime Minister.
4 To the electorate, they represent the public face of the department at public meetings, via visits, meetings and performances on the media. At Health, Alan Milburn is regularly to be seen opening hospital extensions and launching new initiatives on health care and provision.
5 Ministers usually take at least one 'red box' home with them at night, filled with paperwork on issues which may require decisions to be taken.

The government: its hierarchy of ministers

Prime Minister (1)
Cabinet ministers (21–24) – e.g. Chancellor of Exchequer
ministers of state (30) – e.g. Department of Trade (4 in 1998) each covering a specific policy area
parliamentary under-secretaries (35) – junior ministers in a department
parliamentary private secretaries (47) – governmental backbench MPs, chosen by a minister, as assistants. They are unpaid, but are members of the government.
whips (23) – the party managers
law officers (4)

NB: Numbers of office holders – other than the Prime Minister – are approximate.

The minister–civil servant relationship

It is unusual for a former professional to be put in charge of a department, although Estelle Morris, formerly at Education, was once a practising teacher. 'Amateur' ministers meet 'professional' civil servants in a relationship once characterised in the phrase 'civil servants advise, ministers decide'. In recent decades, it has been recognised that senior civil servants are involved in decision making every day and that no minister could possibly have oversight of every decision in his or her department.

Ministers often believe that their civil servants are obstructive over policy proposals. They may bring in special advisers, often political advisers, but as we see on pp. 218–19 their presence can cause tensions within the department.

Individual ministerial responsibility

Ministers are collectively responsible for government policy (see Cabinet collective responsibility p. 192). They are also individually responsible for the work of their departments.

The constitutional position concerning the relationship of ministers to civil servants is clear. Convention states that ministers with a portfolio are accountable to Parliament for all the actions or otherwise within their department. Civil servants (officials) are unelected, neutral and anonymous; they administer policy and carry out the work of their political masters, the ministers. Ministers are elected, partisan and high profile, and they 'carry the can' for decisions and actions of the department. The convention has two virtues. Officials are kept out of the political arena and therefore any incoming ministers of either party can have confidence in their impartiality. The public and especially their representatives in the House, the MPs, know to whom they should address any doubts and anxieties about any aspect of departmental policy; in other words, the doctrine pinpoints responsibility.

The implication of individual ministerial responsibility was that a minister should resign over a mistake made by civil servants. For example, in 1954 the Conservative minister, Sir Thomas Dugdale, resigned over the Crichel Down affair. Crichel Down was farmland taken over by the Ministry of Agriculture during the Second World War and not returned to its original owner. Ironically, much of the 'maladministration' had been made under the previous Labour government. Again, following the Falklands invasion by Argentina in 1982, the Foreign Secretary, Lord Carrington resigned. Although he had personally been engaged in high-profile diplomatic initiatives, as a man of honour he felt that a failing of his department to chart the Argentinian threat had caused a difficulty for the government.

Rarely do ministers resign over maladministration or mistakes made by their department. The two above stand out, whereas in usual circumstances ministers survive errors and controversies, as long as they have the goodwill of the Prime Minister and their colleagues. When ministers do resign, as many have in the last two administrations, it is more often because of some financial or sexual misconduct. Examples include the following:

- 1998 Ron Davies (Welsh Secretary) resigned over sexual impropriety on Clapham Common.
- Peter Mandelson (Trade and Industry) resigned over his acceptance of an undeclared loan from the Paymaster-General, whose affairs were being investigated by Mandelson's department. The Paymaster-General resigned as well.
- 2001 Peter Mandelson (Northern Ireland Secretary) resigned over the granting of a passport in the Hinduja affair, following allegations that he had intervened in the handling of the application and had then misled the House over the matter.

The restructuring of government in recent years, with the creation of Next Step agencies, has had an impact on the convention of individual responsibility. In the 1990s, various crises occurred in the running of the prison service, including a breakout from Parkhurst. The Home Secretary, Michael Howard, sacked the head of the executive agency overseeing prisons, rather than accept responsibility himself. He claimed that day-to-day operational matters were not the responsibility of the Home Secretary, whose remit was to deal with broad policy issues and lay down the guidelines for the service.

The civil service

Structure

The civil service is the governmental bureaucracy. Government departments are run by ministers who are elected politicians, but they are administered by professional and permanent paid officials. Many of these are clerical or managerial staff, distributed in government offices up and down the country. The ones who concern us most are those who belong to the top administrative grades, often referred to as the 'mandarins' or, collectively, as 'the higher civil service'.

These 750–800 senior officials are based mainly in the large Whitehall departments. The top civil servant is the Cabinet Secretary, but in a typical department there will be a Permanent Secretary at the helm, and below this rank a number of Deputy Secretaries, Under Secretaries, Assistant Secretaries, Senior Principals and Principals. Many of these are still public school/ Oxbridge educated and they are drawn from a narrow stratum of society – this 'bias' has been the subject of many enquiries.

Higher civil servants have a number of key functions, among them:
- advising ministers;
- preparing and drafting discussion documents and legislation;
- acting as a secretariat for ministerial meetings;
- preparing ministerial answers to questions asked in Parliament or by the public;

- implementing government decisions.

There are now well under 500,000 civil servants, a marked drop on the number two decades or so ago. The fall is partly due to rationalisation – a streamlining of the way departments are run. The reduction is also caused by the reclassification of some jobs and the privatisation of many former public services.

Traditionally, the civil service is run according to three interlinked features which are still important but no longer carry the force they once did:

Permanence

In Britain, civil servants are career officials prepared to serve a government of any colour. They do not change at election time, as they do in the USA. This permanence is associated with experience and continuity, so that an inexperienced incoming government will be able to count on official expertise. Permanence, coupled with confidentiality, means that civil servants can speak frankly to ministers, without fear of dismissal. It makes a civil service career seem attractive. The other side of the coin is that permanence means 'no change at the top' which may well stifle fresh thinking and new initiatives, a point which worried Sir John Hoskyns (see p. 216).

Neutrality

Officials are required to be politically impartial. They must carry out decisions with which they personally may disagree and not involve themselves in any partisan activity. If they were to do so, this would make it difficult for them to remain in office. Some critics suggest that neutrality puts it too strongly, for they are expected to further the policies of the elected government, be 'neutral on the government's side'.

Anonymity

Ministers are answerable for what happens in their departments (see Individual Ministerial Responsibility, p. 213) and the role of civil servants is to offer confidential advice, in secret. If officials became public figures, this would endanger their reputation for neutrality, for they could become identified with a particular policy. They might then be unacceptable to a new administration. Identification might also prevent them from offering frank advice to ministers; if they knew that they could be named they might feel the need to be very discreet. On the other hand, does anonymity conceal poor advice and shield officials from the consequences of any inadequacy?

Change under Margaret Thatcher

Margaret Thatcher was instinctively suspicious of the civil service. She saw in it a potential obstacle to her vision. In her view, a large bureaucracy went hand in hand with the 'big government' of the consensus years, which she so despised. She wanted to roll back the frontiers of the state. This involved curbing a civil service, which had become unnecessarily large and was urging or pursuing misguided policies. Moreover, she was suspicious of the power and type of senior civil servants, some of whom might use their permanence and expertise to develop their own view of what was needed, rather than assist in carrying out the wishes of the government of the day. They were excessively powerful. They were also sometimes poor managers, ill-equipped for the task of running a large department. They often lacked training in management skills, many being generalist all-rounders rather than expert administrators. Overall, her aim was to make the civil service more 'business-like' and cost-effective.

She did not begin her term of office with a grand review of Whitehall, being initially more concerned with cost-cutting changes; in 1979, she had a simple target, a 3 per cent reduction in staff expenditure (thereafter, she set targets for staff numbers). Among later initiatives, she tried to bring in people at the top who were 'one of us'; several early retirements enabled her to sweep away several long-serving 'mandarins'. She also brought in outside advisers such as Sir John Hoskyns, a businessman who was not sympathetic to the existing bureaucracy. He thought it needed some fresh thinking, and wanted more exchanges with the business world. Another adviser was Sir Derek Rayner, joint managing director of Marks & Spencer, then a firm with a reputation for efficient management. He had a reputation for staff economies, having reduced staff costs at Marks & Spencer by 5 per cent, by cutting out unessential paper work and other modest economies. Like Hoskyns, he also challenged the attitudes and outlook of many senior officials and was responsible for cost-conscious policies and efficiency savings. It was his Financial Management Initiative, which set targets for departments and their staff; he wanted clear objectives and a means of recognising whether they had been attained. With strong Prime ministerial backing, he appointed Sir Derek Ibbs to run the Efficiency Unit; Ibbs effectively took over the work which Rayner had done, examining progress on the efficiency scrutinies which his mentor had put in hand. Ibbs was dissatisfied with the rate of change and in 1988 produced the very influential report, 'Improving Management in Government: The Next Steps'. It wanted the creation of a slimmed-down, better-managed civil service.

The Next Step executive agencies

Ibbs argued that the civil service was too vast and complex to be managed well as one organisation. Departments varied and needed their own systems of management. Accordingly, he recommended a division of work. New agencies would be responsible for 'blocks' of executive work (operational matters), and a smaller 'core' civil service would work in the departments to 'sponsor' the agencies and to service ministers with policy advice and help. He suggested that it was unrealistic to expect ministers to be managers as well as politicians. It would be better if they concentrated on the areas for which they were elected and left management to the specialists in the agencies.

In practice, this meant that in a department such as Social Security (DSS), there would be a core department of around 2,800 dealing with policy and personal advice to ministers. In addition, there would be six agencies, which in order of size are:
- The Benefits Agency (assesses and pays out benefits);
- The Child Support Agency (assesses/collects maintenance payments);
- The Contributions Agency (ensures collection of National Insurance);
- The Information Technology Agency (provides computer services for department);
- The War Pensions Agency (provides pensions for war veterans);
- The Resettlement Agency (ran hostels for homeless, until closure, 1996).

All government departments are affected in this way; for instance, the Defence Department has 21 agencies. Gradually, throughout the 1990s, the functions of departments have been handed over to these new bodies, so that there are now about 150 of them. Most civil servants work in them, rather than in departments. The agencies are headed by appointed chief executives, often very well-paid individuals brought in from the business world.

But there are concerns about these agencies.

- **Cost**. The new chief executives are paid much more generously than the equivalent civil servants; e.g. the Prison Service head initially got £133,000.

- **Policy/administration**. Can you really separate the two things? Don't you need to know the possible pitfalls of implementation when a policy is being devised?

- **Fragmentation**. Might not the civil service become too fragmented? Coordination once relied on officials having experience and a network of contacts across Whitehall. Movement between highly specialised agencies into different ones or into core departments might be difficult. Would high flyers really want to join an executive agency instead of advising ministers on policy?

- **Accountability**. This was the main anxiety and it has proved difficult. The agencies and their chief executives are not accountable to Parliament or the electorate, as government ministers and their departments used to be. When the Child Support Agency ran into initial difficulties, it was easy for the minister to say it was not his concern. This issue came to a head over the Parkhurst/Sir Derek Lewis affair. Michael Howard would not resign as Home

Secretary, for he distinguished between operational decisions for which Lewis was responsible and policy decisions, which were his responsibility.

Further change under Tony Blair

Under the Major government, the Next Step agencies were given additional responsibilities on matters such as pay levels and recruitment. The incoming Blair administration accepted the idea of such agencies. It now looked as though Whitehall was in a state of continuous upheaval. The old days of hierarchical departments staffed by permanent officials had long gone.

Like his predecessor, Tony Blair wished to deliver effective public services. He was anxious to achieve 'performance targets' and was more interested in reaching them than in worrying about the means by which this might happen. Thus cutting waiting lists for hospital appointments was a goal, as was cutting class sizes in infant schools. Ministers were less interested in the department or agency which delivered the outcome, than in ensuring that it was attained. Tony Blair wanted to see the civil service act as an efficient enabling body, in the same way that councils had become enabling authorities in the 1980s. The White Paper *Modernising Government* (1999) discussed the role of central and local government, and the role of the private sector in service delivery.

To improve policy coordination and implementation and get away from the 'short-termism' of traditional governmental thinking, Tony Blair established the Performance and Innovation Unit in the Cabinet Office. Specifically, it was to examine cross-governmental policies, sorting out departmental disputes. The Prime Minister is committed to 'joined-up' government, and uses Lord Falconer and others to ensure that officials plan for the future and work with those in other departments.

To open up government, the Prime Minister is keen on changing the culture of senior civil servants. He suspects that many are resistant to new thinking and doubts the quality of some of them. He and his advisers make the comparison with the Labour party machine at Millbank and want to see the same efficiency in Whitehall. Above all, he fears 'departmentalitis', the idea that civil servants have adopted a policy view and keep to it whichever party is in power. To break the stranglehold of traditional attitudes, he is keen to see new people brought in from outside the service. His fondness for political advisers illustrates his enthusiasm for changed thinking.

The debate about the use of political advisers

Tony Blair increased the number of political advisers in Number 10 from 38 to 74 when he came to office in 1997. Most ministers have a supply of advisers, often party workers who have been drafted in to assist them in their work, though some are 'special advisers' with a particular area of expertise. Appointed for the lifetime of a government, they become temporary civil servants and are bound by the civil service code. The role of such advisers is to add a political dimension to the advice ministers receive from civil servants; and to act as a source of independent advice – a help for ministers who are suspicious of possible civil service obstructionism.

There has been much recent debate about the number and influence of advisers. One criticism is that they may assume more influence than the minister, as happened in the case of Alan Walters, a special adviser on economic policy to Margaret Thatcher in the late 1980s. Under New Labour, there has been concern that political advisers have undermined the functions of the civil service and involved individuals within it in much-publicised disputes. Some have been accused of 'briefing' against other ministers in the government, or against those who oppose a policy of their department. For example, Charlie Whelan, one of Gordon Brown's team, briefed against Peter Mandelson; Jo Moore in the Department of Transport briefed against the American Bob Kiley, who was advising the Mayor of London on the future of the London underground.

Permanent civil servants are wary of advisers, because they assume some of their responsibilities, undermine their influence and introduce a different type of thinking into the department. Other critics dislike the way in which political advisers may 'spin' stories, seeking to massage 'bad news' or 'bury it' by making pronouncements on days when there are serious issues dominating the headlines.

The Neill Committee recommended in 2000 that their number should be limited to a maximum of 100. Neill rejected the view that special advisers have broken Whitehall rules or that there has been an unhealthy 'politicisation' of the civil service, but wanted to ensure that they operate to a code of conduct which sets out the relationship between special advisers, officials, ministers and the media.

A note on quangos

Quangos are quasi-autonomous non-governmental organisations. 'Quasi-government' means 'government at arm's length'. In recent years, there has been considerable debate about what is and what is not a quango, and also about their proliferation. Broadly, the category includes:
- tribunals – e.g. those handling benefit appeals;
- advisory bodies – e.g. enquiry teams which investigate specific problems and help in the formulation of policy, such as the Overseas Profit Board;
- executive bodies – e.g. those bodies which regulate a part of the law, such as the Commission for Racial Equality;

- NHS Trusts – as established in the 1990 reform of the health service;
- others, such as the Urban Development Councils set up to renovate particular areas of the country.

Defenders of quangos suggest that:
1 They contribute expertise and are an effective means of administering certain policy areas.
2 They are at arm's length from government and therefore a decision can be made away from the field of political battle.
3 They may involve members of the public and provide an opportunity for participation.
4 They can be a source of speedy advice, as with the Nolan Committee.
5 They can allow for productive partnerships, as between government and various interests, such as Housing Action Trusts.

Critics point out that:
1 Quangos are unelected and unaccountable, but in receipt of public money.
2 Appointments are made in secret by ministers who may appoint 'like-minded' people to them.
3 Meetings are often held in secret, and minutes made inaccessible.
4 They are often remote and unknown to the people they are supposed to serve.
5 There are too many. In spite of pledges to curb their growth, they continue to have a key role.

FURTHER READING

J. Burnham, *Whitehall and the Civil Service*, Politics Association/SHU Press, 2000.
N. McNaughton, *The Civil Service*, Access to Politics series, Hodder & Stoughton, 2000.

USEFUL WEBSITES

Whitehall departments have their own websites giving details of their aims, policies, current news and initiatives, etc.

Examples include:
Education and Skills **www.dfes.gov.uk**
Health **www.doh.gov.uk**
Home **www.homeoffice.gov.uk**
Defence **www.mod.uk**

SAMPLE QUESTIONS

1 (a) Define the term individual ministerial responsibility.

(b) Why, and in what circumstances, do ministers resign?

(c) How have the roles of ministers and civil servants changed since 1979?

2 (a) Distinguish between a 'career civil servant' and a political adviser.

(b) Why, historically, has it been considered important that the civil service was permanent, anonymous and politically neutral?

(c) How has the civil service been restructured since 1979 and with what effects?

14

Parliament: the role and operations of the House of Commons

AIMS OF THIS CHAPTER

➤ To outline the business and functions of the Commons.

➤ To consider its role in the legislative process.

➤ To examine the background and work of MPs.

➤ To assess the issue of MPs and standards in public life.

Proceedings and organisation of the House

The Speaker presides over sittings of the House of Commons. In 2000, Betty Boothroyd – the first woman to hold the position – resigned, and was replaced by Michael Martin, the current occupant.

The role of the Speaker in the Commons is unique: he or she is an elected MP, but may not speak on behalf of his constituents in the Commons. The Speaker, along with the Deputy Speakers, chairs the proceedings in the House and so must remain impartial. The Speaker may only vote in the event of a tie and then is usually guided by the precedent of previous Speakers in similar cases. The Speaker ensures that the standing orders of the House – rules of procedure – are followed, calls upon MPs to speak, and has various sanctions at his disposal to ensure order. For example, an MP may be suspended from the House for serious indiscipline and the Speaker may suspend proceedings totally in the event of general disorder. As John Major said in 1992 about the qualities Betty Boothroyd would need as Speaker: 'She needs a quick mind and a ready wit . . . She will sometimes need the wisdom of Solomon and, if I am strictly honest, she will sometimes need the patience of Job.'[1]

The Chamber

(See Figure 14.1.) The seating arrangements of the Commons chamber are indicative of some of the key characteristics of the conduct of the House. The importance of parties and the adversarial nature of debate is emphasised by the governing party sitting to the right of the Speaker and all of the opposition

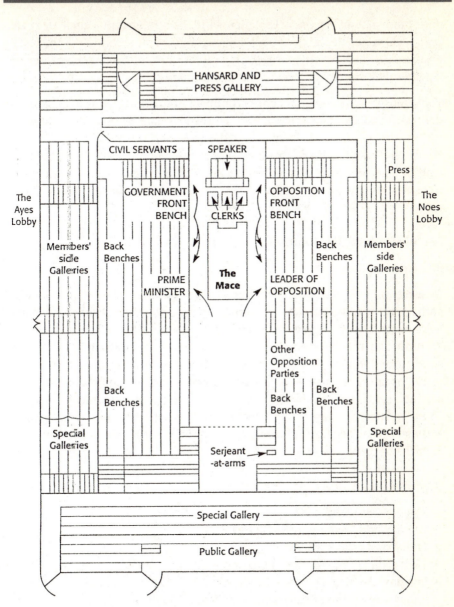

Figure 14.1 The layout of the House of Commons

parties to his left. The gap between the two blocks of seats, facing one another, is – in line with tradition – wider than the length of two sword blades.

The Prime Minister and the leader of Her Majesty's Opposition, Chancellor of the Exchequer and Shadow Chancellor occasionally confront one another at the despatch box (placed at the table by the mace). Competition and alternatives are thus very much a part of the proceedings. It is worth noting that in most other assemblies or parliaments seating is arranged in a circle or semi-circle, which has the merit of allowing members to sit according to their real position on the Left–Right spectrum, rather than forcing them to decide whether they are 'for' or 'against' the government.

The atmosphere in the Commons is for much of the time not as it appears on the television news at Prime Minister's Question Time. Certainly the House is full on this occasion. In fact, when the chamber was rebuilt after it was bombed in 1941, it was deliberately kept too small to seat all MPs in order to lend atmosphere for major debates. However, the Commons is most often characterised by rows of empty green benches when debate takes place, especially after key party figures have spoken.

The business of the House

Annual

Between general elections, meetings of the House are divided into annual parliamentary sessions usually running from October to October (or early November). Each session is divided by a recess or holiday at Christmas, Easter, Whitsun and the summer. The summer recess is especially long with MPs absent from July to October. When the House returns in the autumn, the session is not prorogued – i.e. formally closed – until any unfinished business for that session is completed. The state opening of Parliament with the Queen's Speech, marks the 'official' start of the session. Occasionally, Parliament may be recalled during a recess. This was the case in autumn 2001 after the terrorist attacks.

Weekly and daily (from January 2003)

- Monday 14.30 to 22.00
- Tuesday and Wednesday 11.30 to 19.00
- Thursday 11.30 to 18.00
- Wednesday Prime Minister's Questions 12.00 to 12.30
- Monday, Tuesday, Thursday Other Ministers' Questions 11.30 to 12.30
- Friday – occasional sittings, e.g. for Private Members' bills

The House sits for approximately 120 days per year. This is comparable to legislatures in other countries, including USA and France. The hours of business per day have now also been much reduced from the previous pattern.

Organisational matters

The business for each week is arranged by the Chief Whips (see p. 225) of the government and opposition. The Speaker is then informed about the main speakers for each party who would like a chance to express their views in each

> **Meetings in Westminster Hall**
>
> In December 1999, meetings parallel to those in the main chamber became possible. They are open to all MPs. and take place in the Grand Committee Room, which is part of Westminster Hall. The MPs sit in a semi-circle. Meetings are usually chaired by a Deputy Speaker, and are held on Tuesday and Wednesday mornings, and Thursday afternoons. Meetings here are low key.
>
> On the one hand, these meetings allow opportunities for debates on issues for which there would be little or no time in the main chamber. But they can be regarded as a distraction from events in the main chamber and as a means by which government ministers can sideline issues and 'by-pass' Parliament.

debate. This procedure is known as 'arranging business through the *usual channels*'. Each Thursday, the Leader of the House (Robin Cook, following the 2001 election) announces the business of the House for the next fortnight.

Each party in the Commons has a team of parliamentary business managers – a Chief Whip – and a number of assistants. The term 'whip' is derived from the 'whippers-in' who manage the hounds at hunt meetings. The government Chief Whip is formally a Treasury Minister with a seat in the Cabinet and an official residence at 12 Downing Street. There is also a Chief Whip in the Lords with a smaller number of assistants. Party discipline is much less strict in the Lords

- The whips are responsible for party discipline and ensuring a good turnout for voting in divisions of the House.

- The 'documentary whip' is the printed sheet of instructions sent to MPs each week by their party whips office. The importance of each division is shown by underlining it. A *three-line* whip means attendance is essential. A two-line whip means that MPs must attend unless 'pairing' has been arranged by government and opposition whips, i.e. MPs from each side are to be 'paired' and be absent for a specific division or divisions. A one-line whip requests attendance.

- For a critical division, party whips use a variety of measures to ensure support especially if a backbench revolt is likely (this is where backbench MPs vote against the party line or abstain). These include the prospect of punishment. An MP who votes against the party line will at least be questioned by the whips, will be likely to damage his 'career' prospects or may even be expelled or suspended from the parliamentary party. This is known as having the whip withdrawn. This happened to Peter Temple-Morris, Conservative, in 1997 when he opposed his party line on the single European currency. He subsequently 'crossed the floor' and joined Labour.

- **The usual channels**: government and opposition whips arrange the weekly business of the House and inform the Speaker.

- A **'Good Career Move'**: the job of an assistant whip is unpaid but responsibility for managing a number of MPs enables a whip to 'network', learn secrets and gain 'friends' within the party. The Chief Whip of each party will not only advise the leader about party members – rebels or otherwise – but also on those whips who are efficient. Many whips have gone on to hold high office, e.g. John Major.

Functions of the House

Although the role of the Commons is vital to the legislative process, much of the business of the House is not directly connected with legislation. Time is spent on debates on vital issues like the economy, and Question Times for the Prime Minister or ministers. On average about 30–40 per cent of the time of the House is taken up with bills. Therefore it is essential to understand that the Commons is not just involved in law making.

The functions of Parliament are most important to the Commons as it contains MPs, the representatives of the people. The functions of the Commons can be categorised in a variety of ways, such as:

Legitimisation

The function of legitimisation operates on two levels.

- **Latent Legitimisation**. Robert Packenham[2] reminds us that historically the Commons has met regularly without interruption since the seventeenth century. This has produced throughout society a wide acceptance of the government's right to rule. This is reinforced by the fact that government ministers who are mostly drawn from the House, continue to fulfil their functions as constituency MPs. Via this element of fusion the overall function of government is conducted through Parliament and through the Commons in particular.

- **Manifest Legitimisation**. This is the overt giving of assent to bills, government decisions, and, ultimately to the continued existence of a government. In 1979, the Labour Government of Prime Minister Callaghan lost office when it was defeated on a vote of confidence. A general election followed. *Legitimisation had been denied*.

Representation

This too operates on a number of levels.
- Each of the 659 MPs represents a constituency – on average, 60,000 voters. When the result of the constituency election is declared, the MP in his acceptance speech pledges to represent all the people in his constituency not just those who voted for him. Thus the MP may pursue matters of

concern to his constituents – individually or collectively – via written or oral questions to ministers, by lobbying ministers and by other means.

- The collective voice of MPs, given that the House provides good geographical representation, provides a useful indicator of the views of the public on important subjects such as the National Health Service and other issues that are of most and least concern.

Legislation

Legislative proposals – mostly government bills – are passed by the Commons. The other parts of the legislative process are important but this is the vital one for government. As MPs mostly vote on party lines, a government with a good majority may reasonably expect to pass its Bills. However, MPs do rebel. Even Margaret Thatcher's succession of large majorities did not prevent backbench revolts. For example the Shops Bill, a manifesto promise to introduce Sunday opening was defeated in 1986. At the same time, backbench opposition, even if not successful, is soon picked up by the media and is a source of embarrassment to government.

Recruitment and training of ministers

Ministers are usually drawn from Parliament and, by convention mostly from the Commons. MPs serve their 'apprenticeship' as potential ministers in the Commons and gain recognition in a variety of ways. These include strong performances in debates and serving on a select committee. Competition is fierce, especially since 1997. Over 400 Labour MPs were returned after both the 1997 and 2001 general elections. From this number the Prime Minister has about 100 posts to fill. There is competition too in the other parties to become 'shadow' spokespersons who are seen as an alternative to the government team.

This recruitment and training is vitally important given the increasingly powerful position of the Executive. Reputations are advanced mostly in the Commons during debates although such skills do not necessarily ensure competence as a government minister. Nevertheless, Gordon Brown as shadow Chancellor, and Tony Blair as shadow Home Secretary, from 1992 to 1994, both advanced their reputations.

Forming and sustaining government and opposition

The formation of government and the opposition is decided by general elections. The government and leaders of the opposition parties argue that their respective MPs owe their place in the House to their party. Hence, MPs in the Commons are there to support their parties, the party leadership and party policy, except on issues where a **free vote** takes place.

Much of the debate in the Commons is intensely party political. Many observers argue that the Commons and Parliament as a whole, no longer functions as a major forum for the debates of current political issues. Governments make policy, not Parliament, so the Commons is invited to comment and vote. A wide variety of issues may be debated in a week and MPs have some

free votes
These occur where MPs may vote according to their own particular view on an issue rather than supporting the party line. The March 2002 vote on banning fox hunting is an example.

methods of introducing any issue of their choice. However, it is rare for a debate on whatever issue or Bill to have a significant impact on policy. Indeed, some MPs despair of the grip that the parties have over the proceedings in the Commons and the 'strait-jacket' that they each have to wear. In the words of Tony Wright MP, 'what exists is Government and Opposition, locked in an unending election campaign on the floor and in the committee rooms of the House of Commons'.[3] Some observers also criticise the debates in the above context. As Philip Norton writes: 'the term "debate" is itself a misnomer. Members rarely debate but rather deliver prepared speeches which often fail to take up the points made by preceding speakers.'[4]

However, when a government has a small majority, backbench MPs may have an effect on contentious matters. For example, the government of John Major in 1993 had great difficulty in securing a majority for the Maastricht Treaty partly because the Conservative government had a small majority but also because of the detrimental opposition to the treaty by a group of Conservative backbenchers, known as the 'Euro-sceptics'. This was only achieved after a vote of confidence was demanded by John Major; if the government had then been defeated, a general election would have been called. As Major put it in his *Autobiography*, 'the longest white-knuckle ride in recent British politics was over'. Such occasions are rare, especially now that we are living in times of large parliamentary majorities.

Yet this does lead to another significant point. When governments frame their legislation they do need to be careful that it is reasonably acceptable especially to its own back-benchers. In this way, limits are placed on proposed policy while the whips play a crucial role in reconciling government objectives with its party's objections. In December 2001, David Blunkett attempted to introduce new anti-terrorism laws subsequent to the terrorist attacks on New York (see p. 259) to the accompaniment of objections not only from New Labour, but also MPs in other parties and civil rights groups. The latter arises from a 'landmark event' but it is important for a government, via its ministers and backbench support, to win the argument as well as the vote even when they hold a huge Commons majority.

Debate and political education

The issue of debate has essentially been covered in the previous section. However, debates on the stages of each bill, current issues, Minister's questions and especially Prime Minister's Questions are all repeated in the broadsheet newspapers and to some extent on television and radio. **Hansard** contains the verbatim reports of the daily proceedings in Parliament. These are scarcely read by the public but edited extracts often appear in the broadsheet newspapers too. When Parliament is in recess, the absence of political news leaves a gap that newspapers find especially hard to fill. This is particularly the case during the long summer recess. The first few weeks of this period when MPs and ministers take their holidays is sometimes referred to as 'the silly season' when trivial stories on other issues achieve an otherwise unwarranted coverage.

> **Hansard**
> The name of the official reports of proceedings in Parliament. They are named after Luke Hansard (1752–1828), printer of the *House of Commons Journal* from 1774. The first official reports were published from 1803 by William Cobbett, a journalist and subsequently a radical politician. Cobbett was imprisoned from 1810 to 1812 during which time he sold the business to his printer, Thomas C. Hansard, the son of Luke Hansard. The publication of the debates stayed in the family business until 1889 and is now the responsibility of Her Majesty's Stationery Office. The name Hansard was officially adopted in 1943.

Financial control

Public expenditure has been scrutinised more effectively since 1971 with the introduction of a White Paper, a debate, and an Expenditure Committee with greater powers than its predecessor the Estimates Committee. The introduction of select committees in 1979 (see p. 271) has also led to increased influence by the Commons. The Chancellor's budget proposals, especially over taxation, come under close scrutiny also and often in an informal way.

Scrutiny and influence

These functions of close and careful examination of legislation and attempting to influence the form which the law will eventually take have already been covered on p. 228. The Commons may be influenced by the strength of its argument, by vociferous opposition (especially from back-benchers on the government side) or by successfully defeating a part or the whole of a bill. Scrutiny and influence are also key functions of the House in relation to government actions that may not be part of the legislative process such as the handling of unforeseen events like the foot-and-mouth crisis in 2001 or the arrival of large numbers of asylum seekers. Closely linked to this function is that of accountability.

Holding the Government to account

Accountability involves the scrutiny of government actions and making those responsible answerable to a higher authority – the people, or the representatives of the people, their MPs. This issue will be considered in far more detail in Chapter 16. However, for the moment, it is important to be aware of 5 methods by which government is held to account:

- Question Time: to the Prime Minister and to ministers;
- select committees;
- party committees;
- HM Opposition;
- the media, especially **the broadcasting authorities** responsible for the televising of Parliament.

The legislative role of the Commons

When a party has been elected and forms a government, it decides when and how its manifesto promises will be introduced and enacted. This is done mostly in the form of public/government bills. Some types of government bill are introduced in every parliamentary session – e.g. the Finance Bill which contains the main provisions of the Budget. Other bills are brought in response to an event or crisis. The stages in the legislative process are as follows.

Consultation

Initially, this may take place while the political party is in opposition prior to the proposed bill being written into the election manifesto. Consultation then takes place between the government department concerned and other departments (particularly the Treasury), outside organisations such as interest/pressure groups, party policy committees and experts in the field. During this consultation advice from lawyers is also sought. A more formal consultation involves the issue of a **Green Paper**, an outline proposal inviting the views of interested parties. Sometimes the government may avoid the initial consultation stage, or follow it, by issuing a **White Paper**, a statement of government policy and intent. This may be debated in parliament. A White Paper reads like a draft bill.

the broadcasting authorities
The BBC was established as a public body in 1927 but radio coverage of Parliament did not begin on a regular basis until April 1978. In 1985, television coverage of the House of Lords began. In 1988, the Commons voted to allow television coverage on an experimental basis. Coverage of the Commons became permanent in July 1990. This covers not only proceedings in the House but also the select committees. Since 1992, continuous live coverage of the Commons has been available on cable television.

The BBC's charter required it originally to broadcast on radio a daily account of proceedings in both Houses. Post-1945, this has been done via 'Today in Parliament' while a re-edited version was introduced, 'Yesterday in Parliament'. The latter, in 1998, was moved from the FM waveband to long-wave only, despite protests from MPs.

Occasionally during the consultation process, a public inquiry is set up with a judge presiding if the reaction of the general public needs to be considered further.

Stages in Parliament

House of Commons

The **First Reading** is a formality in which the minister responsible introduces the bill into the Commons. Copies are then circulated to all MPs

The **Second Reading** is a debate on the principle of the bill, not its details, after which a division is taken.

In The **Committee Stage** a standing committee (see box, p. 232) considers the bill in detail. This is where amendments may be suggested and voted on. If this stage proves time-consuming, the government may introduce the 'guillotine', a dramatic form of time limit which halts further discussion after a fixed period has elapsed. The outcome then is that early clauses may be debated at great length while later clauses are only superficially considered or not debated at all. Sometimes, before this stage, a device known as a 'Kangaroo' is imposed whereby selected clauses are debated fully while others are totally ignored. Time is saved by hopping over many clauses like a kangaroo.

The **Report Stage** is one in which the amended version of the bill is discussed in the Commons.

The **Third Reading** is the debate on the bill in its final form followed by a division.

Lords (see Chapter 15)

The bill then goes to the House of Lords where the same series of stages are followed. There are some points that must be made here concerning the Lords and its role:

1 A bill may be introduced into the Lords first after which it must proceed through the Commons.
2 In the Lords, the committee stage is taken by the whole house with votes taking place over the amendments but not the principle of the bill.
3 The Lords may amend bills, and send them back to the Commons. The Commons may accept or reject amendments or even return the bill to the Lords for further deliberation.
4 Following the Parliament Acts of 1911 and 1949, the Lords cannot delay the passage of a bill for more than one year.

Royal Assent

Once a bill has been passed in both the Lords and the Commons it formally receives the Royal Assent. Historically, the monarch signed the bill but now no longer does so. By the Royal Assent Act 1967, Commissioners of the Assent Office perform this function.

Commencement order

This is the date when the act becomes the law which may be some time after it has received the Royal Assent or may take effect immediately. Once passed by Parliament and given the Royal Assent, a bill becomes an Act, sometimes known as a statute, more usually as a law.

Implementation

This is fulfilled by the ministries concerned and all persons working on their behalf.

Standing committees

These consist of a small group of MPs who scrutinise bills at the committee stage in the Commons and propose amendments in their report to the House. The party strength of MPs in these committees is in proportion to their numbers in the Commons overall (compare with Select Committees). Standing committees are:
- not permanent – they are formed to scrutinise a bill and are then disbanded;
- identified by letters – A, B, C, etc. – so when Standing Committee A has completed the scrutiny of a bill it is disbanded and a new A committee is appointed to deal with another bill;
- staffed by from sixteen up to fifty members, but eighteen is the norm;
- reflect party strength.

At any one time, depending on the volume of bills being processed, there may be up to five standing committees in operation. One standing committee – C – deals with private members' bills.

The purpose of a standing committee is to render the bill 'generally more acceptable' by examining it in detail, clause by clause, and suggesting proposals for amendments. It therefore has some influence. A standing committee cannot however, reject a bill or amend it in such a way that it undermines its principles.

Although the system of standing committees is seen as a good one, it is nevertheless open to criticism for the following reasons:
- Discussion follows adversarial party lines.
- Time constraints: the early stages are often debated in great detail but the later stages might be neglected.
- The use of guillotine and kangaroo.
- Activity of the whips – they marshal members to 'toe the party line'; Government back-benchers are often told to remain silent.
- MPs regard service on these committees as a chore.

Types of bill

Public bills

Almost all bills passing through Parliament are public bills; they concern the general public as a whole. Most public bills are initiated by the government and so are referred to as 'government bills'. Further, they may also be 'money bills', i.e. a special type of government bill that the Lords may not amend.

Private bill

These apply to a specific area or organisation, certain individual or group interests, or a particular section of the population. For example, they may be promoted for large capital projects on behalf of private companies or local authorities – e.g. the Felixstowe Dock and Railway Act 1987. Such bills have sometimes been a means of avoiding public inquiries. The Transport and Work Act 1992 restricted the scope of private bills and ensuing public inquiries. Very few private bills come before Parliament.

Private members' bills

These are bills that are introduced by backbench MPs. Only a limited amount of Commons time is devoted to such bills, and only a limited number become law. There are three ways of introducing a Private Member's Bill.

1 **Ballot bills**. MPs may enter their names in a ballot at the start of a parliamentary session. Twenty names are drawn. Twelve Fridays in each parliamentary session are set aside for such bills. Lack of time and low attendance (i.e. less than a quorum) are particular problems. Success rate for this method is higher than the following two.

2 **Ten minute rule bills**. An MP is allowed ten minutes to outline his case for a new piece of legislation. As such, they are unlikely to succeed but do gain publicity and may be taken up by one or more of the parties.

3 **Standing order 58 bills**. Under this rule, the MP gives the Speaker a day's note that he will introduce a bill but it has to be without debate. Most bills of this type fail.

Hybrid bills

These are bills of both private and public interest, for example the Channel Tunnel Act 1987. When a bill is introduced to Parliament, it is the Speaker who decides on its classification.

The work and backgrounds of Members of Parliament

A legislator who helps to hold the Executive to account

MPs are elected to the House of Commons. They debate and vote on bills in the chamber and in standing committees. They are constrained by party discipline from speaking or voting against the party on a two-line or three-line whip. Sometimes backbenchers do vote against the party line but risk being disciplined by the whips and having their promotion prospects damaged. MPs also pursue particular policy interests, may have particular expertise on certain topics and so may make an important contribution to particular debates. Three examples:

1 Jack Ashley (formerly a Labour MP) who was deaf, campaigned on behalf of the disabled throughout his Commons career.
2 Chris Mullin (Labour) takes a special interest in Home Affairs and chaired the Home Affairs Select Committee in the first 'New Labour' government.
3 Ian McCartney (Labour), now Minister for Pensions, has frequently spoken about drugs following the death of his adult son from drug addiction in 1999.

Constituency

MPs maintain close links with their constituency, typically going home there at weekends, holding 'clinics' for their constituents and helping them with their problems. Many MPs regard this role as the most important part of their work. Participation in community activities as well as providing individual help in the constituency can produce a more immediate feeling of 'making a difference' which is frustratingly absent for many in the Commons. There is also another obvious motivation for gaining a reputation as a good constituency MP; it improves prospects for re-election.

In theory, liberal democracy does not recognise the concept of 'political party', sees the relationship between MP and voter as paramount and ignores the dominating impact of the national party on the MP's work (see p. 235). One peculiar outcome of this arises when an MP defects to another political party, such as occurred in the following examples between 1992 and 1997:

• Alan Howarth – Conservative to Labour
• Emma Nicholson – Conservative to Liberal Democrats
• Peter Turnham – Conservative to Liberal Democrats
• Peter Temple Morriss – Conservative to Labour
• Shaun Woodward – Conservative to Labour

These MPs were not obliged to resign their seats, having been voted in on another party's ticket.

It would be wrong to underestimate the amount of useful work that an MP can do in his constituency as well as the amount of work that comes to him ordinarily. Having been elected for the first time as an MP for Exeter in 1997, Ben Bradshaw expressed his anxiety at the sheer weight of correspondence that confronted him daily. Extra time soon became available in the early months of the New Labour government of 1997. Enabled by their party's huge majority, groups of 50 or more Labour MPs were told to go home and work in their constituencies for up to two weeks.

The uncertainty and insecurity of political careers has never been better illustrated by famous (or infamous) defeats for prominent MPs at general elections and it is the voters in their constituencies that cause this to happen. For example:

- Chris Patten (Conservative party chairman) – defeated at Bath, 1992. High office in John Major's government had been likely.
- Michael Portillo (Conservative Minister of Defence) – defeated at Enfield Southgate in 1997. With John Major's resignation as leader of the Conservative Party, Portillo would have been his most likely successor.

Party

The MP's political party role is the dominant one. He will have risen through the ranks of the party, been selected by his local constituency party to stand as their candidate, and will owe his election win to the local party and to the national leadership's manifesto pledges. He may like to think that he has garnered a large personal vote, rather than a large vote for the party he represents, but in most cases he would be disappointed. If his party wins the general election, it has a mandate to fulfil its manifesto pledges and so he, in turn, is expected to vote according to the party line.

At Westminster, both the Labour and Conservative parties have backbench organisations for their MPs. For Labour, it is the Parliamentary Labour Party (PLP), and for the Conservatives the 1922 Committee. These both hold weekly meetings and have committees that cover major policy areas. Within each party there are groups or factions for like-minded members. The Campaign Group in the Labour party, of which Tony Benn was a leading member, is one example, while in the Conservative party the Way Forward Group – formed after Margaret Thatcher's enforced resignation – is another. Such groups form a focus for pressure to be exerted on the party leadership. MPs also spend time in debates supporting the party line and making contact with the media.

Traditionally, it was the Conservative party that was renowned for its unity and the loyalty of its MPs to the leadership. By contrast, Labour indulged itself with bitter disputes aired in public. The change in the Conservative party was gradual but Sir Geoffrey Howe's resignation speech in the Commons on 13 November 1990 when he attacked Margaret Thatcher's leadership with bitterness and wry humour, was an obvious turning point. Howe had served

Thatcher as Chancellor and Foreign Secretary and his speech provoked the leadership contest that produced Thatcher's resignation. Since then, under Major and Hague, disunity has been rife especially over Europe. By contrast, Labour has become much more disciplined. This has been especially the case since Tony Blair became leader in 1994. In general terms, most Labour MPs toe the party line. However, there are some notable exceptions.

The job description of Members of Parliament: a summary

Aims of the job. To represent, defend and promote national and party interests, and further the interests of constituents wherever possible.

Principal accountabilities
1 to support government or opposition to sustain parliamentary democracy;
2 to hold the executive to account;
3 to debate, amend and review legislation;
4 to support and further the interests of their constituency;
5 to assist/advise individuals and groups within their constituency;
6 to contribute to formulation of party policy;
7 to promote public understanding of party policy in constituency, via media nationally, etc.

Nature and scope. MPs work may be divided into three broad areas:
1 legislator and holding the Executive to account;
2 constituency work (a) representing, promoting and defending its interests, and (b) helping individual constituents and groups;
3 support for the party.

Salary and conditions – paid by the Treasury
Gross annual salary: £55,188
Living away from constituency, i.e. in London   £19,722
Office and staff paid for: £72,310
Incidental expenses: £14,000
Free travel: first class by train and plane to and from constituency and London; on international trips; and for partners of MPs entitled to a number of free trips to London each year.

Job security: if in a marginal seat, poor; if in a safe seat – excellent.

Adapted from *Daily Mail*, 16 December 2002.

Career politicians

The modern trend is towards 'career politicians'. In the past, this was less common with MPs pursuing other careers simultaneously, in areas such as the law or business. Nevertheless, this trend of maintaining a significant and separate career has been in decline. MPs may also have links with outside bodies, such as pressure groups, but since the 'Cash for Questions' scandal and the Nolan report (see p. 248) such activities have come under closer scrutiny. Many realise that involvement in other work may lead to allegations of a conflict of interests. As a result, there is now a growing expectation that being an MP should be a full-time job especially now that their salary and conditions have improved. Today, MPs seem to average about twenty years in the Commons which is much longer than in many countries with similar political systems.

Given the lack of career structure and job security, some MPs – mainly, but not exclusively, on the Conservative side – do maintain other career interests. They recognise that the promotion prospects of MPs are limited and highly competitive, certainly in comparison with some professions (the party leadership and especially the whips constantly assess each MPs potential). Defeat at a general election is always a possibility. At the 1997 election, 126 Conservative MPs lost their seats. Many MPs hope to become Ministers but competition is fierce. Labour returned 412 MPs to the Commons in 2001 but Tony Blair only had approximately 120 ministerial posts to fill, from those of Cabinet rank (22) down to the most junior and unpaid members of the government, the personal private secretaries. There is also competition to become a 'shadow spokesman' in Her Majesty's Opposition – at the moment within the Conservative Party. And there are some jobs which carry prestige but remain unpaid notably chairing a select committee.

Unlike many professions, there is no sensible career structure until an MP joins a government, at whatever level. Even more frustrating is the experience of being constantly in opposition and not in government. Tony Blair was first elected to Parliament in 1983, having served in opposition for fourteen years, and as Prime Minister perhaps his top priority from 1997 to 2001 was that he and his party should be returned for a further term of office.

Are full-time MPs a good thing?

In as much as it avoids the allegation of conflict of interests and enables MPs to tackle their ever-growing postbag, many commentators would applaud the trend. They might wonder how any MP can combine two or more roles and suggest that at least one career might suffer in the process. The House needs experienced and dedicated MPs to run its select and standing committee structure, and constituents have a right to expect that their elected representative is busy on their behalf.

On the other hand, defenders of 'part-timeism' might say that MPs who perform other jobs bring experience of the world beyond Westminster to their task. This prevents the House from becoming a sort of monastery, cut off from everyday life and ensures that members are 'in touch' with everyday life. Some would say that until parliamentary salaries are much higher than at present, it is difficult to attract professional and business people into the Commons, for they would lose much of their income if they left a lucrative career at the Bar or in business.

This trend towards careerism has one other spin-off, which is to make MPs less independently-minded than some have been in the past. A career politician is far more likely to toe the party line, and listen to the party leadership since their job security and promotion depend on the party. Many political commentators and MPs of long-standing, such as Paddy Ashdown before his retirement in 2001, deplore the lack of idealism and principle in the Commons in contrast to previous generations. A good example of this is illustrated by the words of one Labour MP soon after the government proposed a cut to the lone-parent supplement to child benefit in 1997 following which, 47 Labour MPs voted against, 14 abstained and a junior Scottish Office minister resigned. He said that he voted with the government while voicing his concerns to ministers in private. He argued that as a new MP he would lose future credibility if he abstained or voted against the party line. This seemed a reasonable position at the time. However, his name does not appear in the chart of 'Rebels' over the next three years (see box p. 239).

How socially representative are Members of Parliament?

Historical perspectives

Members with an upper-class background retained considerable power in Parliament and Cabinet through the Conservative party well into the 1960s. However, the reduction in the numbers of aristocrats, large landowners and Etonians has made the party less 'upper crust'. That an ex-grammar school student, Edward Heath, a comprehensive school student, William Hague, and a non-graduate, John Major, became leaders would have been unthinkable before the Second World War. That they did was not just a consequence of the introduction of leadership elections in 1964, but a consequence of social change within the party and in society at large.

The changes in the socio-economic background of Labour MPs have been even more eventful. The Commons in the nineteenth century was filled almost entirely by men of the upper and middle classes, hence the demand for working-class representation and the creation of the Labour Party. Before the Second World War, a large proportion of Labour MPs had working-class backgrounds. Since 1945, the proportion of Labour MPs who are graduates has risen from 32 per cent to 67 per cent in 2001. Further, of the '2001 intake' of Labour MPs only 12 per cent came from working-class backgrounds (see chart on occupations).

Labour rebels 1997–2000

Between December 1997 and May 2000, 108 labour MPs voted against government proposals. On several occasions, an additional number of Labour MPs abstained. The issues were:

- December 1997 – cuts to lone-parent benefit;
- June 1998 – university tuition fees and maintenance grants;
- July 1998 – newspaper pricing;
- May 1999 – disability benefits;
- June 1999 – legal aid;
- April 2000 – pensions;
- April 2000 – freedom of information;
- May 2000 – part privatisation of air traffic control.

On these eight issues some of the well-known rebels were (number of times rebelling in brackets): Tony Benn (8), Jeremy Corbyn (8), Dennis Skinner (8), Diane Abbott (5), Gwyneth Dunwoody (5), Tam Dalywell (5).

Source: Adapted from the Guardian Companion to the General Election, 2001.

Social class (based on occupation)

The majority of MPs come from a narrow stratum of society. If you compare, for example, the occupations of MPs in the Commons following the 2001 general election with the Market Researcher's (see Table 14.1); this evidence shows that most are from classes A and B. Only 16 per cent have a background in manual work of whom 54 out of 56 represent Labour. The occupational profile of Labour MPs in 2001 is much the same as in 1977 with the largest categories being public-sector professionals, such as administrators, teachers, journalists and lawyers. The Conservatives, on the other hand, remain very much the party of private-sector professionals and businessmen. The largest professional element is the law; the Conservatives had 93 candidates from this occupation of whom 31 were elected.

Table 14.1 Analysing class: the market researcher's view

Class	% heads of household (1991)
A Upper middle class (e.g. professional, higher managerial, senior civil servants)	3
B Middle class (e.g. middle managers)	16
C1 Lower middle class (e.g. junior managers, routine white collar or non-manual workers)	26
C2 Skilled working class (e.g. skilled manual workers)	26
D Semi-skilled and unskilled working class (e.g.. manual workers)	17
E Residual (e.g.. those dependent on long-term state benefits)	13

Source: National Readership Survey, NRS Ltd, July 1992–July 1993.

Table 14.2 Occupation of MPs, 2001

Occupation	Labour	Conservative	Liberal Democrat
Professions			
Barrister	13	18	2
Solicitor	18	13	4
Doctor/dentist	2	3	3
Architect/surveyor	1	4	1
Civil/chartered engineer	5	1	1
Accountant	2	3	1
Civil servant/local government	30	2	3
Armed services	1	11	–
Teachers			
university	18	1	2
polytechnic/college	31	–	1
school	49	6	9
Other consultants	3	2	–
Scientific/research	6	–	–
Total	179 (43%)	64 (39%)	27 (52%)
Business			
Company director	5	18	6
Company executive	10	31	7
Commerce/insurance	2	6	–
Management/clerical	12	2	1
General business	4	3	–
Total	33 (8%)	60 (36%)	14 (27%)
Miscellaneous			
Misc. white collar	73	2	1
Politician/political organiser	44	18	4
Publisher/journalist	32	14	4
Farmer	–	5	1
Housewife	–	2	–
Student	–	–	–
Total	149 (36%)	41 (25%)	10 (19%)
Manual workers			
Miner	11	1	–
Skilled worker	37	–	1
Semi/unskilled worker	3	–	–
Total	51 (12%)	1 (1%)	1 (2%)
Grand total	412	166	52

Education

On average, MPs have experienced a much higher and more privileged level of education than the rest of the population, as these figures show:

- Following the 2001 general election, 549 MPs (87 per cent) had been educated at a university.

- The Conservative party continues to draw a significantly higher percentage of MPs from public schools. Members from Eton have dropped since 1992, although the College still produced more MPs than any other school. The party now draws more widely from less grand independent schools (64 per cent).

- The most significant change in educational background has been with Labour MPs. In 1945, 32 per cent were graduates but by 2001 it had risen to 67 per cent. While the majority of Labour MPs are graduates from redbrick universities, the majority of Conservative MP graduates are from Oxbridge.

- The Liberal Democrats have a high percentage of graduates and a modest percentage of MPs from public schools.

Table 14.3 Education of MPs, 2001

Type of Education	Labour	Conservative	Liberal Democrat
Elementary +	2	–	–
Secondary	46	3	4
Secondary + poly/college	83	9	8
Secondary + university	213	48	22
Public school	2	6	1
Public school + poly/college	4	10	3
Public school + university	62	90	14
Unknown	–	–	–
Total	412[a]	166	52
Oxford	43	42	9
Cambridge	22	37	5
Other universities	210	59	22
All universities	275 (67%)	138 (83%)	36 (70%)
Eton	2	14	2
Harrow	–	–	–
Winchester	–	1	–
Other Public schools	66	91	16
All public schools	68 (17%)	106 (64%)	18 (35%)

[a] Does not include the Speaker

Age

Most MPs are middle-aged. Although the voting age was reduced from 21 to 18 in 1969, the minimum age at which a person can stand for election is 21.

In 2001, the median age of newly-elected Labour and Conservative MPs was 40 and 38 respectively, whilst the median age for all MPs was 50 for Labour and 48 for the Conservatives. Only 5 MPs were under the age of 30 including David Lammy (born July 1972), the youngest in the House who first entered the Commons after a by-election victory in 2000. The unusual intake of 11 under 30s (10 were Labour) in 1997 was more a reflection of the size of Labour's win rather than any change in candidate selection policy. All three parties are reluctant to select candidates under 30 preferring a 'safe pair of hands' of around 40. MPs of 40 or more often seem remote and out of touch with young people.

Table 14.4 Age of MPs as at 1 January 2001

Age on 1 Jan 2001	Labour	Conservative	Liberal Democrat
20–29	4	1	–
30–39	39	25	14
40–49	152	64	14
50–59	165	57	23
60–69	44	18	1
70–79	8	1	–
Median age			
1992	50	48	47
1987	48	50	46

Why are many MPs middle-aged and middle class?

Party selection panels obviously want their candidate to win and they look for the person with the most ability and experience – previous political experience either as a local councillor or a good performance in a previous election campaign are valuable. Young candidates may be politically inexperienced simply because they are young. A university education and professional experience ensure a trained mind not only able to win the seat but also able to cope with the diversity of work that confronts all MPs. Little wonder, then, that most MPs come from the professions and the world of business. All this partly helps to explain the long-term shortage of female, Black and Asian MPs.

Women MPs

Women have been able to stand for election to the Commons since 1918 but the number of female candidates selected to do so by the three major parties has traditionally been low. At general elections from 1945, female candidates formed a tiny minority of the total number fielded by the three parties. The consequence was that before 1992, the total number of women MPs never reached fifty. In addition, all three parties would often select a female candidate for a seat that was unwinnable.

The reasons for this were many and varied. According to the British Candidate Survey of 1992, the amount of time that applicants could devote to politics was highly significant – four-fifths of candidates spent over twenty hours per week. Women were still viewed as having the primary responsibility for children and the home and, viewing themselves in the same way, seemed to have less time. A further factor is financial. Often, potential candidates have to campaign for selection in a number of constituencies incurring costs such as loss of earnings, accommodation and childcare. Training in public speaking, dealing with the media, and the many skills needed to campaign effectively can be bought but such programmes are again expensive. The financial aspect often rules out women on low incomes who would otherwise be excellent candidates. Finally, it is also clear that some local party selection panels are prejudiced, believing that politics is a masculine career and that women candidates lose votes.

Table 14.5 Women candidates and MPs, 1987–2001

	Labour		Conservative		Liberal Democrats[a]		Other	Total
	candidates	MPs	candidates	MPs	candidates	MPs	MPs	MPs
1987	93	21	46	17	105	2	1	41
1992	138	37	59	20	144	2	1	60
1997	155	101	66	13	139	3	3[b]	120
2001	148	95	93	14	140	5	4	118

[a] Includes all woman MPs elected for Liberal and SDP parties.

[b] Includes the then Speaker, Betty Boothroyd, who was a Labour MP before being elected speaker.

Between 1989 and 1997, the Labour party took positive action to increase the number of women MPs. At the 1993 Annual Conference, it was decided that there should be all-women shortlists in 50 per cent of vacancies in 'winnable seats', requiring a 6 per cent or less swing to Labour. However, following a legal challenge by two male Labour party members under the Sex Discrimination Act, an industrial tribunal found this to be illegal. The Labour party changed the rules but the 35 women already selected via all-women shortlists remained and stood at the 1997 general election. The huge swing to Labour at the election meant that two-thirds of the party's women candidates were returned. The overall number of women MPs from all three parties doubled compared with 1992 (see table 14.5).

Emily's list (Early Money is Like Yeast – it makes the dough rise) was an idea from the USA taken up by women in the Labour party. Essentially it aims to raise money each year to support women who wish to seek selection to be candidates for election to the Westminster or European Parliament. Other organisations, like the Fawcett Society, which aims to have 300 women in the Commons, are active in this field.

The Conservative Party have continued to oppose Labour's methods of achieving a greater number of women MPs. Leading women in the party were particularly vociferous. Ann Widdecombe dismissed 'Blair's Babes' as sub-standard. Julie Kirkbride MP challenged the Labour party's assumption that women MPs were there specifically to represent women rather than the whole population. Some on the Conservative party argued for quotas but were defeated.

The number of women MPs fell from 120 to 118 in 2001. Labour did not expect to make gains and only selected women in 5 of the 16 Conservative marginals vulnerable to a 2 per cent swing to Labour. The Conservatives only selected women for 9 of their top 84 target seats. The Liberal Democrats selected women in only 5 of their 23 target seats likely to swing 5 per cent towards themselves. Thus, the parties in 2001 basically did not place women in winnable seats.

Ethnic Minority MPs

White Britons form the largest ethnic group in the country. Ethnic minority groups include African-Caribbean groups, Asian groups, such as Indian, Bangladeshi and Pakistani, and White Britons of Irish descent. The problems of identification have become clouded, with the growth of mixed marriages and partnerships. Nevertheless, skin colour, race and the issue of racism are never far away from any consideration of **ethnicity**.

> **ethnicity**
> An ethnic group has the following characteristics in common: descent, geographical origin, language, cultural identity, history, religion and literature.

Essentially on the issue of ethnic minority MPs, we are considering the black and Asian communities. The 1991 population census showed that 5.5 per cent of the total population was black and Asian, yet the 2001 general election returned just 12 black and Asian MPs. This is 1.8 per cent of the total number of MPs, a significant under-representation.

Figures from 1991 Population Census of Britain

Total population – 54.81 million
White population – 51.80 million
Black and Asian population – 3.01 million = 5.5 per cent of total

---

Why are there so few ethnic minority MPs?

There are many factors at work here. Discrimination is one, in so far as selection panels reject ethnic minority candidates on the assumption that those who stand lose votes. Also, as the table 14.6 shows, Labour consistently attracts far more support from black and Asian people than other parties, so its activists might argue that there is no need to increase the number of ethnic minority MPs. Other factors, like time, finance, educational and occupational backgrounds – similar to those affecting the shortage of women candidates – are also at work.

Table 14.6 Black and Asian candidates and MPs in general elections, 1987–2001

| | Labour | | Conservatives | | Liberal Democrats | | Other | | Total |
	candidates	MPs	candidates	MPs	candidates	MPs	candidates	MPs	MPs
1987	14	4	6	–	4	–	–	–	4
1992	9	5	8	1	6	–	–	–	6
1997	13	9	10	–	19	–	–	–	9
2001	22	12	16	–	28	–	–	–	12

Source: Adapted from D. Butler and D. Kavanagh General Elections 1987, 1992, 1997 and 2001.

Table 14.7 Black and Asian voting for the two main parties, 1987–2001

	Labour	Conservative
1987	72	18
1992	81	10
1997	78	17
2001	73	12

Source: Adapted from S. Saggar 1998 'Immigration, Race and the Election', in A. Geddes and J. Tonge, Labour's Landslide, Manchester University Press, 1997; and R. Worcester and R. Mortimore, Explaining Labour's Second Landslide, Politico's, 2001.

Does it matter that MPs are socially unrepresentative of the nation?

That MPs are overwhelmingly white, male, middle aged and middle class is hard to contest. Opinions vary as to whether this matters. Some say that it *does* matter:

- It is dangerous in a democracy if groups with less wealth, power and influence are under-represented. If people feel excluded and see the House as having an elite membership, then they may regard it with contempt or indifference, and feel alienated from the political process.

- An unrepresentative House lacks legitimacy, because it will be seen to be biased in its composition.

- As long as minorities are under-represented, there are likely to be fewer debates on issues affecting them, and the quality of debate will be poor as many white males may not take the discussion seriously.

- If all the parties claim to believe in opportunity, a society in which all people prosper on the basis of merit alone, then it is hypocritical for Parliament not to reflect these ideas in its composition. The achievement of a more balanced membership would provide more role models for other members of minority communities, and send a signal to those striving for equal opportunities in other workplaces and institutions.

Those who claim that a more socially representative House is *not* important point out that:

- MPs do not need to be like the rest of the population to represent them. It is important that members represent and understand the views of their constituents, but for them to do this the House does not need to be a microcosm (mirror image) of the nation. What is important is that MPs have an ability to empathise with the poor, disadvantaged and others unlike themselves. You don't have to inhabit a slum to know that slums are a bad thing, even if your recognition of the full horrors might be more acute if you did so. Neither do you need to be Asian, black, female or gay to appreciate that discrimination is hurtful, wrong and damaging to society.

- It is not reasonable to expect that membership will be in exact proportion to the size of various community groups; the process of election means that the outcome is unlikely to be exactly representative.

- It is actually rather encouraging that educationally the background of MPs is higher than that of the whole nation. The overall level of attainment is above average, with a large number of members having been to university. Even if any illiterate people wished to stand for Parliament, which is unlikely, they would almost certainly be totally unable to cope with the level of work involved.

MPs and standards in public life

From 1994, a series of scandals involving MPs and ministers led to the appointment of the Nolan Committee (see p. 248), and its Report, the appointment of a Parliamentary Commissioner for Standards in 1995 (currently held by Sir Philip Mawer). The scandals, either sexual or financial, contributed partly to the Conservative general election defeat in 1997. From 1997, scandals – similar or alleged – have continued. The term for all of this has become known as **sleaze**.

sleaze

From the mid-1990s, this was the popular term referring to sexual immorality or corrupt and improper behaviour by public officials, MPs and ministers in the Conservative government. The term is no longer connected to the Conservative party alone.

Links exist between the Conservative party and business, and the Labour party and trade unions. This has long been the case and as long as such information is known to all other members and available to any who deal with them, then it has not caused many problems. After 1975, they were required to list their interests in a voluntary Register of Members' Interests, but some failed to make the necessary disclosures.

MPs have access to privileged information through the Commons Library, ministerial contacts and/or parliamentary questions. If they have served as ministers, they are privy to even more political and potentially lucrative knowledge and contacts, a point well understood by lobbying organisations and business interests outside. Provided that the member declares the interest in debate, he or she may work as an adviser/consultant to a company and be paid.

Sexual immorality is one area of temptation for MPs but is not usually as politically dangerous as scandals surrounding finance and the granting of favours. In the 1990s and today, there is much concern about questionable or corrupt practices especially for financial gain. MPs are not held in the high esteem which they once were, and some critics feel that they are too easily tempted by the attractions of meeting socially with 'the great and good' members of society, often in the most lavish of surroundings, only to return to their tiny flat in London or modest house in their constituency.

Lobbying an MP is a long-established practice. However, from about 1980, the number of firms whose sole business was lobbying began to appear. By the middle of the 1990s there were about 60 of them in Britain, almost all focusing on Whitehall and the Palace of Westminster. By the mid-1990s they were reputed to have a combined turnover of many millions of pounds.

> **lobbying an MP**
>
> This is where constituents, pressure groups, companies and others are allowed to enter the Member's Lobby in the House of Commons in order to gain access to their MP.

Ian Greer Associates – annual turnover of approximately £3 million – was one of the most well known of these firms. Along with Coca-Cola, it had such clients as Taylor Woodrow (construction) and British Airways.

It is important to remember:

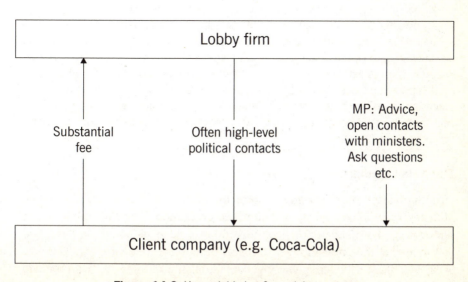

Figure 14.2 How a lobbying firm might operate

1 Work done by MPs on behalf of some special interest is legitimate. However, it is only legitimate if the MP's interest is known beforehand.
2 Prior to the **'cash for questions'** scandal (1994, see below) an MP providing expertise was deemed to be entitled to a fee.
3 The Register of Members' Interests 1975. By this regulation, MPs were supposed to declare an interest in speaking in Commons debates. However, they did not have to do so when asking parliamentary questions as long as they had declared their interests in the Register.

'Cash for questions' July 1994

The *Sunday Times* in July 1994 set up an undercover operation aimed at exposing the abuse of parliamentary privilege by MPs of which there had been many rumours. One journalist posing as a businessman, approached 10 Conservative and 10 Labour MPs, offering £1,000 for tabling a written question to a minister. Two Conservative MPs, (Graham Riddick and David Tredinnick) agreed, and asked for the money to be sent to their homes. Strictly speaking they would not have been guilty of misconduct if they had declared their payments in the Register of Members' Interests, but when the *Sunday Times* printed the story there was public outrage. Both MPs apologised to the House and were suspended for two weeks.

Later in 1994, the *Guardian* alleged that Conservative ministers had tabled parliamentary questions for money – in particular on behalf of Mohamed Al Fayed, the owner of Harrods. The ministers were Tim Smith, Neil Hamilton and Jonathan Aitken. Smith resigned immediately. Hamilton and Aitken clung to office for as long as they could, tried to sue the media – Hamilton combined with Ian Greer – and eventually had to drop their cases. Hamilton and Greer dropped theirs in September 1996. Aitken pursued his case further, but was eventually found guilty of perverting the course of justice and perjury in 1999. Hamilton, the MP for Tatton in Cheshire, stood again in the 1997 general election but was sensationally defeated by the BBC war reporter Martin Bell ('The Man in the White Suit') as an anti-corruption candidate – both the Labour and Liberal candidates withdrew from the contest when Bell stepped in. The Downey report subsequently found 'compelling evidence' against Hamilton (see section on the Nolan committee). He, in turn, took Mohamed Al Fayed to court for libel and lost. The media had focused on the lavish hospitality at Al Fayed's expense enjoyed by Hamilton and his wife at the Paris Ritz Hotel, owned by Fayed. Soon afterwards, he declared himself bankrupt. He and his wife Christine now make occasional appearances on television.

The Nolan committee

Five days after the *Guardian* reports on Smith and Hamilton the Prime Minister, John Major, set up a Committee on Standards in Public Life under senior judge Lord Nolan. This commission on sleaze, as popularly described by the media, took much longer to report than many first expected. This was because it had a wide remit, was given an initial 'life' of three years but seemed to have a long-term future, and it was to make a number of reports. Another factor that also took up time was the degree to which some MPs were unwilling to reveal their private business interests.

When the first report was published, many Conservative MPs were outraged at the proposed regulations on MPs' behaviour (May 1995). The proposals were considered by the Commons again in the autumn. Ultimately they were passed in 1996:

The Nolan Code of Conduct

- This led to the appointment of an independent Parliamentary Commissioner for standards to administer a code of conduct for MPs; deal with complaints against MPs; keep register of MPs' outside interests.
- MPs are compelled to disclose origin and amounts of earnings; not allowed to table questions on behalf of outside interests in return for payment.
- New Commons Committe on Standards and Privileges was set up to enforce the rules.

Sir Gordon Downey was the Parliamentary Commissioner for Standards until 1999 and was succeeded by Elizabeth Filkin (see below).

1997 to present

Lord Nolan and his successor Lord Neill had created a clear code of conduct for MPs, ministers and civil servants. Nevertheless, it was to be a system of self-regulation by the Commons. If it were to succeed, it would not only require the compliance of MPs and ministers in the code but also require their support for the Parliamentary Commissioner.

Tony Blair, prior to the 1997 general election, had promised to be ruthless with any cases of sleaze. However, this did not mean that such cases did not occur.

Cases of sleaze: complaints against politicians

John Major (former Prime Minister) – that he failed to declare outside income.

John Reid (Northern Ireland Secretary) – that he used House of Commons money to pay his researcher and son Kevin to carry out work for the Labour Party.

Keith Vaz (former Foreign Office Minister) – that he took cash for favours from businessmen and recommended one for an honour.

John Prescott (Deputy Prime Minister) – that he failed to register benefits from his low rent on a London flat in June 2000 after being frequently urged to do so by Filkin.

Postscript: Elizabeth Filkin – Parliamentary Commissioner for Standards

Elizabeth Filkin was appointed to the above post in February 1999. Sir Gordon Downey, although not popular, was respected by most MPs as a Whitehall insider, 'but Filkin, Downey's successor as watchdog, soon turned out to be more terrier, than labrador'.[5] Between 1999 and December 2001, it is clear that she carried out her duties rigorously. Her investigations are amongst the following.

Problems for the Blair government and the Parliamentary Commissioner, 1992–2001

1997
- July: the Downey Report was published. Five MPs, including Neil Hamilton and Tim Smith, were found to have broken parliamentary rules by accepting money from Mohamed Al Fayed.
- November: the Labour Party promised to return £1 million donation to Bernie Ecclestone, President of the Formula One Association. This followed revelations that Labour would exempt Formula One from its ban on tobacco advertising.

1998
- January: Robin Cook, Foreign Secretary, announced that he would marry his secretary, Gaynor Regan, after divorcing his wife.
- February: the cost of refurbishing the Lord Chancellor's official residence was reported to be £650,000.
- July: the Parliamentary Standards and Privileges Committee cleared Paymaster General Geoffrey Robinson. It was alleged that he had not registered a payment of £200,000 by the late – and disgraced tycoon – Robert Maxwell.
- December: Trade and Industry Secretary, Peter Mandelson, and Geoffrey Robinson both resigned. Mandelson had received a loan from Robinson of £373,000 to buy a London property and had not declared it.

1999
- March: Fiona Jones, Labour MP for Newark and her agent were convicted in court of falsifying election expenses at the 1997 general election. They were later cleared on appeal.
- October: in a Cabinet re-shuffle, Peter Mandelson returned as Northern Ireland Secretary.
- November: Jeffrey Archer, Conservative party candidate for London Mayor, stood down after press revelations that he asked a friend to provide him with a false alibi in his successful libel action against the *Daily Star*. The paper alleged that Archer had slept with a prostitute (Archer was tried, found guilty and imprisoned in 2001).

2000
- March: Ken Livingstone, independent candidate for London Mayor, was found guilty by Parliamentary Standards and Privileges Committee of not declaring income of £158,000 for speeches and newspaper articles.

2001

- January: Peter Mandelson, Northern Ireland Secretary and close colleague of the Prime Minister, was forced to resign again. He had misled the Commons about his intervention to assist Srichand Hinduja's application for a British passport in 1998. Mr Hinduja and his brother later had given £1 million to the faith zone of the Millennium Dome.

In December 2001, Ms Filkin disclosed that she had been consistently obstructed in her post, and that in some of those cases referred to the House of Commons Standards and Privileges Commission the MPs had been given far too much latitude. She also felt that some powerful figures at Westminster had used their power and influence to undermine the case against them. Her post was for a three-year contract from February 1999 and was therefore due for renewal. The Commission had not given her a new contract but told her to re-apply. The new job was to be for four days per week, not three, and there was to be a 25 per cent salary cut from the previous one of £76,000. Ms Filkin made her complaints clear to the Speaker in a letter to the media. It was clear that she would not reapply. In the Commons, the Speaker, Michael Martin, was dismissive of her criticisms. Subsequently, the Wicks Committee into standards in Public Life was set up to hold an inquiry into Ms Filkin's departure. On 6 and 7 December 2001, Peter Riddell wrote:

> The House of Commons is an inward-looking, narcissistic and deeply complacent institution which has an infinite capacity to damage itself. Yet . . . the Commons is sometimes capable of change . . . Ms Filkin is certainly not faultless . . . The real question is whether independent scrutiny of MPs conduct is any longer possible. The pressure on Ms Filkin and, above all, the attempt by the Commons Commission to downgrade the post suggest that MPs are, to say the least, resistant to such scrutiny. MPs need, for once, to consider how others see them . . . the Commons can no longer take its reputation for granted.

REFERENCES AND FURTHER READING

1 *Guardian*, 28 April 1992.
2 R. Packenham, quoted in P.Norton (ed.), *Legislature*, Oxford University Press, 1990.
3 Tony Wright, 'Does Parliament Work?', *Talking Politics*, Vol. 9, 3, Spring 1997.
4 P. Norton, *Politics UK*, 4th edition, Longman, 2001.
5 The *Sunday Times*, 6 December 2001.

P. Hennessey, *The Hidden Wiring* (Chapter 6, Parliament), Indigo, 1996.
P. Riddell, *Parliament under Blair*, Politico's, 2000.

USEFUL WEB SITES

House of Commons **www.parliament.uk/commons/hsecom.htm**
This page provides a wide variety of useful information including
information about the House of Commons and MPs, the committee
system of the House of Commons, select committees of the House
of Commons and House of Commons publications on the Internet.

SAMPLE QUESTIONS

1 Define 'parliamentary government'.

2 Outline the main functions of the House of Commons.

3 How representative are MPs?

The House of Lords

15

AIMS OF THIS CHAPTER

➤ To establish the composition of the House of Lords before and since the 1999 reform.

➤ To assess the functions of the Lords.

Main changes in the twentieth century: a checklist

- **Parliament Act, 1911**. Lords only able to *delay* legislation for up to two years after second reading of a bill. Lords' power over 'money' bills effectively removed. 1945 'Salisbury Doctrine': Lord Salisbury, Conservative Leader of the Lords, proposed that the House should not defeat a government Bill at second reading if it was a proposal to meet a manifesto commitment.
- **Parliament Act, 1949**. Lords power of delay reduced to one parliamentary session.
- **The Life Peerages Act, 1958**. Men and women could be appointed to the Lords just for their lives.
- **The Peerage Act, 1963**. Hereditary Peers could relinquish their title and become eligible for the House of Commons.
- **Wakeham Commission, 1998**. Started to draw up proposals for Reform of the Lords.
- **House of Lords Act, 1999**. Ended automatic right of most hereditary peers to sit and vote in the Lords; 92 to remain.
- **2000 Wakeham Commission Report published**. A scheme for phase two of Labour's reform of second chamber.
- **November 2001**. Government's further proposal on Lords Reform in the light of the Wakeham Commission.

Types of peers, 1 November 1999 (before reform): 1326 in all

27 Law lords:

26 Lords spiritual: 26 bishops of the Church of England (including the 2 archbishops i.e. of Canterbury and York).

1273 Lords temporal; two types:
1 758 hereditary: Those who inherited a title and automatically became members at the age of 21.
2 515 Life: Those who gained their title under the Life Peerages Act 1958. This made it possible for men and women to be elevated to a non-hereditary peerage for their lifetime. Appointments made by the Prime Minister.

Table 15.1 Party strength in the House of Lords, 1 November 1999
(before reform)

Party	Life Peers	Hereditaries	Spiritual	Total
Conservative	173	310	–	483
Labour	175	19	–	194
Lib Dems	50	23	–	73
Cross-bench	128	226	–	354
Other	12	69	26	107
Total	538	647	26	1,211

Types of peers after reform: 1 December 1999: 670 in all

26   Archbishops and Bishops
27   Life Peers (under Appellate Jurisdiction Act, 1876)
525   Life Peers (under Life Peerage Act, 1958)
92   Peers under House of Lords Act, 1999

Table 15.2 Party strength after reform: 30 December 1999

Party	Life Peers	Hereditaries	Spiritual	Total
Conservative	181	52	–	233
Labour	179	4	–	183
Lib Dems	49	5	–	54
Cross-bench	132	31	–	163
Other	7	–	26	33
Total	548	92	26	666

The unreformed House of Lords: before 1999

(See boxes above and Tables 15.1 and 15.2 for before and after the 1999 reform.) Prior to the Life Peerages Act, 1958, the House consisted of the Lords Spiritual and the Lords Temporal (hereditary peers and the Law Lords):

1 **Lords spiritual**. These were the Archbishops of Canterbury and York and 24 bishops, all from the Church of England.

2 **Law lords**. Under the Appellate Jurisdiction Act, 1876, the Law Lords were appointed to carry out the judicial business of the House. They serve as the highest court of appeal in Britain.

3 **Lords temporal – hereditary**. Before the House of Lords Act, 1999, there were 647 hereditary peers. The discrepancy of the total number i.e. 758 (see Table 15.1) is explained by leaves of absence and those peers without a Writ of Summons. The Lord Chancellor grants a Writ of Summons only when a hereditary peer has proved to him that he is a legitimate heir to the title. Legitimate heirs under the age of 21 were also excluded.

NB: Between 1901 and 1958, the numbers of peers increased, because of the creation of hereditary peers. In 1901, the total composition of the Lords was 591. In 1950 it was 847. However, the Life Peerages Act, 1958, was to further increase its size.

4 **Lords temporal – life**. The Life Peerages Act, 1958, provided for the creation by the monarch (on the advice of the Prime Minister), of life peers and peeresses. Women were therefore enabled, for the first time, to become members of the House of Lords.

Traditionally, the Lords had been dominated by the Conservative Party even though some Labour peers were created. One of the objectives of the 1958 Act was to secure a greater balance of representation. This was achieved by the convention enabling recommendations for life peerages to be made by opposition party leaders to the Prime Minister of the day.

Table 15.3 Creation of life peers by Prime Ministers since Life Peerages Act, 1958

Harold Macmillan (1958–63)	90
Sir Alec Douglas-Home (1963–64)	29
Harold Wilson (1964–70)	143
Edward Heath (1970–74)	48
Harold Wilson (1974–76)	83
James Callaghan (1976–79)	60
Margaret Thatcher (1979–90)	216
John Major (1990–97)	171
Tony Blair (1997–2001)	248

Note: Creation of hereditary peers by prime ministers. *Before 1958, this was common practice among Prime Ministers. It continued from 1958 to 1964. In 1964 Harold Wilson stopped the practice. After 1983, Margaret Thatcher created three 'hereditaries'.*

Developments in the unreformed House of Lords 1958–99: the success of the 1958 Act?

The key development was in the creation of life peers so that by 1999 their numbers were approaching those of the hereditary peers. Defenders of the second chamber claimed that they brought a new expertise to proceedings. Among their ranks were not just former ministers and MPs, but many people who had achieved success in other careers, such as David Puttnam, the former film producer, and Victor Feather, a former Trades Union Congress General Secretary. This expertise or experience was not confined to life peers but has been largely associated with them.

Life peers have come from a more varied social background. Nevertheless, even by November 1999, the Lords was not socially representative of society as a whole. A study in the 1980s[1] showed that the majority of peers came from upper middle-class occupations such as the civil service and law.

High achievers with a particular expertise are likely to be at least of middle age. Hereditary peers who were young were small in number too. By January 1999, a majority of members were aged 65 or more. As former Prime Minister Harold Macmillan (Lord Stockton), put it in 1985: 'If, like me, you are over 90, frail, on two sticks, half deaf, and half blind, you stick out like a sore thumb in most places, but not in the House of Lords.'[2]

Work rate in the Lords

The creation of life peers certainly stimulated the House to greater activity. In the 1950s, attendance averaged less than 100 per day, the House hardly ever met for more than three days per week, and on average for three to four hours per day. By July 1998, attendance averaged over 400 per day, the House met for usually four days per week, and on average for about seven hours per day. From 1957, peers were paid an attendance allowance; rates in 1998 were up to £112 per day plus £33.50 per day for secretarial expenses. Such remuneration, especially among the former 'high-achiever' life peers, could not have been a prime motivation. Members of the House of Lords have never been paid a salary – except for those who are government ministers.

The 'injection' of life peers into the Lords certainly had other positive outcomes. During the 1950s divisions (voting) were infrequent – on average ten to twenty per year. By the 1980s and 1990s it averaged nearly 200 per year. This increased activity was also reflected in defeats for government: Labour 1974–79 had 362 and Conservatives 1979–97 had over 250. Governments were vulnerable to adverse votes from a combination of parties: not just opposition but also cross-benchers and some of their own supporters. From 1985 to 1989, the Lords gained exclusive television coverage before it was introduced into the Commons, thereby enhancing public awareness of their lordships.

These were some of the more positive outcomes of the 1958 Act regarding work rate. Nevertheless, critics of the 'reformed' Lords could point to a number of serious limitations. By 1990, the nominal membership of the Lords was about 1200. However, only about 800 attended one or more sittings each year with about 500 contributing to debates. In the 1989–90 session, there were 147 sittings but only 36 members attended 140 or more. Moreover, there was the pro-Conservative bias already mentioned. Even hereditary peers who did not take the Conservative whip often had a conservative social background and many life peers who sat on the cross-benches frequently voted with the party.

Functions of the House of Lords

Legislation

The constitutional position, functions and powers covering legislation are essentially contained in the Parliament Acts of 1911 and 1949 and the 'Salisbury Doctrine', 1945. As we see from the checklist (see p. 253) the powers of the Lords have been trimmed in the twentieth century. Since 1949, the delaying powers of the Lords have amounted to a maximum of one year.

In 1945 the Conservative Leader of the Lords, Lord Salisbury proposed the following response to the post-war Labour government's legislative programme. The Lords would not oppose at Second Reading any Bill that was a clear manifesto commitment, such as a national health service or nationalisation of essential industries. Salisbury's reasoning was clear; the Lords were not elected whereas Labour had gained a huge majority in the Commons; the Conservatives dominated the Lords but it would be folly to challenge Labour's legislative programme. Fears that the Lords might set the Salisbury Doctrine aside as a general election approached led the Labour government to pass the 1949 Act.

In this context, the Lords legislative work has three elements.

Revision of bills from the Commons

This work takes up about 40 per cent of the House's time and is extremely important. Revision by the Lords is usually valuable because bills passed by the Commons may need clarification, and have often received insufficient consideration in the Commons due to pressure of time.

The main work of the Lords takes place at the committee and report stages. The committee stage is usually taken on the floor of the House, and a detailed debate of amendments takes place, often with those peers with a specialist expertise enthusiastic to take part. With less time pressure than the Commons, detailed scrutiny of the Bill is possible with all amendments debated. The report and third reading provide opportunities for more consideration.

Introduction of government bills

These are usually not controversial. They enable the Lords to be kept busy early in the parliamentary session, before more contentious bills have been passed by the Commons.

Introduction of private peers' bills

In the short parliamentary session 1996–97, four such bills that originated in the Lords became law.

In addition, the Lords has a significant role to play in the scrutiny of European Union legislation. In particular, the Lords Select Committee on the EU examines and reports on proposals and draws particular attention to matters of policy or principle. All the evidence suggests that this work has been better done by the Lords than the Commons.

The power of delay

Defenders of the Lords have often claimed that it is important for the second chamber to have a power of delay over legislation, to enable ministers and those involved to have a chance to reflect on the issues involved. In effect this usually means the defeat of a government bill as a whole, or in part, or, more typically, the support of a large number of amendments. Historically, this happened most to the Labour governments from 1974 to 1979, which suffered from a weak position in the Commons; from a small majority until 1976 followed by a minority until 1979, and the permanent Conservative majority in the Lords. Nevertheless, the Conservative governments of the 1980s also suffered significant defeats and delays, although not in the same numbers. Between 1979 and 1987, the Lords blocked approximately 100 items of Conservative legislation, such as the sale of council houses built for the elderly (1984 and 1986) and the retention of corporal punishment in state schools (1986) which was against the spirit of a European Court ruling. Between 1997 and 1999 the Lords attempted to defeat Labour government measures on thirty seven occasions, all of which were overturned in the Commons where New Labour had a majority of 179. In 1998, the Lords temporarily succeeded in forcing the government to drop the lowering of the age of homosexual consent from eighteen to sixteen. This element was dropped so that the rest of the Crime and Disorders Bill would not be delayed. However, a separate bill about homosexual consent was reintroduced in 1999 – this was an obligation under a ruling of the European Court of Human Rights.

David Blunkett (Home Secretary) and the Anti-Terrorism,
Crime and Security Bill

This was introduced in response to the 11 September 2001 terrorist attacks in
the USA, and as part of Britain's contribution to the 'War on Terrorism' experienced a rocky journey in the Lords, as the timeline shows.

Timeline: 11 September to 13 December 2001
- **11 September**. The World Trade Center collapses, killing more than 3,000
  people, after it is hit by two hijacked passenger planes. Hundreds die as
  another hijacked plane crashes into the Pentagon. Another hijacked plane
  crashes in Pennsylvania, most likely on its way to another high-profile target.
- **16 September**. Tony Blair says that Britain is 'at war with terrorism'.
- **19 September**. Britain and the USA are said to be drawing up secret plans
  to launch a 'ten-year war on terrorism'.
- **21 September**. Three men and a woman are held by anti-terrorist detec-
  tives after raids in Britain.
- **25 September**. It emerges that eleven of the hijackers stayed in Britain
  during 2001 before going on their suicide mission.
- **28 September**. An Algerian pilot, Lotfi Raissi, appears in court for extradition proceeding in connection with the terror attacks.
- **29 September**. The FBI questions Zacarias Moussaoui, who had lived in
  South London, about the attacks. Sources say that he was to have been the
  twentieth hijacker, but had been arrested in Minnesota for immigration
  violations on 17 August.
- **31 September**. Tony Blair announces emergency legislation to speed up
  extradition cases, crack down against abuse of the asylum laws and give
  police power to monitor bank accounts in cases where they believe the
  money may be financing terrorism.
- **16 October**. MPs first show opposition to plans to extend the law against
  inciting racial hatred to create a new offence of provoking religious hatred.
- **29 October**. Geoff Hoon, the Defence Secretary warns British Muslims who
  want to join the Taliban, that they face jail on their return to Britain.
- **16 November**. Legislation giving the government sweeping powers to
  detain terrorist suspects without trial is heavily criticised by the all-party
  Joint Committee on Human Rights. The Anti-Terrorism Bill, they say, is
  being rushed through Parliament and may not be justified by the current
  international situation.
- **19 November**. The Labour-dominated Home Affairs Select Committee says
  plans to make incitement to religious hatred a crime are unworkable and
  should be dropped.
- **20 November**. David Blunkett, the Home Secretary, is barracked from all
  sides as he dismisses protests that the Commons was given too little time to
  debate details of anti-terrorist legislation.

- **21 November**. Mr Blunkett agrees to place a time limit of November 2006 on measures to detain terrorist suspects without trial.
- **27 November**. Mr Blunkett rejects cross-party calls to drop incitement to religious hatred from the Anti-Terrorism Bill.
- **6 December**. Conservative and Liberal Democrat peers unite to pass five amendments restricting new police powers allowing access to bank, tax, communications and other records.
- **10 December**. Mr Blunkett writes in *The Times* of his 'anger' and 'irritation' at the 'sabotaging' of the Bill.
- **11 December**. The House of Lords blocks the creation of new offences of incitement to religious hatred and backs a move to allow controversial measures to lapse in one, two or five years.
- **12 December**. Tony Blair appeals to MPs to pass the Anti-Terrorism, Crime and Security Bill when it returns to the Commons. MPs vote overwhelmingly in favour.
- **13 December**. The House of Lords votes for a second time to block incitement to religious hatred by 234 votes to 121. The Anti-Terrorism, Crime and Security Bill becomes law after the Government dramatically abandons its attempt to make a new criminal offence of inciting religious hatred. MPs cheer as the Home Secretary announces he is giving way to peers.

(*Source*: adapted from *The Times*, 15 December 2001.)

Recruitment

The government recruits a relatively small number of ministers from the Lords. At least two peers sit in Cabinet, the Lord Chancellor and Leader of the House. There may be up to four, but this is a rarity. Between ten and fifteen government ministers are drawn from the Lords and seven whips (including the Chief Whip), are appointed. Ministers speak on behalf of particular departments. However, as there are fewer ministers than the departments, some whips are assigned this responsibility.

For Prime Ministers, there are certain advantages in recruiting ministers from the Lords. Peers have fewer demands on their time, as they do not have a constituency, and may be particularly able on the evidence of their previous experience. People from outside Parliament can be given life peerages and appointed to government office at the same time. Here are two examples.

- Charles Falconer (Lord Falconer of Thoroton): a lawyer appointed as Solicitor General in 1997. He later took on responsibilities regarding the Millennium Dome.
- Gus Macdonald (Lord Macdonald of Tradeston): a Scottish television executive appointed as a junior minister in the Scottish Office in 1998. He

subsequently became a high-profile transport minister, especially after the Hatfield Rail Crash in 2000.

Scrutiny of the executive

Scrutiny of the executive in so far as legislation is concerned has already been considered on pp. 257–8. If, and until, there is an element of elected representation in the Lords then, strictly speaking, it would be inaccurate to say that the Lords can hold the executive to account. However, it does scrutinise the executive in various ways, notably: on the floor of the House, via Questions and Debates; and away from the Chamber, via Select Committees.

Questions

The first thirty minutes of each daily sitting of the Lords is used for up to four questions to Her Majesty's Government. These are 'starred questions' – questions which are non-debatable, are asked in person by a peer of whoever represents the government (the relevant minister or whip). The peer may ask for four or five supplementaries. This combination of time and up to four questions, with four to five supplementaries, allows for greater scrutiny of a particular issue.

The other type of question is 'unstarred', these are written questions on which a short debate may take place. Debates on such questions usually take place at the end of the day's sitting; the dinner hour!

Debates

Debates are held on specific policy matters or on topical issues. Their lordships are by no means as bound to party ties and disciplines as MPs are, nevertheless party allegiances are still strong. Some have argued that the level of debate, partly because of the expertise of the participants and the reduction of partisanship, is of high quality. This is particularly the case on one day per month when two debates – the topics are chosen by ballot – take place and may last for up to two and a half hours. For example in March 1999 Lord Campbell of Croy initiated a debate on motor-vehicle crime.

Overall the impact and influence of debates, especially on the executive, is mostly minor. What does create an impact is when a government bill is scrutinised, debated and, in whole or part, is defeated for example the Anti-Terrorism Bill in December 2001.

Judicial function

The House of Lords is the supreme court on criminal matters for England, Wales and Northern Ireland. The Lords is also the supreme court on civil matters for the whole of Britain. Note the exception for Criminal Law in Scotland.

The right to appeal to the House of Lords has to be applied for and granted by the Court of Appeal (often the scene of television news interviews – in the Strand, London). An example is the case of Diane Pretty who suffered from Motor Neurone Disease: she wanted her husband to have legal permission to help her die without the fear of prosecution – the Court refused, as did the Lords when she appealed. Appeals in the Lords are heard by a panel of between five and ten judges drawn from the Appellate Judicial Committee.

The House of Lords: a summary

- The House of Lords is the Second Chamber or Upper House in a bi-cameral system, with the House of Commons as the Lower House.
- At the beginning of 2003, it is the unelected part of Parliament consisting mostly of life peers and 92 remaining hereditary peers.
- Under the Parliament Acts of 1911 and 1949 it has the following powers: to delay legislation for one year; absolute veto over any bill proposing an extension to the life of Parliament.
- It derives some traditional authority from its long history, its use of professional expertise and careful use of its legal powers.
- Given all the above, it acts as a 'guardian of the constitution' not just over the five year life of Parliament but also over 'hasty' or 'ill-considered' legislation especially where the government has a week mandate. It is a revision chamber mostly and the delaying power may not just be used as a blocking tactic but as a means of facilitating greater scrutiny.

NB: The issues surrounding reform of the Lords are discussed in Chapter 17.

REFERENCES

1 N. Baldwin, 'The House of Lords: behavioural changes', in P. Norton (ed.) *Parliament in the 1980s*, Blackwell, 1985.
2 *Observer*, 19 May 1985.

SAMPLE QUESTIONS

1 Briefly, what is the composition of the House of Lords?

2 Describe the functions of the House of Lords.

3 Why has there been so much debate about the House of Lords since 1997?

For question 3 read the section on recent reform of the Lords in Chapter 12.

USEFUL WEB SITES

House of Lords **www.parliament.the-stationery-office.co.uk/ pa/ld/ldhome.htm** The House of Lords home page provides information on House of Lords publications in the Internet, including private and public bills, general information about the House of Lords and further information about members of the House of Lords.

AIMS OF THIS CHAPTER

➤ To assess the apparent decline of Parliament.

➤ To assess the ways in which Parliament attempts to hold the executive to account.

➤ To focus particularly upon the role and function of Select Committees.

In December 2001, proposals for further reform of the House of Lords and for the reform of the House of Commons became a matter of public and parliamentary discussion. Concern about the position of Parliament within the British system of government has been the source of debate since 1945.

The central issue has been Parliament's decline in strength vis-à-vis the Executive, even though Parliament is regarded formally as the sovereign body within the constitution. In particular the focus has been on: Parliament's ability, (a) to hold the Executive to account, (b) to restrain the Executive effectively, and (c) to scrutinise the Executive effectively.

Given the statutory reduction in the powers of the House of Lords in 1949, following those of 1911, anxiety about the performance of the Commons became paramount. Reform of the Lords, often the source of heated debate in the past, became less pressing.

Parliament's 'Golden Age'

If Parliament has declined, this presupposes a previous position of strength. For this, we return particularly to the period 1832–67 (between the first and second Reform Acts) and the years which followed. This era has sometimes been described as the 'Golden Age of the Back-Bencher', because it was a time when many MPs were only too willing to assert their independence and there was much cross-voting in the House of Commons; this was before two large and disciplined political parties began to dominate the Commons, from the end of the nineteenth century onwards. Governments depended on the collective support of a Commons in which MPs could censure ministers, force their resignation, organise the proceedings of the House and shape policy in debate. In the legislative process, MPs were able to scrutinise and amend bills partly because they had more time, but mostly because governments were so dependent on their collective good will.

The passing of the 'Golden Age': traditional explanations

A party system and a mass electorate

The growth of a mass electorate along with the development of a disciplined party system perversely did not help to strengthen the Commons but weakened it. The parties came to dominate, because governments saw the need to advance an overall policy programme, for disciplined MPs to support the party line in the voting lobbies and to ensure that they retained a parliamentary majority. Of course there may have been many MPs who have been 'independent-minded' since 1900, but the trend to party loyalty in the voting lobbies has been apparent in the key divisions of every party session.

Fusion and the power of the Prime Minister

Writing in 1867, the political commentator Walter Bagehot, the author of a famous textbook on the Constitution, wrote that 'the efficient secret of the English Constitution may be described as the close union, the newly complete fusion, of the executive and legislative powers . . . The connecting link is the Cabinet.' He felt that much of the meaningful work of real government was conducted via this fusion. However, the growth of the party system has combined with this fusion to undermine the sovereignty of Parliament and the position of back-bench MPs, while enhancing the powers and patronage of the Prime Minister (see pp. 195–6).

Expansion of Central Government and the civil service

Because of the expansion of government activity in the twentieth century, with the growth of the welfare state and the development of a managed economy, much of the detail of legislation has been passed in the form of 'delegated legislation'. Parliament consents to a broad framework and the details are worked on by civil servants working in government departments. This undermines the position of the Commons especially, for much of the resulting legislation is subjected to less scrutiny than was the case at the turn of the twentieth century.

The influence and impact of the media

Televising of the House of Lords began in 1985 and of the Commons in November 1989. To some extent this seemed to direct more public attention back to the floor of the House after television, radio and the newspapers had distracted attention away from it. However, television interviews and discussions with leading politicians are more instantly informative than live coverage of the Commons or newspaper reports and articles.

Another trend, especially in recent years, is typified by the following account which shows a downgrading in the impact that Parliament makes in the media age:

> Sir Politic Would-Be wakes up to the *Today* programme (Radio 4) to hear a cabinet minister interviewed about a government policy initiative due to be announced later in the day, a Green or White Paper, or a new Bill. Later, the main opposition spokesman is also questioned, together with a Liberal Democrat . . . Sir Politic then looks at his morning paper, where details . . . have been widely leaked by advisers to the minister . . . (in fact) to every paper. The agenda has been set for the day, to be followed by the *Evening Standard* and the lunchtime news programmes. The formal statement in the House of Commons is almost an anti-climax and Sir Politic wonders whether it is worth turning up as he knows what is going to be said and his own comments will not be reported in the press.[1]

In the above example, Peter Riddell shows how the executive is so media-conscious that Prime Minister and ministers seize the initiative by setting the political news agenda for the day by making announcements outside Parliament first. Important statements and policy initiatives are sometimes announced outside Parliament with no repetition in Parliament. This circumvention of Parliament has further reduced its standing, diminished the role of the typical MP (e.g. Sir Politic) and enhanced the status of the executive.

The European Union

Britain's membership of the European Community/Union since 1973 has led to many vital decisions affecting Britain being made away from Parliament. Political decisions taken by EU institutions have affected Britain economically and socially, as in the case of the Common Agricultural Policy and the adoption of the Social Chapter in the Maastricht Treaty, 1997.

Control over finance

Control of government finance, once held by the Commons until it was gradually weakened from the late nineteenth century, is now almost completely in the hands of the executive. The Lords influence over finance ended with the Parliament Act, 1911.

The Commons is now just left with approval or otherwise of the budget proposals and the government's estimates for spending by each government department for the following year. Only very occasionally is the government defeated on a financial matter, as in 1994 when Conservative back-benchers voted against an increase on VAT for fuel. A large overall majority for the government avoids such embarrassment.

Pressure groups

Pressure groups have grown in number and influence, to the detriment of the Commons, in at least two ways. Firstly, since 1979 (with the exception of the Major government, 1992–97), five governments have had good or massive overall majorities and have been confronted by a weak, some would say unelectable, opposition in the Commons. Given this power of the Executive over the Commons, many interests in society have worked through pressure groups to advance their claims; in the case of powerful groups, they are in direct contact with ministers and civil servants in Whitehall. For example, Charter 88 was established to campaign for constitutional and Parliamentary reform.

Secondly, given the growth of government responsibilities and powers, it has often consulted with and gained advice and information from pressure groups in the drafting of new legislation. The combination of ministers, civil servants and representatives from pressure groups has been to the exclusion of the Commons. MPs only see the proposal at the Green or White paper stage.

Referendums

Some argue that the use of referendums has undermined the sovereignty of Parliament. There were four in the 1970s, and four more in the period 1997–98 (as described on pp. 282 and 287). These referendums were approved by Parliament in the first instance via statute law, but the final decision was effectively taken out of its hands.

Public disaffection with politics and politicians

This, of course, is not just about Parliament but government too. The evidence of opinion polls, declining turnout in local and European elections, and especially the turnout of 59 per cent in the 2001 general election all suggest growing indifference or disaffection with political processes in Britain.

Even though we have listed several key points in Parliament's decline, it is essential to be aware that most are rooted in the fusion of Parliament and government and the extent to which government now dominates.

Some recent factors in Parliament's decline

Many factors seem to undermine Parliament today, among them:
- 'elective dictatorship'- especially with a majority of 165;
- a 'presidential' Prime Minister;
- a Prime Minister's 'department' (with around 80 special advisers);
- the by-passing of the Commons to deliver policy statements.

The effectiveness of Parliament

Peter Riddell[2] reminds us that 'Parliament itself does not govern . . . Parliament's role is to create, sustain and hold government to account, but not itself to govern'. Among the main functions of Parliament, we have mentioned are:

- the creation of governments and sustaining its majority;
- scrutiny of the executive and its agencies;
- approval of the government's expenditure and tax proposals;
- legislation – making the law;
- deliberation – consideration and debate;
- representation.

The creation of government and sustaining its majority

This is one function that Parliament does well. It is very rare for a government to be turned out by a vote in the Commons. Concerns about the effectiveness of Parliament rarely focus on this function at all. Bernard Crick, however, pointed to the importance of this function and the educative aspect of parliamentary deliberations, rather than voting in the division lobbies: 'The voter does not expect his MP to turn out the government he has elected; but he expects him to ask the right kind of questions and to help him know what is happening.'[3]

Approval of the government's expenditure and tax proposals

In financial matters, Parliament's effectiveness is severely limited. The House of Lords' influence lies in the past. The formal processes dealing with the Budget proposals and the 'estimates' for spending by government departments rarely produce change, though as we have seen, in 1994, the government withdrew its proposal to increase VAT on fuel. The Public Accounts Committee subsequently can investigate spending by departments.

Legislation – making the law

There is little time for private members' legislation. With government bills, Parliament at best revises legislation. Parliament is dominated by the government's agenda. Some bills receive far too little time, because of use of the guillotine. Parliament has to give its approval to change the law, but most measures have been drawn up either by the British government or by the European Union.

The House of Lords, with more time and weaker party discipline, can be effective. A longstanding argument in favour of the Lords is the presence of professional expertise. For example, in November and December 2001, the

Anti-Terrorism Bill was revised due to the presentation of two reports of the Joint Committee of both Houses on human rights (see pp. 259–60).

The Commons does have successes too. Backbench revolts, even if they do not defeat a bill, may well embarrass the government. Examples in recent years include:
- 1996 – the second VAT rise on domestic fuel;
- 1997 – lone-parent benefit – 47 Labour MPs voted against;
- 2000 – part-privatisation of Air Traffic Control; 46 Labour MPs opposed the government's plans.

The Commons, of course, also provides a positive role in the process by which bills are debated and amended. A party-disciplined Commons is vital so that the executive may create the laws it promised at the general election. However, substantial amendments are infrequent.

Scrutiny of the Executive and its agencies

Scrutiny and control of the executive is carried out in many ways, among them:
- Her Majesty's opposition;
- Opposition days;
- Backbench rebellions;
- Question Time to ministers;
- Prime Minister's Question Time;
- departmental select committees;
- the **Ombudsman**;
- government defeats in the Lords;
- the work of cross-benchers in the Lords;
- the quality of argument via professional expertise in the Lords.

Ombudsman

This literally means a 'grievance man' in Swedish. The Ombudsman or Parliamentary Commissioner for Administration is appointed by the Prime Minister. His job is to seek redress of grievances for bureaucratic abuses like delay, neglect and incompetence.

Deliberation

There is more potential and time for careful and efficient deliberation in the Lords than in the Commons. MPs often do not stay in the Commons for a whole debate; they may speak, leave to do other work, and return to vote. They usually know how they intend to vote from the start of the debate. Rows upon rows of empty benches do little for Commons' credibility.

Representation

The effectiveness of representation is limited by:
- the unrepresentative composition of the Commons produced by the simple plurality voting system;
- public perceptions of sleaze, involving MPs and ministers;

- unrepresentative pressure groups having disproportionate influence;
- the Lords still having no elected members, making it unrepresentative and unaccountable.

What can be done to make Parliament more effective?

Parliament's present capacity to scrutinise and control the Executive as well as represent the people is limited. Some modest reforms have been proposed and implemented. However, the following changes might be on the list of those who want radical change:

- a system of PR for elections to the Commons;
- a fully elected Lords;
- increased power for **select committees**;
- an entrenched Bill of Rights;
- a demand that the Prime Minister should appear before the Public Accounts Committee at the end of each parliamentary session.

Several of these measures have been mentioned elsewhere, but much of the attention of parliamentary reformers centres on the role and performance of the system of select committees. Defenders of the present system would point to

> **select committees**
> Committees of both the House of Commons and the House of Lords. In the Commons, they monitor the work of the main government departments. In theory, their members are chosen by the Commons. In practice, they are chosen by the whips. Essentially, their function is to scrutinise the work of the Executive and to hold it accountable to Parliament.

the importance of their impact since their introduction. Critics feel that they lack essential powers and that, with further reform, they could do more to strengthen Parliamentary scrutiny of the Executive.

Select committees

Historically, select committees are a well-established means of Parliamentary scrutiny. However, for most of the twentieth century, their use was very limited. Before 1979, there were two long-established select committees: the Public Accounts Committe and the Estates Committee.

1 **The Public Accounts Committee (PAC).** This was first set up in 1861, and is a permanent committee. It scrutinises public expenditure after the taxpayers' money has been spent. Parliament votes on the allocation of this money, and the PAC checks that it has been spent according to the wishes of Parliament. This committee still exists today.

2 **The Estimates Committee (from 1971, the Expenditure Committee).** This committee was set up in 1912 to examine how policies could be administered in the most cost-effective way. It was established in 1971 when the Expenditure Committee was set up with wider functions, but this in turn was abolished when the departmental select committees were set up in 1979 which, since then, have examined the spending of the appropriate department.

In the late 1960s, a number of select committees were established covering some departments and policy areas, such as agriculture and abortion, respectively.

Departmental select committees

In 1979, following the return of a Conservative government at the general election, Norman St John-Stevas (now Lord St John of Fawsley), the Leader of the House of Commons, presented the proposals for departmental select committees to Parliament. In 1980, fourteen such committees began their work. The number has varied over the years, reflecting the occasional restructuring of government departments. After the 1997 general election, for example, there were sixteen. There were also seventeen non-department select committees created, mainly for domestic matters, e.g. Catering, Committee on Standards and Privileges.

Composition

Each committee consists entirely of backbench MPs, typically eleven. No whips or ministers may sit on them. The number of MPs from each party roughly reflects their total number in the Commons. The procedure for selecting MPs for each of these committees became controversial in mid-July 2001 (see Case study, p. 275). The whips draw up a list of MPs for each committee; this, in turn, is approved by a selection committee of the Commons as a whole. This is usually a formality.

The chairmanships of these committees are shared between the parties. In theory, it is the members of each committee who elect the chairperson. In practice, it is the party whips who negotiate these appointments. Some chairs have proved to be good at asking 'awkward and difficult' questions, among them Chris Mullin (Labour Chairman of the Home Affairs Committee, 1997–99).

Neither the chairman, nor any member of the select committees is paid for this work which is in addition to their work as MPs. Each committee has the support of a small administrative staff. The expenditure of these committees is controlled by the Commons, not the Treasury or the whips.

Work and powers

Each committee runs for a whole Parliament, i.e. from one general election to the next. They usually meet once a week, set their own agenda, and decide what they wish to consider. They examine particular subjects by taking oral and written evidence in public. Their work, often in the case of major inquiries, may require travelling abroad to compare the experience of other countries, or to gather fresh ideas to add to the policy-making process in the

UK. In 2000, for example, after several months of such work at home and abroad, the Select Committee for the Department of Science and Technology, chaired by Dr Michael Clark (Conservative) reported on cancer prevention, treatment and cure, with recommendations that formed the basis for a Labour government initiative.

In gathering evidence, select committees have the power to send for 'persons, papers, and records'. Sometimes, this may not be as easy as it sounds, given the traditions of government secrecy. Witnesses, from ministers, top civil servants and special advisers, may be interviewed; the Chancellor appears before the Treasury Committee once per year. The permission of the Commons as a whole is required to *compel* ministers to attend, but most do.

On completion of their investigations, the committees produce a report for Parliament and government. The 1992–97 Parliament produced 453 reports on a wide variety of subjects, ranging from food safety to the prison service. Most reports are agreed by the whole committee, but occasionally members divide on party lines, as happened with the Employment Committee's report about the treatment of miners who were sacked during the strike of 1984–85. The government must acknowledge receipt of these reports, but responses are variable (see below).

Assessment

The views of academics and political commentators have been, on the whole, favourable, but with reservations about the limitations of select committees. Peter Hennessy has been impressed by their performance:

> I rate the establishment of the so-called departmentally related Commons Select Committees in 1979 as not just the most significant parliamentary development of the post-war period, but the single most important clawback in terms of the relative influence of the legislative and the executive since . . . 1902. I use the word 'influence' deliberately. It is not the same as 'power'. Governments govern; Parliament does not, even though without the consent of Parliament no government can exercise power for long.[4]

Andrew Adonis is similarly impressed: '[They have] enhanced the profile and reputation of the House of Commons among policy formers and the media.'[5]

Professor the Lord Norton of Louth has acknowledged their strengths 'of value to the House and to MPs individually. They have acted as a means of speciali-sation, as deterrents, as agents of open government, as safety valves, and as policy influences . . . '[6] However, he also points to the limitations of select committees: 'The committees stand accused of having inadequate resources, an amateurish approach, limited powers, little linkage with the floor of the House, limited influence, and of wilting under the pressure of political inter-ference and of other demands on MPs' time.'[7]

Essentially, the key issue is: To what extent do select committees influence the executive, and hold it accountable to Parliament and public?

Great expectations. Having taken decades to come, the St John-Stevas proposals raised huge expectations, but could not guarantee radical change. This would depend on the MPs who sat on these committees.

Fusion of Legislature and Executive. Given the lack of a separation of powers in the UK's central government, in particular the fusion of legislature and executive, and the increasing power of the latter over the past two decades, these committees were much needed. Indeed, by the late 1980s, they had established themselves as important contributors to the parliamentary functions of scrutiny, investigation and influence (rather than power) over the Executive.

Independence/asking the right questions. Although their membership is proportionate to party members in the Commons, these committees can be refreshingly non-partisan and independent in their questioning and thinking. MPs take their work on these committees seriously, and the majority seem to see themselves as true representatives of Parliament in their scrutiny of government departments. As Joe Ashton (the former Labour MP for Bassetlaw), once said on a television series, *The Great Palace*, about the Westminster Parliament: 'MPs are very good at asking questions. They may not be very good at answering them, but they are very good at asking them.' Certainly, some select committees have worked well in the fairly recent past asking the 'difficult' questions, for example the Health Committee chaired by Nicholas Winterton (Conservative) 1991–92 and the Transport Sub-Committee, chaired by Gwyneth Dunwoody (Labour) 1997–2001. The former drew attention to problems in the internal market within the NHS following reforms in 1990. The latter was scathing about the deficiencies of Railtrack following the Hatfield Rail Crash (2000).

Lack of evidence/asking the wrong questions. Select committees are often denied vital evidence. There were several important examples in the 1990s. Perhaps the most striking was the enormous difference in the limited material available to the first select committee on Trade and Industry's inquiry into the Iraqi 'Supergun' affair and those available some time later to the Matrix Churchill trial, concerning the same issue, when the judge ordered a full 'discovery of documents'. In 1998, the Foreign Office resisted the Foreign Affairs Select Committee's request to see telegrams concerning its part in the restoration of the government in Sierra Leone. Without sufficient documentation, committees often appear amateurish when questioning well-prepared ministers.

The last two points are just some of the features that produce variability of the effectiveness of select committees. There are other considerations.

- insufficient time, resources and professional staff;
- civil servants may only speak as advised by their ministers;
- some committees have avoided the most controversial of issues in order not to undermine their consensuality. 'The Environment, Scotland and Wales committee's failure to tackle the poll tax question is the most glaring example' Hennessy.[7]
- Chris Mullin (Chairman of the Home Affairs Select Committee 1997–99) has pointed to the faults of some MPs, regarding poor attendance. He cited three rules: read papers beforehand; ask short questions; keep your bum on your seat throughout the session.

Impact. Each committee issues a report to Parliament and government. However, these reports do not have to be debated in the Commons. Given the sheer number of them (e.g. 453 in the 1992–97 Parliament), there is just not enough time. However, some mechanism is required whereby the Commons has some time to consider recommendations and carry them forward. Governments are not bound to accept them, they can be ignored or taken up later. Sometimes, the recommendations of a select committee are not acted on, despite government assurances to the contrary. For example, Menzies Campbell (Liberal Democrat) sat on the Defence Select Committee in the early 1990s which issued a report pointing out over 50 faults on the standard issue rifle used by the British Armed Forces; the Defence Department subsequently assured them that all was well. Some years later, the same faults identified by the committee became public knowledge, for example the fact that they were unusable in freezing conditions .

By-passing Parliament? When departmental select committees were introduced in 1979, Michael Foot, then the Leader of the Labour Party, opposed them. He argued that they shifted attention, focus and energy away from the Commons. Certainly, there have been occasions when this seems to have been the case. Matthew Parris pointed to the events of the previous few days when activity on the committee corridor had produced the political headlines:

> Jeff Rooker . . . junior agriculture minister . . . slammed by MPs on the Agriculture Committee over his efforts to ban Vitamin B6 . . .

> He noted that Clare Short had been attacked by the International Development Select Committee for her department's performance over the Sudan and that the Prime Minister's Press Secretary, Alastair Campbell, had similarly faced inquisition, in public, by the Public Administration Committee.[6]

There is a danger that investigation by committee becomes a substitute for discussion on the floor of the House, in which all MPs have a chance to be involved. Some critics see the use of committees as a further way in which the chamber is being by-passed.

Summary

Most analysts agree that select committees have done little to change the balance of power between executive and legislative, but the combination of media attention they attract and the more specialised knowledge gained by MPs who have served on them makes them very worth while. They have, and do, provide more information, detailed scrutiny, and public criticism of government, and, especially where media attention is strong, help to make the Executive more accountable. They also have made government more open.

Reformers suggest that they can be made more effective, by giving them larger budgets, more powers, more access to documentation and greater powers to interrogate ministers (even the Prime Minister), as well as civil servants.

A case study: the appointment of select committees, July 2001 –
a government defeat

Wednesday 11 July

Meeting of Parliamentary Labour Party. Concern expressed over the following:
1 The removal of Gwyneth Dunwoody (chair of Transport Sub-Committee), Donald Anderson (Chair of Foreign Affairs Select Committee), and Derek Foster (Chair of Employment Sub-Committee). All three had chaired these committees 1997–2001, all were independent-minded, and all were omitted from the lists for approval by the Commons.
2 Chris Smith (former Culture Minister) to be appointed as new chairman of the Foreign Affairs Committee.

The removal of Mrs Dunwoody caused particular anger. Initially, the Parliamentary Labour Party (PLP) voted down the list. When the new Chief Whip, Hilary Armstrong, said that she would take their concerns on board, it was approved.

Monday 16 July

> The two Labour MPs axed as the heads of Commons watchdog committees called on Labour MPs yesterday to rebel against government attempts to silence friendly criticism.
>
> Supporters of Gwyneth Dunwoody and Donald Anderson, who chaired the transport and foreign affairs select committees in the last Parliament, will try to reinstate them in the Commons tonight. Senior figures in all parties joined protests yesterday over the Government's handling of the committees.
>
> Gordon Prentice, the Labour MP for Pendle who has put down one of the motions, predicted yesterday that 50 colleagues would take on the government whips . . .
>
> . . . Mrs Dunwoody, MP for Nantwich and Crewe, acknowledged that the Government's huge majority made it difficult to defeat. Ministers' actions, however, had been 'too blatant' to let them get away with it, she said.
>
> Lord St John of Fawsley, who oversaw modernisation of the select committee system as Tory Leader of the Commons in 1979, denounced the Government's

actions as 'sinister and dangerous . . . The essence of these committees was that they should speak not for a party but for the House of Commons as well.' Lord St John said ensuring that appointments were in the control of the Commons rather than the government had been an integral part of the reforms. Referring to the appointment of the former Culture Secretary, Chris Smith, in Mr Anderson's place, he said: 'They were never intended as a consolation prize for failed former ministers.' . . .

Mrs Dunwoody said that recent parliamentary reports had called for MPs to be given the power to make select committee appointments rather than government whips and it was an invincible argument. (Adapted from 'Axed watchdogs call on Labour MPs to rebel', Philip Webster, Political Editor, The Times, Monday 16 July)

With the vote to take place later in the day, there seemed little chance of a Government defeat.

Afternoon. Tony Blair in his first major speech since the general election defied both Trade Union opposition and that of many in the PLP by insisting that private companies would be used, where appropriate, to run and improve public services. This goaded some Labour MPs into a defiant mood.

Evening. Free vote (customary) on appointments to select committees:
1 Vote on membership of new transport committee (excluding Mrs Dunwoody), for 221, against 308. 124 Labour MPs voted against.
2 Vote on membership of new foreign affairs committee, for 232, against 301. Over 100 Labour MPs voted against.

Subsequently, the Chief Whip, Hilary Armstrong, revised the lists and Mrs Dunwoody and Mr Anderson resumed the chairs of their respective select committees. The House Modernisation Committee, meeting the following day, agreed on a comprehensive review of select committees as its first priority.

Reasons for New Labour's first ever defeat in the Commons since its election in 1997

1 Labour backbenchers had become increasingly restless following the June election results and the formation of Blair's government because many had been passed over for promotion, and many were unhappy about Blair's insistence on private companies becoming more involved in public services.
2 Backbenchers on both sides of the House wished to revive pressure for modernisation over scrutiny, resisted by the previous Leader of the House, Margaret Beckett, but likely to be viewed more positively by her successor.
3 Since 7 June, there had also been a sense that the Conservative Party, Her Majesty's Opposition, had been distracted by its leadership election. Clearly, a considerable number of Labour MPs believed that the Commons should assert itself.

REFERENCES

1 Adapted from P. Riddell, *Parliament under Blair*, Politico's, 2000.
2 As note 1 above.
3 B. Crick, *In Defence of Politics*, Continuum, 2000.
4 P. Hennessy, *The Hidden Wiring*, Indigo, 1995.
5 A. Adonis, *Parliament Today*, Manchester University Press, 1993.
6 P. Norton, 'Select committees in the House of Commons: watchdogs or poodles?' *Politics Review*, Vol. 4:2, November 1994.
7 As note 4 above.
8 M. Parris, *The Times*, 26 June 1998.

Constitutional change 1997–2001: future possibilities 17

AIMS OF THIS CHAPTER

➤ To assess the process and impact of devolution for Scotland and Wales.

➤ To consider reform of the House of Lords now that Phase One has been accomplished, the Wakeham recommendations and the government's response to them and various other suggestions for the future of the House of Lords.

➤ To outline the 'modernisation' reforms proposed for the House of Commons.

➤ To outline the Freedom of Information Act, Human Rights Act and the increased political role of judges.

➤ To outline the issue of reform for elections to the House of Commons.

By the time New Labour won the general election in 1997, a whole series of concerns about the workings of the British constitution were being much discussed. These included:

- fears about parliamentary sovereignty and the impact of Britain's membership of the European Union, especially after the ratification of the Maastricht Treaty;
- corruption and sleaze associated with the House of Commons;
- the fairness of the electoral system;
- the future of the second chamber;
- the erosion of civil liberties;
- the increasing number of unelected quangos.

As a party of renewal, New Labour could not avoid the belief that the constitution was in need of modernisation and its 1997 manifesto reflected this in detailed pledges. Labour would:

- end the hereditary principle in the House of Lords;
- hold referendums on devolution for Scotland and Wales and, if the issue was supported, set up assemblies in both parts of the UK;
- draw up a Freedom of Information Act;
- incorporate the European Convention on Human Rights into British Law;

Key developments

1997

- **Cabinet Committee on Constitution** set up. Included Paddy Ashdown and other Liberal Democrats.
- **Referendum (Scotland and Wales) Act**. Legal basis for establishing a Scottish Parliament with tax-varying powers and a Welsh Assembly.
- **Referendum in Scotland**.
- **Referendum in Wales**.
- **Jenkins Commission**. Lord Jenkins chairs commission to examine alternative electoral systems for elections to House of Commons.

1998

- **Good Friday Agreement**. Created an elected assembly for Northern Ireland.
- **Referendum in Northern Ireland and Eire** on Agreement.
- **Government of Wales Act**. Established Welsh Executive/Assembly.
- **Greater London Authority (Referendum) Act**. Subsequently, London voted for creation of a Greater London Authority led by a mayor.
- **Human Rights Act**. Incorporated the European Convention of Human Rights.
- **Northern Ireland Act**. Established devolved Assembly/Executive.
- **Wakeham Commission**. Lord Wakeham chairs commission to examine options for reform of the House of Lords.
- **Scotland Act** Established Scottish Parliament with tax-varying powers.

1999

- **European Parliament Elections Act**. Allowed 1999 and subsequent elections to European Parliament to be conducted on a 'regional list' system.
- **Greater London Authority Act**. Established the GLA through elections for Mayor and Assembly.
- **House of Lords Act**. Ended automatic right of hereditary peers (with the exception of 92) to sit and vote in the Lords.

2000

- **Wakeham Commission**. Report on the Lords widely perceived as cautious.
- **Freedom of Information Act**. Allowed new rights of access to official documents.
- **Local Government Act**. Allowed for executive mayors and other changes.
- **Political Parties, Elections and Referendums Act**. Established a new elections commission to oversee contents.
- **Representation of the People Act**. Allowed voting experiments.

Adapted from *Did Things get Better?* Penguin, 2001.[1]

- hold a referendum and, if the issue was supported, set up a directly elected strategic authority for London, with an elected mayor;
- hold a referendum on the electoral system to the House of Commons.

All this and other items amounted to the largest, most radical and formidable package of constitutional reforms proposed by any political party in the twentieth century.

Devolution

Devolution is the process of transferring power from central government to subordinate regional institutions, the passing of powers or duties from a higher authority to a lower one. As such, devolved bodies form an intermediate level of government between the central and the local level. It occurs in a unitary state in which sovereignty resides in a central Parliament. In theory, this transfer of power is reversible, in that the central government can take back all the powers it has devolved.

By contrast, federalism involves the existence of two distinct levels of government. Neither level is legislatively or politically subordinate to the other (federalism is derived from the Latin *foedus* meaning 'pact'). Both levels of government, a central (or federal) level, and regional (or state) level, have powers which the other cannot take over. Both have legislative and executive authority. In a federal state such as the USA, sovereignty is shared between central and regional government.

Devolution has been on the agenda in the United Kingdom for several decades, because of the development of nationalist pressures in Scotland and Wales.

Nationalism in Scotland and the failure of devolution in 1979

National identities in Scotland and Wales were both preserved into the twentieth century, despite their subservience to England over hundreds of years. In the early twentieth century, parties developed to articulate the nationalist case. In 1925, the Welsh Nationalist Party, Plaid Cymru, was formed. In 1934, the Scottish National Party (SNP) was formed. Even though the SNP, for example, returned an MP in a by-election in April 1945, only to be defeated in the general election in July, it was not until the 1960s that the SNP and Plaid Cymru evolved into fully-fledged political parties. In 1966, Plaid Cymru won a by-election in Carmarthen, and in 1967, the SNP famously won a by-election in Hamilton. Eventually, both parties were to achieve a significant breakthrough in the general elections of February and October 1974. After the latter election, the SNP had 13 MPs, and Plaid Cymru 3. Prior to this, in 1968, the Labour government set up the Kilbrandon Commission to investigate the possibilities of devolution, but its findings were inconclusive, although both the Labour and Conservative parties affirmed their support in principle before the 1974 elections.

The Labour government that was returned in October 1974 had a very narrow majority, so political necessity, given the combined number of SNP/Plaid Cymru MPs, committed ministers to a devolution strategy. The issue divided Labour bitterly. As a consequence of amendments passed during the passage of their devolution legislation, the referendums to be held in Scotland and Wales in 1979 were to be subject to the vital condition that at least 40 per cent of each electorate had to vote in favour of the package Labour offered each country.

REFERENDUM ON DEVOLUTION FOR SCOTLAND: 1 MARCH 1979

Yes

1,253,502, 51.6% of those voting, 32.85% of the electorate

No

1,230,937, 48.5% of those voting, 30.78% of the electorate

Turnout

62.9%

RESULTS OF REFERENDUM ON DEVOLUTION FOR WALES: 1 MARCH 1979

Yes

243,048, 20.2% of those voting, 11.9% of the electorate

No

956,330, 79.8% of those voting, 46.9% of the electorate

Turnout

58.8%

The results of each referendum disappointed those who favoured devolution. Their case was lost. In Scotland, the 'yes' vote was well below the 40 per cent required. In Wales, devolution suffered a huge defeat, of almost one to four against. These two results together destroyed the credibility of Labour's proposals and led to motions of no confidence in the Labour government, first by the SNP, and then by the Conservatives. When Labour lost the latter vote, defeat precipitated a general election which the Conservatives won. Devolution was not on the Conservative agenda. However, the issue refused to go away.

Devolution in Scotland

Successive Conservative secretaries of state for Scotland found themselves administering a country in which they had less than one third of the votes cast in each general election. In the Scottish Grand Committee, which was set up in 1981 to deal with non-controversial Scottish legislation, the Conservatives were in a minority, but in 1995 the Secretary of State made the position very clear. He declared that 'the absolute Westminster veto over Scottish business remains . . . the Scottish Grand Committee is not a Scottish Parliament.'

This was the correct constitutional position, but its expression fuelled Scottish discontent, as did the introduction of the controversial poll tax into Scotland in 1989, one year before its introduction in England. In 1989, a Scottish Constitutional Convention was set up to translate what was seen as widespread support for devolution into concrete proposals. The SNP refused to participate as political independence was not part of the Convention's remit; so did the Conservatives. Those who did participate – Scottish Labour and Liberal Democrat MPs, and representatives from local government, the Scottish TUC, the Scottish CBI, the churches, and several other bodies – reported firstly in 1990, and then most spectacularly in 1995. These two reports, 'Towards Scotland's Parliament', and 'Scotland's Parliament, Scotland's Right', laid out a plan for devolution which formed the basis of the Scotland Act of 1998.

The Scottish referendum 1997

Before the 1997 general election, New Labour and the Liberal Democrats signed a pact on constitutional reform, which included a united policy towards devolution. In September of the same year, a referendum was held on devolution for Scotland. The referendum asked two questions of the electorate, on separate ballot papers. No minimum percentage of the electorate was required for devolution to be confirmed, just a simple plurality of votes. The detailed results are given in the box below. Briefly, on a satisfactory turnout, three-quarters of those who voted supported the proposal of a Scottish Parliament, and two-thirds supported the proposal that it should have tax-varying powers.

1997 Scottish referendum results

Q 1: Do you agree that there should be a Scottish Parliament?

	Votes	% of votes cast	% of electorate
Yes	1,775,045	74.3	44.7
No	614,000	25.7	15.5

Q 2: Do you agree a Scottish Parliament should have tax-varying powers?

	Votes	% of votes cast	% of electorate
Yes	1,512,889	63.5	38.1
No	870,263	36.5	21.9
Turnout	60.2%		

As a result of the referendum, a bill was drawn up to provide for a 129–strong Scottish Parliament from which an executive would be formed. The resulting Scotland Act was passed in 1998.

A Scottish Parliament

This was to be elected for a fixed term of four years, with 129 members. It was to have tax-varying powers of plus/minus 3p in the pound, and the power to spend block grant allocation from Westminster. It would have the power to create its own primary legislation in the following policy areas:

1 home affairs and the judiciary;
2 education, culture and sport;
3 health and community care;
4 environment and planning;
5 local government and housing;
6 social services;
7 agriculture and fishing;
8 implementation of EU directives.

Powers to be retained at Westminster

- defence;
- foreign policy;
- constitution of the UK;
- macro-economic and monetary policy and taxation;
- nationality, immigration and passports;
- employment law;
- social security benefits and pensions;
- some health issues, e.g. abortion;
- relations with the EU.

A Scottish executive would include the following: First Minister, Deputy First Minister, and senior and junior Ministers.

In the 1999 elections, the overall turnout was a modest 56 per cent. The electoral system employed was a hybrid one, with 73 MSPs elected by First Past the Post and another 56 by a list method. Although Labour gained 56 MSPs, it was nine short of a majority. The SNP came second overall, but it was, ironically, the Conservatives who benefited notably from the use of a regional list system. The Liberal Democrats mustered 17 MSPs. However, it was not just the four main parties who gained MSPs. The Greens gained their first representative outside a local council through a regional system in the Lothians. Secondly, the Scottish Socialist Party gained an MSP similarly in Glasgow. Thirdly, the rebel Labour MP Denis Canavan was elected as an MSP for the Falkirk West constituency too.

As a result, Labour formed a coalition administration with the Liberal Democrats. It has survived under three different Labour First Ministers.

Table 17.1 The Scottish elections, 6 May 1999: MSPs elected

	Elected by simple plurality	Elected by regional list	Total
Labour	53	3	56
SNP	7	28	35
Conservative	0	18	18
Liberal Democrat	12	5	17
Others	1	2	3
Total	73	56	129

The newly-elected Scottish Parliament, 1999

The Scottish Parliament provides a good example of devolution in practice. It has the power to create and pass its own primary legislation (see p. 00). In its first legislation programme, 1999–2000, the Scottish Executive introduced bills on such areas as school standards, the establishment of national parks in Scotland, transport, and the environment. In all, eight bills were to be introduced. For some, this seemed like a light burden for one year; Westminster usually passes nearer twenty in a similar period. For others, devolution had produced seven Scottish bills, more than would have been passed by Westminster in a year.

There are, nevertheless, a number of key policy areas in which the Scottish Parliament has little power, or, indeed, no power at all. The Scotland Act, 1998, included eighteen pages to detail the reserved powers, over which Westminster retained control. In addition, because the Scottish legal system is distinct and separate from that of England and Wales, some of the reserved powers are not under the exclusive control of the Westminster Parliament. There will be a need for continuous dialogue and negotiation over the details of some policies and their implementation in Scotland.

The Scottish Parliament is also responsible for implementing European Union legislation and has established an EU Committee to scrutinise such proposals. (*NB*: There is a strong focus on committee work in the Scottish Parliament.) In this case too, there is much need for dialogue with Westminster, as the committee's views are channelled back to London, and become part of the UK's position in the EU Council of Ministers.

As we have seen, the concepts of devolution and reserved powers in this instance do not involve an entirely clear-cut and simple division of responsibilities.

The Edinburgh–Westminster relationship: an amicable separation, or a potential divorce?

The following are some early considerations regarding the impact of devolution for Scotland, and in particular, its impact on relations between Edinburgh and Westminster:

Parliamentary sovereignty

In theory, devolution in a unitary state does not undermine parliamentary sovereignty. Hence, devolution for Scotland should not undermine the sovereignty of the Westminster Parliament, nor should it undermine the integrity of the UK. However, even though the division of responsibility for specific areas of policy between Edinburgh and London has initially been made clear, the potential for difficulties in the future is also apparent even at this early stage. For example, some have questioned whether the idea of tax-varying powers is compatible with the traditional concept of sovereignty being indivisible.

A 'new model' of government

There has been a conscious attempt to reject the Westminster model. A different electoral system, more sociable working hours, and the use of electronic voting methods are just part of the evidence for this. However, possibly even more significant in this rejection may be the development of a less Executive-centred, more open and responsive system. As such, the Scottish Assembly and Executive may have a strong case for possessing greater legitimacy than the Westminster Parliament. At the very least, this would effectively curb any proposal by central government for reducing Edinburgh's powers.

Independence?

The 'de facto' sovereignty of the Westminster Parliament could be further threatened if proportional voting increases SNP representation. It is already the official opposition party in Scotland, and if it were eventually to gain a majority of seats and exercise power, it could claim that independence was a logical progression for Scotland. In this way, there could be pressure for the Union to come to an end.

The role of Scottish MPs at Westminster

The over-representation of Scottish MPs. Since 1918, Scotland's electorate has been over-represented at Westminster in terms of its size, compared to the rest of the UK's electorate. At the general election in June 2001, it still sent 72 MPs to Westminster. If, as seems possible, the Boundary Commission were to redraw the Scottish constituencies on the same basis as in England, the number of MPs

---

The West Lothian Question

This issue is not new. It was raised by Tam Dalyell, the MP for West Lothian, in the 1970s. He pointed out the problems of devolving powers to particular parts of the country, but not all, while trying to retain a unitary state. Issues such as education in West Lothian, and indeed for the whole of Scotland, would be, and are now, voted on by Scottish MSPs alone. However, Scottish MPs still sit in the Westminster Parliament. Hence, since education legislation for England is still voted on at Westminster, these Scottish MPs may still have a say in English education, while English MPs have no say over Scottish education. This would prove vital, as well as significantly unfair, for a government dependent on the votes of Scottish MPs for its majority to legislate in England. As a group, 72 Scottish MPs could render a government impotent.

This is clearly an anomaly which could lead to resentment by English MPs and feature in any revived sense of English nationalism. The same issue could be raised in relation to Stormont, in Belfast. Northern Ireland now has its own law-making assembly, in which its members decide many issues of relevance to Northern Ireland. But Northern Irish MPs continue to sit at Westminster.

---

would be reduced to between 56 and 60. This, in turn, would have additional consequences for the composition of the Commons, such that Labour's number would be reduced. (In 2001, Labour won 55 out of the 72 seats.)

The roles of Scottish MPs (see also West Lothian Question). Given the Scottish Parliament's remit of policy areas, Scottish MPs at Westminster might not be able to pursue such topics as Scottish health and education. They will be limited to involving themselves in discussion of those areas reserved for the UK Parliament affecting Scotland, plus matters affecting England and Wales.

There are a number of solutions to this imbalance, some of which have been suggested since devolution took place. Parliament could

1 devolve power to the English regions or even create a system of regional government in England;
2 reduce the number of Scottish MPs at Westminster;
3 restrict the voting rights of Scottish MPs. In July 1999, William Hague suggested that Scottish (and Welsh) MPs should be banned from voting on purely English matters at Westminster;
4 create a federal structure;
5 ignore the West Lothian question, given the inconsistencies in the British constitution already.

Position of Secretary of State for Scotland: a suitable case for redundancy?

The position of Secretary of State for Scotland was first established in 1885. Its traditional duties have now been handed over to the First Minister in

Edinburgh. However, there is some scope for a Scottish Secretary to remain, at least in the short term, for the following reasons.

1 A large number of policy areas remain at Westminster, such as air and rail services between Scotland and London, employment legislation and the gas and oil industry in Scotland.

2 The Scotland Act gave the Scottish Secretary the power to block bills from the Scottish Parliament if they infringe upon the UK government's powers.

3 The Secretary of State in the UK Cabinet remains responsible for managing Scotland within the Union.

4 He or she can provide Scotland with a continuing voice in the highest councils of the United Kingdom, ensuring that it gets its viewpoint acknowledged.

Long-term, however, it does not seem that this would be enough. One possibility is the creation of a post of Secretary of State for Intergovernmental Affairs, covering Northern Ireland, Scotland and Wales.

Policy making

Tax-varying powers but not tax-raising powers. The lack of tax-raising powers may hinder the ability of the Scottish Parliament to fulfil its functions in the way it wishes.

Differences with Westminster. Within its tax-varying powers, or even without using them, the executive could switch resources within its £15 billion annual budget. There are already differences of policy over university tuition fees and care for the elderly between Edinburgh and Westminster. It could also develop different policies, for example, regarding roads and primary health care.

Devolution in Wales

Similar nationalist pressures had developed in Wales in the 1960s and 1970s, but in the 1979 referendum it was clear that devolution was not what the Welsh people wanted. Labour had miscalculated its appeal. Labour lost interest for several years, but the Welsh Liberals/SDP and Plaid Cymru continued to support devolution in 1983 and within a few years a campaign for a Welsh Assembly was established. By 1992, the three parties were all supporting devolution and it featured in Labour's 1997 manifesto. Following its electoral success, a referendum was held again. This time, there was a very narrow victory for the pro-devolutionists (50.1–49.9 per cent). It was just enough.

Opinion in Wales had shifted over the previous two decades. Many Welsh people resented the treatment that Wales received in the Thatcher/Major years, particularly the way in which English MPs were appointed as Secretary of State (the number of Conservative MPs in the principality was ever declining, so the

The positions of the political parties on devolution, past and present

Conservatives

The Conservatives have opposed devolution, since the 1970s, with the exception of Northern Ireland, arguing that it would lead to the break-up of the United Kingdom. In 1979 and 1997, they campaigned against devolution for Scotland and Wales. Very few supported it. However, they accepted devolution following the 'yes' vote in each referendum, and now participate in the devolved governments. They remain opposed to any increase in the devolved powers of these governments in the future.

Labour

Since the 1970s, the Labour Party has largely been in favour of devolution. Nevertheless, there were divisions within the party, with opposition coming from major figures on the left, like Neil Kinnock. However, by the late 1980s, it had become much more sympathetic, under his leadership. Years in opposition, three general election defeats, and continued strong support for Labour in Scotland and Wales were strong motivations. In the 1992 general election, Labour strongly supported devolution for Scotland and Wales, and the return of a regional level of government for London. John Smith moved these plans forward, and in 1997 they were part of a package of radical constitutional reforms in New Labour's manifesto. They may still pursue the creation of regional assemblies in England, along similar lines to the Welsh model.

Liberal Democrats

Since the late nineteenth century, when William Gladstone tried in vain to secure Home Rule for Ireland, mainstream Liberals have supported devolution within the UK. More recently, they supported the 'yes' vote in the referendums for Scottish and Welsh devolution in 1979 and similarly in 1998. They advocate an extension to the powers of the Welsh Assembly, similar to those of its Scottish equivalent. They are enthusiastic about regional assemblies for all parts of England too. Overall, they favour the creation of a federal state in the UK. In other words, the concept of the unitary state would be set aside with a federal Parliament at Westminster, along with state and regional Parliaments. This structure would be similar to that in the USA.

Scottish Nationalist Party and Plaid Cymru (Welsh Nationalists)

Not surprisingly, both nationalist parties supported devolution, not so much as ends in themselves, but as the means to an end, independence for Scotland and 'self-government' for Wales.

Summary

- All parties now support devolution for Scotland and Wales, and even the Conservatives agree that there can be no turning back.
- There are considerable variations, however, between the parties, as to the long-term consequences of the new arrangements.
- All parties support political devolution for Northern Ireland.

choice was not a wide one). Like the Scots, the Welsh too had realised that devolution would make them part of a Europe-wide representation for regions and provinces. It would give them a larger voice in Brussels.

As a result of the Wales Act, 1998, Wales received a 60–strong Assembly, rather than a Parliament. It is a weaker body, as its name implies. It lacks primary lawmaking powers, although it is responsible for secondary legislation and is able to flesh out bills already passed at Westminster. Again, elections for the Assembly are conducted under the same Additional Member System, and there is a First Minister and executive, all as in Scotland. In both countries too, there is currently a Labour–Liberal Democrat coalition.

DEVOLUTION IN SCOTLAND AND WALES – SIMILARITIES AND DIFFERENCES

Scotland

Wales

Election by additional member system.

Election by additional member system.

Parliament
Unicameral, 129 members of the Scottish Parliament (MSPs) elected for a fixed term of four years,
First Minister and Executive.

Assembly
Unicameral, 60 assembly members elected (AMs) for a fixed term of four years,
First Minister and Executive.

Powers of the Scottish Parliament
• administrative, financial and legislative devolution;
• primary legislative power to make, amend and repeal laws in specific policy areas;
• tax-varying powers, independent of Westminster.

Powers of the Welsh Assembly
• administrative devolution;
• cannot create its own laws;
• does not have tax-varying powers;
• can govern by secondary; legislation, fleshing out primary legislation passed at Westminster.

The early history of Welsh devolution in practice has been chequered. Minority Labour rule gave way to the present coalition under Rhodri Morgan. There have been leadership problems in both parties, and some dissatisfaction with the conduct of affairs. The key advantage of devolution is that it gives Welsh people some – modest – say in the running of their own country. Decisions are taken nearer to the people, not by a government in London. In Wales, the Assembly has been able to opt for free prescription charges, making it the only part of the United Kingdom where these apply.

The future of the House of Lords

New Labour was elected with a huge majority in 1997 but did not introduce a bill into Parliament on Lords reform until January 1999. Previously, in October 1998, the government announced that a Royal Commission was to be set up under the chairmanship of the Conservative peer, Lord Wakeham, to examine the various options for reforming the House of Lords.

The House of Lords Bill, with its main clause proposing the removal of heredity as a basis for membership, passed through the House of Commons with ease and a predictably large majority. The Lords adhered to the Salisbury convention by not voting on second reading, but the bill was severely held up at the committee and report stages by debate, scrutiny and hostility. There was the potential for the Lords to wreck a whole year of the government's legislation by using up time on this bill (the negotiations that then went on behind the scenes between the Lord Chancellor and Lord Cranbourne are described at the end of Chapter 1). Lord Weatherall, a former Speaker of the Commons, was asked to introduce a compromise in the form of an amendment. This would allow 92 hereditary peers to remain, elected from among the party groups. The compromise was acceptable to ministers, so that the amended bill became law. A House previously based on the hereditary principle was now based on Prime Ministerial appointment. Phase One of Lords reform was complete, but ministers assured interested parties that there would be a Phase Two at a later date.

In January 2000, the findings of Lord Wakeham's Royal Commission were published in a Report entitled *A House for the Future*. Lord Wakeham was determined that his Commission's proposals would be sufficiently practical and realistic, in order that they would be acceptable and implemented. To this end, he and his team opted for a largely appointed house, with a small elected element, offering three alternative scenarios for the balance of membership (see following section). Its functions and powers would be substantially the same as at the present time.

Outline of A House for the Future

- **Powers**: No radical change.
- **Composition**: 550 members approximately. Minority – by election. Majority – by appointment.
- **Election**: three models proposed.

Table 17.2 Three election models

	Nominated members (approx. number)	Regionally elected members	Total members (approx. number)
Model A	485	65 (11.8%)	550
Model B[a]	463	87 (15.8%)	550
Model C	355	195 (35.4%)	550

Source: Adapted from The Guardian, 21 January 2000.

[a] Majority of the Commission supported this model.

Model A: Selected via a proportional 'reading off' from notes cast at a general election in the region.

Models B and C: One third directly elected under regional list proportional representation system at the time of European Parliament elections.

NB: Elected regional members to serve for up to three cycles eligible for reappointment after 15 years.

Appointments commission: To have massive powers over overall composition of the Lords. Composition to reflect political opinion in Britain: 20 per cent of peers in new House to be cross-benchers (mostly appointed), 30 per cent of new members to be women. Aim – gender balance in time. Ethnic minorities – represented in proportion to numbers in Britain. Existing life peers to continue if they wish. Life peers eligible for reappointment after 15 years.

Note: Prime Minister to have no influence over this Commission.

Religions: 16 Church of England archbishops and bishops, 5 from other Christian denominations, 5 from non-Christian faiths.

Law lords: To stay – no change.

Future options for Phase 2 of Lords reform

Philip Norton[2] has suggested that there are four future possibilities: to remove, retain, replace, or reform.

Remove

This would involve the abolition of the House of Lords which would not be replaced by any other reconstituted second chamber. Britain would have a unicameral legislature, with the legislative burden being carried by the House of Commons only. Supporters of this option argue that the Commons would have to be reformed in order to fulfil the functions carried out by the two chambers at present. This was Labour policy in the 1983 election.

Those who *favour* this option put forward the following arguments.
- An unelected second chamber has no legitimacy, while an elected, or partly elected, second chamber might conflict with the fully elected Commons. In any case, much of the work of Parliament has been passed over to the other bodies; the European Union, the creation of the Scotland and Wales assemblies and the revival of a Parliament at Stormont for Ireland.
- The current powers of the Lords are only concerned with delaying bills and ensuring that Parliament is not prolonged more than five years. The power of delay can be nullified by a determined Commons, another safeguard could be put in place over the length of Parliament and the function of further scrutiny could be accomplished by a reformed Commons.
- Britain is still a unitary and not a federal state. It is in federal states, such as the USA, where a second chamber is usually required to counter-balance the first.

- The Law Lords and their work could be accomplished via a properly constituted, and separate, Supreme Court. This would remove the longstanding
  fusion of functions embodied in the Lord Chancellor, in executive, legislature and judiciary, and the Law Lords, in legislature and judiciary.
- Other countries successfully use the option of a unicameral legislative; for
  example Sweden, Denmark, Israel and New Zealand.

Those who *oppose* this option put forward the following arguments.

- Abolition has never attracted much support and in MORI polls in 1998 it was
  the least favoured option. It was not an option of the Wakeham Commission.

- From a purely practical point of view, the sheer burden of legislation is too
  much for an already overworked Commons to efficiently scrutinise. If only for
  this reason a second chamber is necessary. Countries with unicameral legislatures all have total populations of under 10 million. Britain has a population
  of approximately 59 million, entailing far more public business for the
  legislative function.

- The Commons alone would not provide a sufficient constitutional safeguard.
  It would be basically functioning as a safeguard against itself.

- The 'second look' at legislation provided by a second chamber could not be
  emulated in a single chamber. Scrutiny by a second chamber provides a
  valuable method of improving and clarifying legislation.

- A second chamber, without party domination, provides a better forum for
  debate. This would be determined by the reformed composition of the House.

- There is also the 'turkeys not voting for Christmas' argument. Many MPs
  eventually wish to be appointed or even elected to the Lords, depending on
  the nature of the reform, so are unlikely to vote for its abolition.

Retain

This option supports the retention of the Lords as a non-elected assembly.
Before the reform of 1999 and the Wakeham Report, this was very much the
position of the Conservative party. Some Conservatives now hold a different
view (see section on Reform p. 294), while others still favour retention, but
now of the present 'interim' House. This position is held by Philip Norton, an
academic and a peer, and probably the vast majority of other Conservative life
peers.

Those who *favour* retention put forward the following arguments:
- The interim House is infinitely preferable to an elected or partly elected
  chamber because it successfully complements the work of the Commons
  given the different composition of the two.

- The expertise and experience of the peers, especially the life peers, who come from many career backgrounds – academia, commerce, finance, industry, the law and so on – complement the deficiencies of the Commons especially. This, it is argued, is especially the case with the scrutiny of the bills.
- The absence or reduction of party influence, the role of the cross-benchers in holding the balance of power in the Lords and the exercise of independent thinking by peers, are all strong positives given the entrenched party positioning in the Commons.
- An elected House would not only lack the above qualities but would create constitutional issues since it would claim democratic legitimacy with the Commons. For example, a Lords elected at a different time or by a different method, could produce very different party representation from the Commons; such an eventuality could lead to a legislative stalemate. On the other hand, if elected at the same time as the Commons, the Lords would mirror it in composition and merely 'rubber-stamp' the work of the Commons.

The arguments opposing this view are contained in the next section 'Replace'.

Replace

For many, this option involves replacing the present House with a new and wholly-elected second chamber. In their view, to have anything other than an elected chamber is unacceptable. The hereditary principle survived for almost the whole of the twentieth century, and an hereditary 'rump' is still present. However, the government's proposal in its White Paper of November 2001 (see p. 295) of 20 per cent elected members and 80 per cent appointed members would produce a chamber that was almost as unacceptable as its predecessors.

Those who *favour* replacement with a wholly elected second chamber argue as follows.
- A nominated or even a partly-elected chamber lacks legitimacy. A wholly elected chamber would bring popular legitimacy to the House.
- An elected chamber would create additional representation and provide greater legitimacy to the House in two key functions: scrutiny of legislation and holding the Executive to account.
- It would provide citizens with an additional avenue for redress of grievances via their elected representatives.
- Elections could be on a national or regional basis. The latter would provide representation at the centre not only for Scotland, Wales and Northern Ireland but for the English regions.

Those *opposing* a fully-elected chamber argue as follows.

- If both Houses are elected at the same time, the balance of parties would be more or less the same. This would make the Lords superfluous if both Houses are dominated by the same party. This would also undermine the function of the Lords as the 'watchdog' of the constitution.
- If the two Houses are elected at different, or even partly different times, this could lead to the problems of mixed mandates, conflict between the two Houses, a legislative stalemate and even a constitutional crisis. This could mean that an elected government would be prevented from fulfilling its manifesto commitments.
- The issue of accountability may become complicated. If the Lords disagrees with the Commons, who should the voters hold accountable?
- The Lords would lose the professional expertise and experience provided by life peers.

Comparative considerations

In General Studies, January 2001, Meg Russell – Senior Research Fellow at the Constitution Unit, University College, London – made the following observations:
- Of 178 parliamentary democracies worldwide, 66 are bicameral.
- Almost all of the countries with upper houses like the Lords have been reformed. 27 use direct elections, 21 use 'indirect elections.'
- Canada's upper house or senate, among all western democracies, is the only one to be wholly appointed, although some have a small percentage of appointees. Canada's senators are all appointed by the Prime Minister. The senate is powerful, but, because of its composition, is seen as illegitimate and in need of reform.
- The Australian Senate is wholly elected – half at each general election – with representatives from the six states and two territories. Elections are by proportional representation, so that the political balance is different to that of the lower house. Elections too provide for legitimate interventions in the legislative process.

Reform

This option, advocated by the Wakeham Commission and the government White Paper (November 2001), involves an element of election and nomination. Election would provide more legitimacy, nomination would preserve existing levels of expertise and safeguards would be put in place to prevent 'cronyism' (Prime Ministerial powers to appoint people of their own choosing and for party political reasons).

Those *favouring* this option argue as follows:

- The level of professional expertise and experience required to scrutinise bills effectively requires the nomination of appropriate life peers. This level of 'professionalism' has been one of the successes of the Lords since the Life Peerages Act, 1958.

- The combination of election and nomination would ensure a House that is less confined by party politics, more independent in its views, and more likely to maintain its role of watchdog over the constitution.

- Elections might ensure representation for ethnic minorities, women and other groups that have little or no representation at the moment. Nomination could allow for the representation of Nonconformists and non-Christian faiths.

The key issue with the reform option is the proportion of elected members to nominated members. This is a subject of considerable debate. In 1977, the former Prime Minister Lord Home chaired a Conservative commission that recommended two-thirds should be elected. Another Conservative commission, headed by the former Lord Chancellor, Lord Mackay of Clashfern, recommended that only one-third to be elected. Wakeham favoured Model B – 15.8 per cent elected. Ministers favour reform, and have opted for a 20 per cent elected element.

New Labour's Phase Two proposals

In November 2001, the government published a White Paper, *Completing the Reform*, proposing the next stage in the reform of the Lords. In this paper, Lord Irvine stated: 'When we legislated in 1999 to remove most of the hereditary peers, we promised we would complete the job of creating a modern and representative House of Lords, suitable for the twenty-first century. This White Paper fulfils that promise.'

The key proposals in the Paper were:
- the total number of peers to be reduced from 700 to 600;
- 120 members (20 per cent) to be elected;
- 480 members to be appointed as follows: 120 by an independent Appointment Commission, and 360 by the political parties based on their share of the vote at the general election;
- no change to the Lords' power of delay;
- the right to veto secondary legislation to be reduced – members would only be allowed to delay changes and force ministers to think again about their proposals.

These proposals were brought before Parliament in January 2002. Lord Irvine received a hostile reception from a meeting with Labour MPs and fared little better in the Lords. He argued that: the reforms would reduce Prime Ministerial patronage, and that a directly elected or substantially elected chamber would challenge the pre-eminence of the Commons.

Those who *oppose* these reform proposals argued that:

- The independent Appointment Commission would be under the influence of the Prime Minister both in terms of its composition and in its appointment of life peers.

- The fact that 60 per cent (360) of the life peers would be chosen via party patronage would certainly ensure an in-built Labour majority.

- The hereditary principle was to be abolished, only to be replaced by an equally undesirable House.

Lord Strathclyde, the Conservative leader in the Lords, described the proposals as a 'ghastly charade' and warned that existing peers would oppose them as they would undermine democracy. Lord Wakeham viewed the White Paper as a means of promoting political patronage through cronyism and undermining the political authority of the second chamber.

In mid-January 2002, Iain Duncan Smith struck a damaging blow by proposing a solution apparently more democratic than that which ministers were suggesting. He wanted:
- the Lords to be renamed as the Senate;
- the new body to consist of 300 members;
- 80 per cent of the 300 to be elected, regionally.

As yet, ministers have not taken the issue any further. Few Labour MPs feel that they can offer enthusiastic backing to the White Paper and pursuit of the issue is likely to cause party unrest. Tony Blair has remarked that there is no majority in the House for any particular proposal. Some say that he might use this lack of agreement as a reason for letting the matter rest.

Reform of the House of Commons

As a reform-minded Leader of the House of Commons, Robin Cook presented a set of proposals to the Modernisation Committee of the Commons in December 2001. His paper concentrated on the central issue of the standing of the Commons 'as a chamber which is effective in holding government to account, vigilant in scrutiny of legislation and competent in adapting itself to contemporary working practices'.

Various proposals were made to make Parliament operate in a manner appropriate for the twenty-first century, among them:
- more opportunities for select committees to scrutinise bills in their draft form, before they become part of a party battle at the second reading;
- a rescheduling of bills so that the House is not swamped with legislative work in the spring; if necessary, they could be allowed to carry over from one parliamentary session to another;
- renaming select committees as scrutiny committees, as part of a package to make them more effective – membership would be taken out of the

hands of the party whips, a response to the rows in the summer of 2001 over the reappointment of two prominent select committee chairpersons (see p. 275);

- better scrutiny in the chamber itself, by moving Prime Minister's Question Time to mid-day (enabling issues to be aired on the lunch-time news), ensuring that more topical questions are asked of ministers, and staging more but shorter debates;
- a reduction in the length of the summer recess, fewer night sittings and two or three morning sittings.

Cook argued that Parliament has no alternative but to change, not least because it is in long-term decline as an institution. In the light of the low turnout in the 2001 election, it must re-engage with the public. Peter Riddell agreed but threw in a word of caution. He argued that any reforms should make the Executive more accountable to the legislative and should break down the barriers between Parliament and public. Fundamental also was a change in attitude on the part of the MPs and ministers.

More open government and freedom of information

In recent years, many critics have called for greater transparency in the British system of government. They believe that more openness is desirable and necessary, and that democracy works best when citizens are well-informed.

In 1989, a new Official Secrets Act was passed. Ministers claimed that it was liberal in that it provided a narrow definition of official secrecy, but opponents claimed that it tightened secrecy within these narrower confines. Some liberalisation has occurred since then. The Major government promised more **open government** and

> **open government**
> The relatively free flow of information about government to the general public, the media and other representative bodies.

released information about Cabinet committees, rules of ministerial conduct, some Public Record documents and even some data on MI5. The Citizen's Charter, 1991, also promised more open government and more information.

A code of practice produced in 1994 stressed that secrecy must only be maintained when there is good reason for it and that there should be more information to promote policy discussion. In 1997, Labour promised to introduce further reform, but as yet nothing has been done on open government, but the related issue of **freedom of information** has been tackled.

> **freedom of information**
> Refers to free public access to government information and records. Freedom of information is regarded by many people as a pre-requisite for more open government.

Is more open government desirable?

The case for
- Openness is favourable to good government, in that excessive secrecy may undermine faith in the authority and fairness of administration and fuel suspicion that there is corruption, inefficiency or waste.
- The more policies and their implications are disclosed and debated in an open and informed manner, the greater the likelihood of a good decision being made.
- Openness acts as a restraint on ministers and their officials, for they come to accept that their decisions have to be capable of convincing justification.
- For particular groups such as ethnic minorities, the disabled and others, openness might help to allay their fear. Moreover, pressure groups would be in a better position to help them.
- Above all, there is the basic 'right to know'. In a modern democracy, the voters have a right to know more of the attitudes and actions of those who have power over them.

The case against
- Some civil servants see open government as a contradiction in terms. As Sir Humphrey explained in the TV programme *Yes Minister*: 'You can be open, or you can have government.'
- There is a feeling held by many officials (and argued in the discussions surrounding the Matrix Churchill case in 1989) that to reveal documents or oral evidence which provides honest and candid advice for ministers is contrary to the public interest, because it might prevent them from speaking frankly for fear of their views being found out; it might also 'colour the tone of public debate'.
- Open government might slow down the decision-making process. As Lord Bancroft once graphically put it: 'Government is difficult enough already, without having to halt continually while people peer up the government kilts.'

Freedom of information

Many states have freedom of information enshrined in law. It guarantees citizens the right to see a wide variety of documents, both state and personal. State secrets are exempt, but they are more narrowly defined than in Britain. There are occasional practical difficulties, in that documents can go missing, be destroyed or even suppressed, but in general it has worked well in most countries. The Commonwealth offered the closest models for the UK and demonstrated that legislation was compatible with the Westminster system. Australia, Canada and New Zealand all legislated in 1982. Elsewhere, in France, Sweden and the USA, residents have similar rights of access.

In Britain, a campaign for freedom of information was created in 1984 with the backing of many leading, all-party politicians and senior ex-officials. New

Labour, in opposition, talked of reforming the Official Secrets Act and introducing a Freedom of Information Bill. The latter did merit a rather liberal White Paper which pleased most commentators. But then the minister responsible was dropped and the matter fell into the hands of Home Secretary, Jack Straw, whose draft bill in 1999 ran into much criticism. The eventual legislation was slow to materialise, but freedom of Information became law in 2000, originally intended to operate from 2002.

The Freedom of Information Act, 2000

Government has always been able to release information voluntarily if it chose to do so, but in Britain ministers were reluctant to take advantage of the opportunity. Straw claimed that little in his measure barred the disclosure of information. Critics were troubled by two aspects of his proposals.

1 It did not give the future independent information commissioner the power to compel ministers and officials to release secret documents.
2 Government policy processes were not opened up for scrutiny, in the way that they are in the USA.

Taken aback by the tide of opposition, including that of select committees in the Commons and Lords, Jack Straw widened the scope of the Bill by removing the blanket ban on releasing reports and information on city financial scandals and corrupt company directors, and on the release of accident and health and safety reports in the workplace. What he would not do is concede on the issue of policy advice, because to do so 'would weaken ministerial accountability'. He claimed that mandarins would be unwilling to give frank policy advice if they believed that their work would in due course be splattered across the front pages of newspapers.

The Act is historic in that it is Britain's first freedom of information legislation. It is a great improvement on the 1999 draft Bill which so watered down the government's earlier good intentions. But to many observers, including those sympathetic to ministers, it is a watered-down version of what is required. Canada, Ireland, Sweden and the USA all have considerably greater openness.

The protection of rights

By the late twentieth century, some academics, commentators and parliamentarians doubted if the means of protection of rights were adequate. They noted that Parliament which is supposed to be our protector has sometimes been the cause of lapses in our record on freedom. Bills pushed through by use of a governmental majority have trampled on rights, as with the Commonwealth Immigrants Act, 1968, or the Criminal Justice and Public Order Act, 1994. Other laws have seriously curtailed our liberties.

British citizens had been given the right to pursue a grievance against those in authority to Strasbourg, the home of the European Court on Human Rights, in 1966 (several cases were lost by British governments, thus emphasising that rights in Britain could not be taken for granted). But for many campaigners, this was not enough. There was no effective protection of our liberties available in this country. With this in mind, some parliamentarians, legal experts and journalists began to call for the incorporation of the European Convention into British law. Others wanted a home-grown Bill of Rights. By the end of the century, the lone voices of campaigning activists were joined by many others, including several prominent judges. Under John Smith and then Tony Blair, Labour came out in favour of incorporation, a position already supported by the Liberal Democrats.

The European Convention

The Council of Europe was established in 1949 to promote political cooperation between the democratic countries of Europe. A key goal was to work for the 'maintenance and further realisation of human rights and fundamental freedoms'. This was achieved by the introduction of the European Convention on Human Rights, drawn up mainly by British lawyers in the Home Office. It began its work in 1953. Britain was an early signatory and in 1966 the Wilson government gave individual British citizens the right of access to the European machinery. This meant that although the Convention was not part of British law, citizens who felt that their rights had been infringed could take the long road to Strasbourg to gain redress and possibly compensation.

Via the broad phrases of the 66 Articles and several Protocols, the Convention sets out a list of basic freedoms such as:
- Article 2: The right to life;
- Article 3: Prohibition of torture;
- Article 5: Right to liberty and security;
- Article 6: Right to a fair trial;
- Article 10: Freedom of expression.

For each right, the basic statement is followed by a series of qualifications which list the exceptions to it. So that although Article 10 guarantees freedom of expression, this is limited by considerations such as those 'necessary in a democratic society, in the interests of national security, for the prevention of disorder or crime, or for the protection of health or morals, for the protection of the rights of others' etc. The Strasbourg Court has the task of interpreting the Convention in a particular case. Now, with the incorporation of the Convention into British law via the Human Rights Act, British courts have similar scope.

The Human Rights Act, 1998

The Human Rights Act passed in 1998 became operative from October 2000. It provides the first written statement of people's rights and obligations by enshrining the European Convention on Human Rights into British law. It allows them to use the Convention as a means of securing justice in the British courts. Judges are now able to apply human rights law in their rulings.

The effect of incorporation of the Convention is to introduce a new human rights culture into British politics. In general, decisions by Parliament, a local authority or other public bodies must not infringe the rights guaranteed under the Act. Where rights conflict, such as privacy versus freedom of information, the courts will decide where the balance should lie. Judges will have the task of deciding cases as they come before them, in effect creating new law. If courts decide that a statute breaches the Act, they can declare it 'incompatible', but they cannot strike it down. So they cannot overrule Parliament. It will then be for Parliament to amend the law.

There are some concerns that the Act will clog up the courts (particularly in the early stages) and that the chief beneficiaries will be lawyers. The courts are likely to be deluged with all kinds of cases, some of them extreme. In Scotland, where the European Convention is already in force, the vast majority of the early cases failed. But already many groups and individuals are proceding with cases in which the new Act will be tested. Possible areas of interest and controversy in the future include:

- **Health**. Is 'postcode rationing' compatible with allowing patients in Oxford to have a drug but not in Newcastle, if the state has a positive obligation to safeguard life?
- **Law and order**. Are marchers/demonstrators charged with public order offences likely to argue that a conviction would breach their rights under Article 10 to freedom of expression? Should the police continue to use stop-and-search powers that discriminate against ethnic minorities, or is this in conflict with Article 11 on freedom of assembly or Article 14 on anti-discrimination?

The future of rights protection

The passage of the 1998 Act has been a significant step forward in the protection of rights in Britain. It may be that it will prove adequate and win broad support, once it has 'bedded down'. It is not necessarily the end of the road, for as Jack Straw, the previous Home Secretary remarked, it was 'a floor but not a ceiling'. Should there be a demand, it would be possible in the future to move towards a distinctive British bill of rights.

Some libertarian groups are dissatisfied with the Convention in its present form and would like to see additional rights included and the phraseology changed to make it more appropriate to the twenty-first century. Others accept what has been done as good and beneficial, but concentrate on the need to go further and devise a home-grown bill attuned to the British situation today. However, there are many people, most notably in the Conservative party, who disliked the move to incorporate the Convention into British law; they would almost certainly oppose any further move on rights protection.

A key issue in the minds of those who oppose written proclamations of rights is that they have to be interpreted by the judges, whose political involvement has in any case being developing in recent decades (see next section on judicial power).

Growing judicial power

In recent decades, the growing importance of judges and the courts has been one of the most significant political developments. Previously, the role of the courts in British politics had been restricted and sporadic, whereas it is now often said to be central and constant. Today, the power of judges to review the legality of governmental action has become a new, important stage in the public policy process.

Interest in this process of judicial review is a relatively new phenomenon in Britain. It is the process whereby the courts monitor the way in which public officials carry out their duties. It empowers the courts to nullify those actions which are considered illegal and unconstitutional, or in which a decision was irrational or unreasonable, or unfairly reached. The increased relevance of review was apparent when in 1987 government lawyers produced a document for civil servants, entitled *The Judge over your Shoulder*. It showed them how to avoid the pitfalls into which they might tumble. Between 1981 and 1996, the number of applications for judicial review rose from just over 500 to nearly 4,000; in the latter year alone, there were 1,748 immigration applications and 340 concerning homelessness.

Tension between the politicians and the judges

The increasing resort to review and the decisions which judges reached in several cases caused resentment under the Major government. Home Secretary Michael Howard made several important decisions which were considered unlawful by senior judges, on issues ranging from criminal injuries to the exclusion of the Revd Moon from the UK. Tension became acute, for ministers were overtly critical of judges and complained about judicial activism, whilst some judges felt there was a campaign to discredit them. The tabloid press joined in the 'judge-bashing', complaining of the 'galloping arrogance' of the judiciary.

By convention, Ministers adopt a respectful attitude to judges and court judgments. This broke down in the 1990s and there was increasing concern about judges' political involvement, the more so as some of them began to make enthusiastic noises about the European Convention – at a time when

European Court justices were causing Conservative MPs some irritation by their judgments. The limits of judicial power were ripe for discussion, as ministers felt they were stepping out from their specific role and trespassing dangerously into the political arena.

Why do politicians fear this growth in judicial power?

Opponents of a home-grown British bill of rights (or the recent incorporation of the European Convention), often claim that it would remove power from the hands of elected MPs and give it to the judges. Fears about the transfer of power to the judiciary are at the heart of much anxiety about the new Human Rights Act. If today that suspicion is often voiced on the political Right, in the past it was the Labour movement which felt uneasy about judicial power.

Why has the Left been traditionally fearful of judicial power?

Labour suffered from a series of judicial decisions in the nineteenth and twentieth centuries, among them the Taff Vale case in 1900 – and some high-profile cases in the 1980s in which union assets were sequestered. But suspicion has not been based solely on unfavourable verdicts. It has much to do with a feeling that these judgments derive from problems about the selection, backgrounds and attitudes of those 'on the bench'.

Firstly, many judges have formerly practised at the Bar, membership of which has long been thought to be elitist and unrepresentative. Members tend to have professional, middle-class backgrounds, and have often been educated at public school before attending Oxbridge. In other words, they are conservative, wealthy and out of touch. Even if a privileged life-style might not render judges unsuitable to exercise greater political influence, then – it is alleged – the nature of their training and the character of the job they do, tends to give them a preference for traditional standards of behaviour and make them particularly impressed by traditional values in matters of behaviour, family life and respect for the law. They are unlikely to be overly sympathetic to demonstrators, minority activists and those who are strident in seeking justice for their cause.

Secondly, it is the fact that they are appointed which causes particular concern. MPs have to keep in touch with the electorate if they wish to be re-elected, but judges have less need to be sensitive to the tide of popular opinion. They are accountable to no one, remote from present-day reality. As Ewing and Gearty ask: 'Is it legitimate or justifiable to have the final political decision, on say a woman's right to abortion, determined by a group of men appointed by the Prime Minister from a small and unrepresentative pool . . . Difficult ethical, social and political questions would be subject to judicial preference, rather than the shared or compromised community morality.'[3]

Electoral reform

Labour cautiously moved towards acceptance of the principle of electoral reform in the 1990s. As a result of its pre-election agreement with the Liberal Democrats, it was pledged in 1997 to introduce a proportional voting system for devolved and European elections, as well as for the Greater London Assembly and mayor. These pledges have been honoured, so that for the first time in British experience those who write about the need to introduce a different system for voting in Westminster and local elections have British experience upon which they can draw.

In 1999, the devolved elections were held under the Additional Member System (AMS) and the European elections operated under a Closed Party List system. Minority groupings did better than they would have under first past the post, so that the nationalists gained solid representation in the Scottish and Welsh assemblies, and in the European Parliament they and the Greens and the UK Independence Party have a voice.

No action has been taken by ministers on the Jenkins proposal for the use of 'AV-top up' (see pp. 80–1) in general elections. No referendum is as yet planned, and there is no sign that there will be one in this Parliament. Should an alternative system be favoured, there are several possibilities whose strengths and weaknesses have already been discussed (see Chapter 5). The most usually canvassed choices are between some variant of proportional representation and the Alternative Vote. The general case for and against a proportional system is set out below:

Proportional representation

The case **for** proportional representation in Britain is that it would introduce a fairer system which would remove many of the anomalies or blemishes of the existing first past the post method of voting. Under PR:
- Votes are not wasted.
- The number of seats won by each party is broadly in proportion to the total number of votes gained, so that the result is a more accurate reflection of people's wishes.
- Third parties are more likely to gain just representation.
- There is likely to be greater choice, with voters having the chance to choose between candidates from either wing of a main party; in multi-member constituencies, there are more likely to be female and ethnic minority candidates as well.
- The politics of cooperation and agreement would replace adversarial politics, and make government by coalition more likely.
- Coalitions would probably gain more than 50 per cent of the votes cast, and so governments would enjoy greater legitimacy.

The case **against** PR is that proportional schemes have been used on the continent for many years and the problems associated with them depend to some extent upon the system selected. General points are that:

- They encourage a proliferation of small parties; this can result in instability and – at worst – political collapse.
- It is unlikely that one party will be able to form a government on its own, so that most continental administrations are coalitions. These are said to have many disadvantages, among them behind-the-scenes deals as the parties bargain over the formation of a coalition, lack of action because of the difficulty of reaching agreement, threats of/actual withdrawal and excessive power being placed in the hands of small parties who can determine the fate of larger parties.
- They use multi-member constituencies and this means that the traditional link between an MP and his/her constituency is lost.

There is no perfect electoral system appropriate for every country at every time. It is possible to employ different systems for different elections within the same country, so that in Britain the recent use of alternative methods in devolved and European elections does not necessarily mean that change for Westminster elections has to be introduced. At the present time, given Labour's landslide majority, it has little interest in pursuing the matter further.

Postscript: reform of the House of Lords

On 4 February 2003 debates on Lords reform took place in both the Commons and the Lords. They were followed by votes on a number of options (see results below) presented by a Joint Parliamentary Committee.

In the previous week, Tony Blair had come out in favour of an all-appointed House for the first time, contrary to his government's previous policy to implement the Wakeham Report. The Lord Chancellor, Derry Irvine, holds the same view.

Reform of the Lords now looks dead for the foreseeable future.

Table 17.3   Results of votes, 4 February 2003, on reform of the House of Lords

	Commons		Lords	
	For	Against	For	Against
Abolition	172	392		
100% elected	272	289	106	329
80% elected	281	284	93	339
60% elected	253	316	91	318
100% appointed	245	323	335	110
80% appointed	No vote	No vote	39	376
60% appointed	No vote	No vote	60	359
50:50	No vote	No vote	84	322

REFERENCES

1 P. Toynbee and D. Walker, *Did Things Get Better?*, Penguin, 2001.
2 P. Norton (ed.), *Politics UK*, 4 edition, Longman 2001.
3 K. Ewing and C. Gearty, *Freedom Under Thatcher*, Clarendon Press, 1990.
4 As note 2 above.

FURTHER READING

T. Boyd and K. Harrison, *The Changing Constitution: Evolution or Revolution?*, PoliticsAssociation/SHU Press, 2000.

R. Deacon, D. Griffiths and P. Lynch, *Devolved Great Britain: The New Governance of England, Scotland and Wales*, Politics Association/SHU Press, 2001.

G. Thomas, *Parliament in an Age of Reform*, Politics Association/SHU Press, 2000.

D. Watts, *Protecting Rights in Britain*, Access to Politics series, Hodder & Stoughton, 1998.

D. Watts, *British Electoral Systems: Achieving a Sense of Proportion*, Politics Association/SHU Press, 2000.

USEFUL WEBSITES

The Electoral Reform Society: **www.electoralreform.org.uk** This organisation campaigns for proportional representation in the UK parliaments and assemblies.

Charter 88: **www.charter88.org.uk** The site includes information on the organisation's independent campaign for constitutional reform.

The Constitution Unit: **www.ucl.ac.uk/constitution-unit** This deals with constitutional reform, including devolution.

SAMPLE QUESTIONS

1 Outline the cases for and against the reform of elections to the House of Commons.

2 Do the operation of the Scottish and Welsh devolved assemblies have anything positive to offer as a guide to reform of the House of Commons?

3 Why has the Blair Government done so much by way of constitutional reform, yet been so reluctant to bring it to public attention?

4 Why do you think there was more enthusiasm for devolution in Scotland than in Wales?

Index